D0355313

FORTS OF THE WEST

FORTS
of the
WEST

MILITARY FORTS AND PRESIDIOS

AND POSTS COMMONLY CALLED FORTS

WEST OF THE MISSISSIPPI RIVER

TO 1898 *By Robert W. Frazer*

UNIVERSITY OF OKLAHOMA PRESS : NORMAN AND LONDON

By ROBERT W. FRAZER

Mansfield on the Condition of the Western Forts, 1853–54 (editor)
  (Norman, 1963)
Forts of the West (Norman, 1965)
New Mexico in 1850: A Military View (editor) (Norman, 1968)

Library of Congress Catalog Card Number: 65–24196

ISBN: 0–8061–1250–6

Copyright © 1965, 1972, by the University of Oklahoma Press, Norman, Publishing
Division of the University. All rights reserved. Manufactured in the U.S.A.

10   11   12   13   14   15   16   17   18   19   20   21   22   23

To Mike and Marlys Harder

INTRODUCTION

THE AMERICAN WEST has excited the interest and imagination of visitors, writers, and arm-chair travelers since it first came to the attention of the European. What the progenitors of the American Indian thought of it can only be conjectured. They at least peopled it, fought mightily, if unsuccessfully, to hold it in the face of European encroachment, and left a good many descendants throughout its extensive reaches. The history of the West is replete with tales of wonder and of adventure. Most of them had some basis in fact, but a sizable number were cut from whole cloth.

Alonzo Álvarez de Pineda, the first European to lead an expedition which touched the American West, sailed a short distance up the Río Grande in 1519 and thereafter skirted the coast of Texas and Louisiana. He carried back to his superior, Governor Francisco de Garay of Jamaica, a fascinating account of the region he had seen, an account which led to a completely unsuccessful attempt to plant a colony near the mouth of the Río Grande.

Álvarez de Pineda's account was but the first of the tales of the wonders of the West. Cabeza de Vaca, Fray Marcos de Niza, Coronado, Antonio de Espejo, and their successors added to the reputation for wonder. Some accounts were discouraging, some were harrowing reports of misery, starvation, and death. Other accounts were of fabulous cities, strange animals and people, vast inland seas and westward-flowing rivers, and, later, of lost mines and buried treasures, of such natural phenomena as Colter's Hell, and of such amazing revenants as the survivors of the lost continent of Mu, safely ensconced in some hideaway on Mount Shasta. All of the tales, true, half-true, and false, tugged at the imagination. Down through the years the West was explored, its far corners sought out, and the tales and the legends tracked down. Yet the wonder and the excitement remained.

Over the years the cast of characters changed. And this too became a part of the West. The list of typical western figures is surprisingly long. Depending upon the time, the region, or the interest of the individual, the West calls to mind conquistador or mission padre, explorer or settler, *voyageur* or mountain man, prospector, scout, or freighter, timber baron or cowboy, bad man or frontier marshal. Even the mighty buffalo and the lowly burro conjure up visions of the West. The list could be expanded. In the process of developing the western hero, fancy has become entwined with reality. Radio and television, the motion picture, popular song, and fiction have done much to keep the West alive and to perpetuate that which, in many cases, never was. No better example comes to mind than the recent Kansas senator who desired to enshrine Matt Dillon in the Hall of Fame.[1]

Beyond much reasonable doubt, the most typical figure of the West was the American Indian. Ubiquitous, with widely varying culture and attitude, the Indian was present long before the European arrived and is still present, not unchanged, but often retaining to a remarkable degree his beliefs and even his way of life. Except for the Indian, no western figure was more persistent than the soldier. He accompanied Álvarez de Pineda, was cast ashore with Cabeza de Vaca, and participated in all of the early expeditions of exploration. The first settlements in the West, San Juan de los Caballeros and Santa Fe, La Salle's lonely Fort St. Louis on the Texas coast, Tubac, and San Diego, all had their contingents of troops. Spain provided mission guards and established a variety of garri-

[1] *The Wichita Morning Eagle*, February 2, 1961.

soned posts. French soldiers often protected isolated trading-post forts. As the United States moved into the West, the soldier was very much at the fore. The initial exploration of the Louisiana Purchase territory was carried out by military expeditions, those of Lewis and Clark, Pike, Long, and of many others making less extensive examinations. Following its achievement of independence, Mexico continued and even augmented the existing Spanish military establishments. The Republic of Texas added its contingent. Of all the nations to touch the West, only England and Russia, both of which worked through officially chartered trading companies, failed to establish military outposts.

That Indian and soldier spanned the history of the West was not chance. The primary reason for stationing troops in the West was to control the Indian. There were variations and abberations. Posts were established to protect the seacoast and to guard international frontiers. Mexico established posts in Texas to block the illegal movement of persons and goods from the United States into its territory. Spain and France maintained their petty garrisons, face to face on either side of the Arroyo Hondo. For the United States, the periods of the Mexican War and, more particularly, the Civil War saw large numbers of troops in the West engaged in doing something other than controlling Indians. Yet the great majority of western military posts established prior to the Spanish-American War, regardless of their initial purpose, were concerned with the Indians.

Where troops were stationed, facilities to accommodate them came into existence, more often than not erected by the labor of the troops themselves. The sites for most posts, even overnight encampments, were chosen with care. Need, either real or assumed, was an initial consideration for those posts intended to be maintained for any length of time. Under Spain, the establishment of a presidio was a serious matter, requiring, as it did, the approval of the viceroy. The few forts established by Mexico in Texas were erected only after long and careful investigation. United States posts were most often established by order of a department commander, but the exceptions to this practice were relatively numerous. Toward the close of the century, when major posts were constructed by private contractors, the selection of a location often depended upon the willingness of a state to make available a suitable site. Once this condition was met, actual construction awaited the appropriation by Congress of the necessary funds.

However, until the expansion of the railways lessened the dependence of the individual post upon its local area, certain important considerations influenced the choice of site. This was true of the posts established by Spain, France, and Mexico as well as of those established by the United States. Water was essential, and, without exception, western forts were built close to what was considered to be a dependable source, usually a stream, but occasionally a spring or a lake. As long as posts were erected by the labor of the soldiers, a supply of suitable material, not too inconveniently located, was necessary. Workable stone, timber, earth from which adobes could be manufactured, or even brush to be fashioned into jacales would serve. Physically, at least in its early years, a western military post was very much a product of its environment.

Fuel was needed in some form for heating, cooking, and the smithy. In the vicinity of some posts, workable deposits of coal were found, although most posts depended upon wood, sometimes brought from a considerable distance. Lumber was desired for many purposes, but it was often in short supply and frequently unavailable locally. Of Ringgold Barracks, Texas, it was reported in 1856 that it was "well supplied with all things except lumber of this they have only sufficient for coffins."[2] Forage was a further necessity and was

[2] In "Report of the Inspection of the Department of Texas, 1856, by Colonel Joseph K. F. Mansfield," Records of the War Department, Office of the Adjutant General, National Archives, Washington, D. C. (hereafter designated as O.A.G., N.A.).

amply available at most posts, either by cutting the natural hay or by contract, although in the latter case the cost was sometimes excessive. In the early years of Fort Yuma, California, cane and willow bark were gathered along the river, as much as fifteen miles below the post, as a substitute for hay. The nearest natural hay was one hundred miles away.[3] Despite the care taken in choosing a site, more than one post was relocated or abandoned because the water supply proved unsatisfactory, because the location was considered poor from a defensive point of view, or because of the prevalence of disease.

The principal Spanish post was the presidio. By definition, a presidio, in the military sense, is either the garrison of a plaza, *castillo*, or fort, or the town or fort which is so garrisoned.[4] In the present western United States, the Spanish presidios, with one exception, were separate establishments, provided with their own facilities. The exception, Santa Fe, New Mexico, is often and correctly called a presidio. However, the fact that a garrison was stationed for a long or short period of time in a center of population did not mean that the center was officially a presidio. Presidial troops from Santa Fe were stationed at Las Vegas, New Mexico, on various occasions, yet Las Vegas was not a presidio. In addition to presidios, Spain established *castillos, destacamentos*, mission guards, *puestos*, and, by royal decree, designated *plazas fuertes*. The *castillo* was a fortification of the traditional sort, and those few established in the West were all in conjunction with presidios. In general, then, it may be said that the presidio was intended to be a permanent military post and that it corresponded most nearly to a United States Army fort. It is interesting to note that during the period in which Spain was in

[3] In "McCall's Inspection Report, Department of the Pacific, 1852," Records of the War Department, O.A.G., N.A.

[4] In a non-military sense a presidio is also a prison, the assemblage of prisoners therein, and other definitions of similar meaning. See the *Diccionario de la Lengua Española* of the Real Academia Española.

control of Louisiana, forts (*fuertes*) were established by name in that area.

The French established no exclusively military posts west of the Mississippi River. Even the post at Natchitoches was intended to promote trade with the Indians as well as to guard the frontier. Most, perhaps all, of the French trading-post forts were at times garrisoned by small numbers of troops. The major period of French activity west of the Mississippi River, except in the Minnesota area, was concentrated into less than half a century. The number of French posts which had a significant military function was surprisingly small. Following the transfer of Louisiana to Spain in 1762 there was a flurry of activity as Spain sought to strengthen the Mississippi frontier against British and, later, United States encroachment. A number of forts were constructed along the Mississippi River from the mouth of the Missouri to the south. But, in the same period, three of the Texas presidios were abandoned as a result of the recommendations of the Marqués de Rubí, who inspected the Texas posts in 1767.[5] The Spanish efforts were ended when France reclaimed Louisiana in 1800, only to transfer it to the United States in 1804.

With the acquisition of Louisiana, the United States Army became, for the first time, a factor in the Trans-Mississippi West. Existing military posts were taken over, although most were only briefly occupied. At the risk of great oversimplification, it may be said that United States military policy in the Trans-Mississippi West passed through three general phases as far as the establishment of posts was concerned. The first covered the years 1804–45. In this period the army maintained a line of posts in advance of the frontier of settlement, thus providing a military zone between settler and Indian. There were several objectives in view. An effort was made to control the Indians and thus prevent them from committing depredations.

[5] Rubí's recommendations were embodied in the *Reglamento e instrucción para los presidios que han de formar en la linea de frontera de la Nueva España. Resuelto por el en cédula de 10 de Setiembre de 1772* (Madrid, 1772).

There was also a distinct attempt made to protect the Indians, especially those Indians who were being removed from east of the Mississippi, by discouraging wars between Indian tribes and preventing illegal activities by whites. This effort was reflected in the factory system maintained by the United States from 1795 to 1822 in the hope of protecting the Indians from the sharp practices of some of the private traders as well as excluding English and Spanish traders from United States soil. Most of the trading posts established under this system were in connection with military posts.

With the beginning of large-scale migration to the Oregon country in 1842, consideration was given to the establishment of a post near Fort Laramie, then a trading post, or even farther west along the Oregon Trail. However, principal reliance continued to be placed on the use of military expeditions to overawe the Indians. Colonel Stephen Watts Kearny, following the completion of the summer expedition which took him as far as South Pass in 1845, recommended:

> In lieu of the establishment of a military post in that upper country, I would suggest that a military expedition, similar to the one of this season, be made every two or three years. They would serve to keep the Indians perfectly quiet, reminding them of (as this one proved) the facility and rapidity with which our dragoons can march through any part of their country, and that there is no place where they can go but the dragoons can follow; and, as we are better mounted than they are, overtake them.[6]

As late as 1845, on the eve of the Mexican War, there were only fifty-six military posts in the United States. West of the Mississippi were twelve permanent posts, eleven forts, and Jefferson Barracks.[7] This line of posts constituted the military frontier immediately prior to the Mexican War.

[6] Kearny to Colonel Roger Jones, adjutant general, September 15, 1845, in the Report of the Secretary of War, 1845, 29 Cong., 1 sess., *House Exec. Doc. No. 2*, 212.

[7] See *ibid.*, Table D, following p. 220.

The second period of United States western military policy extended from 1845 into the 1880's, although the terminal date varied from one part of the West to another. Immediately following the annexation of Texas, two posts, Forts Brown and Polk, were established on the lower Río Grande in anticipation of the outbreak of hostilities with Mexico. Of the other posts planned during this period, only one, Fort Kearny I, on the Missouri River in Nebraska, was established prior to the outbreak of the contemplated conflict.

The annexation of Texas, the settlement of the Oregon question, and the acquisition of territory resulting from the Mexican War forced a complete revision of western military policy. No longer was it possible to maintain a permanent military zone between Indian and settler. Extensive areas of the newly acquired territory were already settled. From 1846 until the 1880's, the military policy of the United States in the west was devoted to the control of the Indian. In the years immediately following the Mexican War the United States established military posts to protect the areas of settlement in California, New Mexico, Oregon, and Texas. Posts were established along the major overland routes to the West in order to facilitate travel and communications. Although the Treaty of Guadalupe Hidalgo, which concluded the Mexican War, provided that the United States restrain the Indians in its territory from crossing into Mexico to commit depredations, the terms were never fully carried out. This onerous obligation was canceled by the Gadsden Purchase Treaty, ratified in 1854.

The period witnessed a rapid expansion in the number of western military posts, with the greatest number existing during the years 1868–80.[8] Frequent reorganizations were carried out in the number

[8] This does not take into account the posts established by the Union and Confederacy west of the Mississippi in connection with the conduct of the Civil War or the posts maintained by the United States for the purpose of reconstruction following the war. Those posts cannot be classified as frontier military posts, although the very interesting Forts Davis and McCulloch, established in Oklahoma by the Confederates and garrisoned in part by Indian troops, might be so considered.

and geographical extent of the military departments, districts, and divisions.[9] All of the major Indian wars of the West were fought during these years, and most of them led to the establishment of permanent military posts. As settlement moved into the West as a result of the expanding agricultural frontier, the various gold and silver rushes, the cattle industry, and other factors, new areas were occupied, and for these protection was usually provided. The major routes of travel multiplied in number as the emigrant trails were augmented by stage and mail routes, and the ponderous freight wagons hauled goods into the most isolated regions of occupation. Later came the transcontinental railway and the telegraph. Initially the army was called upon to provide protection for the major routes of travel between the Mississippi River and the Far West. Closely associated with this activity was the role of the army in exploring the West, laying out new routes of travel, determining the location and usability of passes, and examining the navigability of western rivers. In the years 1853–56 the army undertook the monumental task of exploring, mapping, and describing the potential railway routes from the Mississippi to the Pacific and from San Diego to Puget Sound. In connection with these activities additional posts, both permanent and temporary, were established. The policy of providing protection for the Indians was continued throughout the period, particularly, as increasing numbers of Indians were induced to settle on reservations. In almost all parts of the West military posts were established on or adjacent to Indian reservations for the threefold purpose of guarding the agencies and protecting and restraining the Indians.

Two principal factors combined to usher in the third and final phase of western military policy. Because the combination was achieved at different times in the various parts of the West, no spe-

[9] The best available treatment of this complicated subject is found in Raphael P. Thian, *Notes Illustrating the Military Geography of the United States* (Washington, D. C., 1881).

cific date can be attached to the termination of the second phase. With the growth of the reservation system the process of controlling the Indians became increasingly a matter of constraining them within fixed limits. As Indian hostilities gradually declined, an increasing number of military posts were abandoned as no longer useful. Equally important was the improvement in transportation facilities, resulting from the construction of railways throughout the West. No longer was it necessary to maintain many of the posts which had served isolated areas or functioned as centers of supply.[10] As early as 1853, Secretary of War Jefferson Davis had stated:

> The multiplication of small posts, however much it may appear to have been called for by the necessities of the service, is of more than doubtful policy. The system is expensive far beyond any good results that are attained by it. It is injurious to the discipline, instruction, and efficiency of the troops, and it is believed that it often invites aggression by that exhibition of weakness which must inevitably attend the great dispersion of any force.[11]

Similar opinions were expressed over the years by secretaries of war and various army officers, yet the multiplication of posts went on. Now it became feasible to concentrate troops in large posts in localities adequately served by rail transportation. From such centers troops could be rushed by rail into or close to trouble spots as the need arose. This, in turn, permitted the abandonment of a large number of small posts.[12] By 1897 the number of western posts had decreased significantly. Fewer than one-third of the remaining posts were in or immediately adjacent to areas occupied by the Indians. Most of those which were, were on the northern plains or in the

[10] Among the once major posts rendered obsolete as depots of supply by the building of the railways were Forts Laramie, Union, and Yuma.

[11] Report of the Secretary of War, 1853, in 33 Cong, 1 sess., *Senate Exec. Doc. No. 1*, II, 6.

[12] The situation in Colorado provides an excellent example. Within four years of the establishment of Fort Logan, on the outskirts of Denver, all other posts in Colorado had been abandoned.

Apache country. In Texas, where, over the years, more forts had been established than in any other state, all of the remaining posts, except for the installations at San Antonio, were along the Río Grande frontier. In California all existing posts were on San Francisco and San Diego bays, except for the troops stationed at Sequoya and Yosemite National parks to protect the natural wonders from vandalism. In four western states—Iowa, Louisiana, Nevada, and Oregon—there was not a single garrisoned post. Only Arizona, California, Montana, Nebraska, Texas, Washington, and Wyoming could boast more than two permanent military establishments.[13] It is true, however, that provisions had been made for additional western posts, some of which were under construction. These included, among others, Fort Lincoln, North Dakota, Fort Mackenzie, Wyoming, and Forts Casey, Flagler, Lawton, and Wright, Washington. These posts were constructed under contract, not by the labor of troops, and had not been garrisoned prior to the Spanish-American War.[14]

The day of the small frontier post was almost at an end. More attention was being paid to the development of coastal defenses, especially on the Pacific Coast. In the interior the posts were larger and, with each passing year, more adequately served by rail transportation. Some of the once small frontier posts, such as Forts Bliss, Leavenworth, Sill, and Snelling, had developed into major installations. The Spanish-American War simply accelerated a process already under way. Some posts were abandoned with the outbreak of the war. From others the garrisons were withdrawn. Most of the rest of the interior posts saw a considerable curtailment in their strength. Yet, the situation in 1897, on the eve of the Spanish-American War, reflected some of the same concerns which had been present in the

---

[13] See *Annual Reports of the War Department for the Fiscal Year Ended June 30, 1897, Report of the Secretary of War* (Washington, D. C., 1897), 104–14.

[14] See the reports of the Quartermaster General in *ibid.*, and for subsequent years.

years immediately following the Mexican War. Major General Nelson A. Miles, commanding the army, reported:

> The condition of the Indian is better to-day than it has been for many years, and during the last year there has been no serious disturbance of the peace. The Indians are making rapid progress toward permanent settlements and semicivilization. It was a wise provision of Congress that authorized the President to detail experienced officers of the Army to act as Indian agents, and I trust this system will be continued. The number of Indian children that are now receiving the advantages of school education is very large, and it is having a very excellent effect upon the condition of the tribes, as well as upon their progress as a pastoral and an agricultural people. Their condition is being benefited in many ways.[15]

Even so, there had been a number of Indian scares during the year and the future behavior of the Indian was a matter which elicited some comment.

Over the years the legal peacetime strength of the army had been increased, but it remained small. According to Secretary of War Jefferson Davis, the legal strength of the army in 1808 had been 9,991 officers and men. Between that date and the Mexican War the legal size of the regular army varied between a low of 6,126 and a high of 12,139. Following the Mexican War it was fixed at 10,120, and then, in 1850, it was increased on a sliding scale which permitted a greater strength for companies stationed at remote posts. In 1853 the legal size of the army was 13,821, but the actual strength was only 10,495.[16] Following the Civil War the legal strength of the regular army was placed at 54,000, but periodically this was reduced until it became fixed at 25,000,[17] something less than twice the permissible strength of the 1850's. In the 1850's four-fifths of the army had been stationed west of the Mississippi; in the 1890's two-

[15] *Ibid.*, 5.

[16] Report of the Secretary of War, 1853, in 33 Cong., 1 sess., *Senate Exec. Doc. No. 1*, II, 11–12.

[17] *Annual Reports of the War Department, 1897*, 7–8.

thirds of the army was in the same area. In almost all of the annual reports of the secretaries of war the complaint was made that the size of the army was too small. However, in 1897, in contrast to earlier years, the army was at virtually full strength, the recruiting service was reported as having unusually good results,[18] and the number of desertions as being lower than at any time during the past decade.[19]

Not only did the United States establish many more military posts than did all of the other nations which, at one time or another, held various parts of the American West; it also, by designation, established a far greater variety. Included were agencies, arsenals, barracks, batteries, blockhouses, camps, cantonments, depots, sub-depots, forts, military prisons, posts, sub-posts, picket-posts, presidios, stations, and at least one stockade and one redoubt. Some of these terms are self-explanatory, or so it would seem, yet in actual practice many were applied in such a manner as to destroy their specific meaning. The designations "arsenal," "battery," and "military prison" were used with reasonable exactness. The term "agency" was applied to a garrison maintained in connection with an Indian agency, while the term "station" usually referred to a garrison located at a station on the mail or telegraph routes. As used (Standing Rock Agency, Plum Creek Station), these were actually place names. Barracks, in theory, were centers in which troops were located temporarily until they could be reassigned. Depots were centers for the storage and distribution of supplies. Sub-depots, though completely separate posts, were subordinate to depots. Arsenals, barracks, and depots were often associated with other posts. For example, Fort Union (New Mexico) and Fort Union Arsenal were located on the same military reservation, Fort Whipple and Prescott Barracks were immediately adjacent, and, for a time, Benicia consisted of Benicia

18 *Ibid.*, 16
19 *Ibid.*, 99.

Barracks, Benicia Arsenal, Benicia Subsistence Depot, and Benicia Quartermaster's Depot. Posts designated batteries, blockhouses, sub-posts, and picket-posts were invariably subordinate to other posts.

Despite the fact that the various categories of posts can be defined, it is difficult to justify the application of the designation in many cases, particularly on the basis of function. Why the post at Monterey should be designated a redoubt and the post at San Francisco a presidio in the years immediately after the Mexican War is difficult to say. Both were intended primarily for coastal defense and the designation "fort" might equally well have been applied to either. Jefferson Barracks existed for 120 years. During that period it performed almost every function that might be demanded of a military post, yet it was always designated a barracks. What logical distinction can be made between Columbia Barracks, Fort Vancouver, and Vancouver Barracks, successive names for the same post? A blockhouse might constitute the principal physical feature of a fort and the fort not be designated a blockhouse.

The problem of nomenclature becomes even more confused in the case of camps, cantonments, forts, and posts. To begin with, "post" is a generic term, including, by definition, all positions at which troops are stationed. Hence a fort, barracks, arsenal, agency, camp, and so on, is also a post. On the other hand, a garrisoned position without other specific desigation was, in some cases, specifically referred to as a post. Examples of this are Post on the Limpia, Post in Navaho Country, New Post near Fort Hall, and Post of El Paso. Here again, however, there is a distinct discrepancy in usage. Many of the posts established by the United States prior to the Civil War, and some thereafter, were simply referred to by the name of the location which they occupied.[20] The establishment, in 1817, of what

[20] For example, most of the posts transferred from France to the United States in 1804 were called by the name of their location: Arkansas [Post], Natchitoches, Ouachita. Following the Mexican War the posts established in New Mexico were similarly called Albuquerque, Cebolleta, Los Lunas, and so on, although more often misspelled than not.

was to become Fort Snelling ushered in a period in which the tendency was to call all new posts "cantonments." This practice had nothing to do with the presumed permanence of a post. The designation became so common that by 1831 there were, west of the Mississippi, three forts, one barracks, and four cantonments. By definition, a cantonment is an impermanent establishment, yet the cantonments, so-called, were not intended to be temporary.[21] To correct this anomaly, General Orders No. 11 was issued by Adjutant General Roger Jones on February 6, 1832, providing that:

> 1. It is the order of the Secretary of War that all the Military Posts designated *Cantonments* be hereafter called *Forts*—and that the works at Old Point Comfort, be called *Fort* Monroe, and not *Fortress* Monroe.
>
> 2. All new posts which may be hereafter established, will receive their names from the War Department, and be announced in General Orders from the Head Quarters of the Army.
>
> 3. Officers and others concerned, will take due notice of the above order, and be governed accordingly.[22]

This order met with compliance so far as the designation of cantonments was concerned, with the result that by the close of 1832 all permanent posts west of the Mississippi, with the exception of Jefferson Barracks, were forts. Between 1832 and the Civil War few posts were designated cantonments, and only one so designated, Cantonment Burgwin, existed for as long as a year. Following the Civil War the designation continued to be applied occasionally. In some cases it was given to a permanent post while the post was under construction. For example, Fort Lewis, Colorado, for which the name had been chosen even before the permanent site was selected, was called Cantonment on the Río La Plata while it was being erected. In gen-

Following the Civil War such designations were rarely used except for the garrisons maintained in the former Confederacy during the period of reconstruction.

[21] Included was Cantonment Leavenworth, now Fort Leavenworth, the oldest fort west of the Mississippi established by the United States.

[22] General Orders No. 11, O.A.G., N.A.

eral, posts designated cantonments in this period were occupied under that name for less than a year. The most notable exception was the Cantonment on the Uncompahgre, Colorado, which was called by that name for six years before it became Fort Crawford.

Once the designation "cantonment" fell into relative disuse, the term "camp" became more common. Yet, as far as any real distinction in the application of the two terms is concerned, it would appear that they were treated as synonyms. During and following the Mexican War there was a rapid expansion in the number of western military posts. Most of these were designated forts or identified simply by the name of the place at which they were located. There were a few interesting exceptions, notably the Presidio at San Francisco and Monterey Redoubt. The number of camps also increased, and by 1855 most new posts were called camps, including those intended to be permanent and eventually to be designated forts. Some camps, particularly those which were subordinate to regularly designated forts, existed for a period of years. At the other extreme were those camps, often identified by a name or a number, which were occupied for a single night.

In theory, the term "camp" came to be the designation for a temporary post and the term "fort" the designation for a permanent post. Yet, in the final analysis, it would appear that a fort was a fort because it was designated a fort. Size, either of the actual post or of the garrison, had nothing to do with it. Defensive strength was not a factor. In fact, the classic concept of a fort as a strongly fortified position would fit very few western posts. Defensive features, such as blockhouses, bastions, and stockades, were completely missing at many western forts. Some forts, actually, were little more than haphazard collections of structures without the slightest arrangement for defense. On the other hand, some strongly fortified posts, such as Alcatraz Island, were never designated forts. The principal distinction, if a distinction existed, was in intent. Impermanent posts were to be called camps and permanent posts, forts. Even this distinction was not made officially until 1878, when it was ordered that:

> As the practice of designating military posts varies in the several Military Divisions, and in order to secure uniformity in this respect, Division commanders are authorized, at their discretion, to name and style all posts permanently occupied by troops, or the occupation of which is likely to be permanent, "Forts," and to style all points occupied temporarily "Camps."[23]

Yet, the fact remains that the oldest military post west of the Mississippi River, the Presidio of San Francisco, has never been called a fort, and Jefferson Barracks, which existed for 120 years, was never anything but a barracks. The oldest operative fort established by the United States in the West, Leavenworth, Kansas, has been in existence since 1827, so the idea of permanence is not entirely misleading. However, at the other end of the scale are Fort Grattan, Nebraska, and Fort Haven, Nevada, neither of which lasted for as long as a month.

Part of the difficulty encountered in attempting to define a fort arises from the fact that many posts began as one thing—agencies, barracks, camps, cantonments, and so on—and later became forts. Conversely, posts which were once forts later became agencies, barracks, camps, depots, sub-posts, or something else. It cannot be said that once a fort, always a fort. This is not a serious difficulty, however, for changes in designation are readily determinable. Another complicating factor is the tendency in official correspondence and documents to refer as forts to posts which were never so designated officially. This problem is further compounded in popular parlance. Almost any military post, excepting only the most ephemeral, is likely to be called a fort by the public. The longer the post remained in existence, the more probable it was that the public would consider

---

[23] General Orders No. 79, November 8, 1878, O.A.G., N.A.

it a fort. Also, once a post had been abandoned, the public frequently elevated it to the rank of fort.[24]

Despite the order of 1832 providing that all new posts would receive their names from the War Department, the sources for the names of forts continued to vary. Some posts were named by the officers who established them, others by the officers who ordered their establishment, still others by the general in command of the army, and some by the secretary of war. In a very few instances the names proposed initially were rejected by the War Department.[25] In other cases posts which were designated forts when first established were later reduced to camps by order of the War Department, including a good many which were still later again designated forts. In addition, there were certain short-lived posts called forts by their establishing officers which were abandoned before any official cognizance was taken of the designation. Many posts also underwent one or more changes of name as well as designaton. An example of this is the Colorado post which began as Fort Fauntleroy, was renamed Fort Wise, and ended as Fort Lyon.

Taking into account only those regular army posts which were at one time or another officially designated forts, the origin of names is not without interest. As would be expected, a majority, roughly three-fifths, were named for army officers. All ranks[26] from second lieutenant to full general were represented except that of lieutenant general. One fort, Grattan, Nebraska, was named for a brevet second lieutenant, and one, Mann, Kansas, for a master teamster. More forts were named for colonels than for officers of any other rank, with brigadier generals, major generals, and captains following in that order. Only one was named for a full general, Fort Sherman,

[24] Another complicating factor is the failure, at times, to distinguish between military forts and trading-post forts or private defensive forts.

[25] Perhaps the most interesting rejection of a name was the refusal of the War Department to accept the designation Fort Racoon for a post in Iowa.

[26] Rank here refers to regular, not brevet, rank.

Idaho. In all cases reference is to the rank held at the time the name was first applied to the post, or, in case of deceased officers, the rank held at time of death.

The second most common source of names was prominent local geographical features. Here rivers and streams predominated, with other forts being named for springs, lakes, bays, towns, elevations, and rapids and one each for a water fall, a cape, a mountain pass, and a national park. Third among sources were men who were or had been in political life. Forts were named for seven Presidents (Jackson, William Henry Harrison, Polk, Fillmore, Buchanan, Lincoln, and Grant) and one Vice-President (Breckinridge), some of whom had been army officers. Two others (Madison and Taylor) were named for men who later became President. Six secretaries of war (Armstrong, Marcy, Conrad, Davis, Floyd, and Rawlins) were so honored, as were three secretaries of state (Madison, Webster, and Seward), and one secretary of the treasury (Cobb). State and territorial governors provided the names for eight forts, while others were named for senators, a diplomat, and a territorial delegate.

At least sixteen forts bore the names of Indian tribes or bands (Apache, Assiniboine, Colville, Coeur d'Alene, Dakota, Klamath, Massachusetts, Mohave, Omaha, Osage, Sisseton, Umpqua, Walla Walla, Washita, Yamhill, and Yuma). It should be noted, however, that not all of these forts derived their names directly from Indian tribes. Some were named for rivers or other geographical features which had given their names to or had been named for Indian tribes. Three were named for United States Navy officers. Two of these were in California—Montgomery, and one which was called successively Fort Du Pont and Fort Stockton. The other was Fort Stockton, Texas. Four were named for civilians: Bidwell and Reading, prominent California pioneers who had served with the California volunteers in the Mexican War; Aubry, who had served the army as a scout; and Washakie, a Shoshoni Indian chief. Finally a number of forts derived their names from sources not fitting any of the above categories. These included four with descriptive names (Defiance, Haven, Supply, and Union). Several were named directly or indirectly for former trading-post forts (Benton, Berthold, Bridger, Hall, Laramie, Lookout, Pierre, Sutter, and Vancouver directly, and Boise, Colville, Spokane, and Walla Walla indirectly). Some of these forts were trading posts purchased by the government for the use of the army, others were named for their proximity to former trading posts, and still others for streams which had derived their names from or given them to trading posts. In addition, there were Forts Ter-Waw, a name of Indian derivation, Massachusetts, apparently named for the natal state of the departmental commander; and Sam Houston, a man so prominent in so many areas that it would be difficult to single out any one as the particular reason for naming a fort for him.

In a rather surprising number of cases more than one fort was named for the same individual. At times the War Department took cognizance of this situation, ordering a change of name because there was already another fort of the same name. Even so, there were two forts named Gaston in California at the same time, although one of them, despite the designation "fort," was a temporary base only. There are several other instances of two forts of the same name in the same state but not at the same time. There are a number of cases of forts which were changed in location yet retained their names, but there are also examples of forts moved as little as six miles and given a new name. If posts other than forts are included, Lincoln, Grant, Winfield Scott, and Nathaniel Lyon received more honors in nomenclature than did any other individuals.

The whole question of the nomenclature of military posts was challenged in 1893 by Brigadier General Richard Napoleon Batchelder, quartermaster general of the army, when he wrote:

A very large number of military posts have been named from the locality where they are placed, some of which, like Angel Island, Alcatraz Island, Davids Island, San Carlos, and Willets Point, are not dignified by any military appelation which is distinctive. A few posts bear the names of Indian tribes distinguished neither for friendliness nor other good qualities.

We have a presidio (Spanish place of defense, garrison, or guard-house), which is a relic of the days of easy conquest.

We have named posts after Presidents and princes, general officers and lieutenants, Christian saints and heathen sinners, Spaniards, Frenchmen, and Englishmen, who were in no way distinguished in, or connected with, the civil or military service of the United States; white men and Indians, cities, towns and villages; after mountain peaks and valleys, and river forks and creeks; the greater number being without significance or dignity.

There are still some fifteen permanent posts known as "barracks," a term erroneously applied to a military post which must of necessity comprise a variety of buildings and quarters for officers, as well as barracks for enlisted men.

It is respectfully suggested that the order of 1878 be amended so as to reserve to the Secretary of War the naming of military posts, and to prescribe the prefix "Fort" for all permanent posts; that the title "barracks" be dropped, and that all purely local names be eliminated from the nomenclature of military posts.

In Batchelder's opinion, military posts should be named for military heroes. He presented a list of thirty-three posts, twenty-two of them west of the Mississippi, the names of which he favored changing.[27] Little came of the proposal. Only one of the western posts which he mentioned underwent a change of name. That was Angel Island, which became Fort McDowell in 1900.

In the brief biographies of military posts presented herein, an attempt has been made to provide certain information: date of estab-

[27] See *Annual Report of the Secretary of War for the Year 1893* (Washington, D. C., 1893), I, 220. Batchelder might have added Forts Omaha, Sidney, Townsend, and Yellowstone to his list.

lishment, location, reason for establishment, name, rank, and military unit of the person establishing the post, origin of post name, present status or date of abandonment, and disposition of the military reservation if a reservation existed. Other pertinent information, such as changes in name and location, has been included. It is recognized that a compilation of this nature must contend with certain problems and that it has definite limitations. For the Spanish presidios an exact date of establishment is available in most instances. For the posts established by France, Mexico, and the Republic of Texas even the year may sometimes be questioned. Official records do not always agree about the date of establishment of some United States posts, particularly in the period prior to 1846. In his report for 1875, Secretary of War William W. Belknap pointed up this fact:

> With the exception of the few official items contained in the archives of the War Department, the only information concerning the early history of our old military posts is gained from vague traditions and personal reminiscences. No records showing when, why, or by whom a military post was established, or who have been its commaders, or the origin of its name, in many instances, can be found by any officer assigned to its command.[28]

Moreover, for United States posts, the date given in various documents may be the date the post was authorized, the date the site was selected, the date the first troops arrived at the site, or the date actual construction of the post commenced. Wherever possible, the date of establishment given herein is the date the site was first occupied by troops.

When it comes to location, there is less diversity of opinion; yet, even for some United States posts, the exact location is disputed. The question of who actually established a post does not always re-

[28] *Annual Report of the Secretary of War on the Operations of the Department for the Fiscal Year Ending June 30, 1875* (Washington, D. C., 1875), I, 5.

sult in a clear answer. The intent has been to credit the commander of the troops first occupying the site with being the establisher. However, in a few cases, this information has not been found. This is particularly true for the posts of the Texas Republic, but also pertains to some of the Spanish, French, and Mexican posts and to a few United States posts. The origin of the name of a post is rarely in doubt, although in a few cases alternate possibilities are given. Where the origin of a name is abundantly obvious, it has not been reiterated. Examples of this are Fort Humboldt, California, located on Humboldt Bay, and Fort James, South Dakota, located on the James River. In only six cases (Forts Cavagnolle, Kansas; Cross, North Dakota; Riley and Lancaster, Texas; Vose, California; and Wayne, Oklahoma) is no origin given or implied in the following post biographies.

The dates of the abandonment of Spanish presidios are not often in question, but those of the French, Mexican, and Texan posts are less decisive. For the United States posts alternate dates are sometimes applicable. In many instances, when the garrison was withdrawn, a caretaker unit or individual remained to conclude the affairs of the post or to protect property. Even after the post was abandoned, the military reservation was sometimes retained for many years. Herein, the term "abandoned" refers to the final withdrawal of the garrison, even though the decision not to regarrison may not have been made at the time.

An effort has been made to include all presidios and military forts west of the Mississippi which were ever, at any time or in any sense, officially so designated. Fort Armstrong, Illinois, has been included even though it occupied an island in the Mississippi and so was west of only a part of the river. Forts established by militia and volunteer units have been included, though without assurance that the listing in this category approaches completeness. French forts offer a problem in that most of them were primarily trading centers, irregularly protected by a small garrison or not garrisoned at all. The forts of the Republic of Texas present a difficulty of another sort. The Texas archives have twice been visited by destructive fires, leaving many gaps in the information available for the period of the republic. Finally, the decision to include a post on the grounds that it is or was commonly called a fort must be arbitrary. Doubtless some posts have been included undeservedly, while others more deserving of inclusion have been omitted. Though arbitrary, the decision to include or to omit has some basis. If a post is frequently shown as a fort on present-day maps or so referred to in present-day writings—and here popular rather than scholarly publications are considered—it has been included.[29] Also, a good many posts were called forts, even though never officially so designated, in official documents or in the correspondence, diaries, and memoirs of the officers and men who were stationed at them. These, too, have been included. Any compilation of factual material of the nature of this undertaking lends itself to errors of fact, sins of omission, and divergent interpretations, even though interpretation enters into it in a minor form. The errors and omissions are regretted; the interpretation must stand on its own.

In the following listing the posts have, for convenience, been arranged alphabetically within the boundaries of the present states. All officers are identified by their regular rank and service unit at the specific date to which reference is made. The one exception is the

[29] Contemporary maps prepared by the military, especially those prepared by officers of the Corps of Engineers or the Topographical Engineers, are usually reasonably accurate in nomenclature and location of posts. The maps in the *Official Atlas of the Civil War* (3 vols., Washington, D. C., 1891–95) as they pertain to areas of the West not actively engaged in the conflict contain some notable inaccuracies. A few examples will indicate the nature of these. Fort Ter-Waw is shown consistently some distance north of the California-Oregon boundary. Fort Bragg, California, is shown as Camp Bragg. Fort Lyon, New Mexico, appears as Fort Fauntleroy. There is no evidence for the change in the designation of Bragg, while there is clear evidence for the change of Fauntleroy to Lyon. Finally, Los Lunas, the proper designation, is shown as Fort Los Lunas. The post, always intended to be temporary, occupied rented quarters and in none of the contemporary writings consulted was called a fort.

brevet second lieutenant, a rank conferred upon graduates of the United States Military Academy at the time of graduation prior to the Civil War. No distinction is made in rank between the volunteer and regular service. Geographical locations of posts are approximate rather than exact.

Finally, I wish to express my appreciation to the many persons who have encouraged and aided me in this undertaking. I wish, also, to acknowledge the grant given me by the University of Wichita Committee on Research.

CONTENTS

ILLUSTRATIONS

MAPS

FORTS OF THE WEST

ARIZONA

APACHE. Established May 16, 1870. Located south of the Mogollon Plateau on the south bank of the east fork of the White River, near the present town of Fort Apache, on what is now the Fort Apache Indian Reservation. Intended to control the Coyotero Apaches. It was situated at the terminus of a military road built into the Coyotero Apache country and was designed to replace Camp Goodwin. Established by Major John Green, 1st U.S. Cavalry. Originally a temporary post known as Camp Ord, for Brigadier General Edward O. C. Ord, the name was changed to Camp Mogollon on August 1, 1870; Camp Thomas, for Major General George H. Thomas, on September 12, 1870; and Camp Apache on February 2, 1871. It became a permanent post in 1873, and on April 5, 1879, it was designated Fort Apache. Abandoned as a military post in 1924, it was turned over to the Indian Service to be used as a school.

ARAVAIPA. See Breckinridge.

BARRETT. Established April 19, 1862. Located at the Pima villages on the south side of the Gila River, a little above the mouth of the Santa Cruz, near the present town of Sacaton. Established by Lieutenant Colonel Joseph R. West, 1st California Infantry, by order of Colonel James H. Carleton, 1st California Infantry, and advanced units of the California Column en route to New Mexico. The fortification consisted primarily of an earthwork at Ammi White's flour mill. When completed, it served as a sub-depot and supply station. The post was named for Second Lieutenant James Barrett, 1st Cali-

3

fornia Cavalry, killed in a skirmish with Confederate troops near Picacho Pass on April 15, 1862. Abandoned on July 23, 1862.

BOWIE. Established July 28, 1862. Located in the Chiricahua Mountains on the eastern approaches to Apache Pass, south of the present town of Bowie. The post was intended to protect travel along the Tucson-Mesilla road and to guard the important spring located nearby against both Indians and possible Confederate action. Established by Major Theodore A. Coult, 5th California Infantry. Originally called a fort, it was later designated Camp Bowie, then again, on April 5, 1879, Fort Bowie. Named for Colonel George W. Bowie, 5th California Infantry. In 1868 the post was moved from its original site to a new location on a nearby hill. Abandoned on October 17, 1894. The military reservation was transferred to the Interior Department on November 14, 1894. In 1896 the land was sold at public auction to local farmers. The post buildings were sold on June 20, 1911.

BRECKINRIDGE. Established May 8, 1860.[1] Located on the north side of Aravaipa Creek at its junction with the San Pedro River. The post was intended to control the Apache Indians and protect the emigrant route across southern Arizona. Established by Captain Richard S. Ewell, 1st U.S. Dragoons. First designated Fort Aravaipa (Aravaypa), then, on August 6, 1860, Fort Breckinridge, in honor of Vice-President John C. Breckinridge. The garrison was withdrawn and the post burned on July 10, 1861, as a result of the invasion of Arizona by a Confederate force from Texas. Reoccupied May 18, 1862, by Lieutenant Colonel Joseph R. West, 1st California Infantry. On May 24, 1862, the name of the post was changed to Fort Stanford, in honor of Governor Leland Stanford of California.

[1] In various sources the date given for the establishment of the post varies from 1856 to 1860. It is highly improbable that it could have been established earlier than July, 1859. The date given herein seems acceptable. See James R. Hastings, "The Tragedy at Camp Grant in 1871," *Arizona and the West*, Vol. I (Summer, 1959), 146–47, note 1.

Fort Defiance

Camp Hualpai

Fort Mojave

Fort Whipple • • Fort Verde

Colorado

River

Río Verde

Fort Apache

Fort McDowell

Salt River

Fort Goodwin
Fort Thomas

Gila River

Fort Barrett

Fort Breckinridge

Fort Grant II

Colorado River

Gila River

Santa Cruz River

San Pedro River

Tucson •
(Fort Lowell)

Fort Bowie

0   50   100
MILES

Tubac and Presidio   Fort Huachuca

Camp Mason
Camp Calabasas

Camp Crittenden
Fort Buchanan

5

The troops were withdrawn on June 29, 1862, and the site was not again permanently garrisoned until after the close of the Civil War. In October, 1865, a camp was established on the banks of the San Pedro River near the site of Fort Breckinridge by Colonel Thomas F. Wright, 2nd California Infantry. On November 1, 1865, it was designated Camp Grant, in honor of Lieutenant General Ulysses S. Grant. In the summer of 1866 the camp was partly destroyed by flooding and was rebuilt on the site of Fort Breckinridge. Camp Grant served to restrain the Apaches, encourage settlement in the San Pedro Valley, and protect travel across southern Arizona. It was never officially designated a fort. The site was considered too malarial and the post was abandoned on March 31, 1873. The military reservation was transferred to the Interior Department on July 22, 1884.

BUCHANAN. Established about March 7, 1857, to replace Camp Moore (see Calabasas). Located on a low plateau on the right bank of the Sonoita River about twenty-five miles east of Tubac and between the present towns of Patagonia and Sonoita. Intended to control the Apache Indians and protect the travel routes across southern Arizona. Established by Major Enoch Steen, 1st U.S. Dragoons. The post was designated Fort Buchanan in honor of President James Buchanan. The site was extremely unhealthful and the post was considered to be the worst situated and most poorly constructed in the Southwest. It consisted of a few scattered buildings, some built of adobe and some of wood, without even a stockade about them, being arranged more like a village than a military post. Evacuated and burned on July 23, 1861, as a result of the invasion of Arizona by a Confederate force from Texas. The Confederates occupied the site for a time, evacuating it in turn, probably on May 4, 1862, upon the approach of the California Column. The United States flag was raised over the post, but all of the buildings had been destroyed and

6

Brigadier General James H. Carleton, commanding the California Column, did not consider it to be of military value, hence it was not regarrisoned. Camp Crittenden (*q.v.*) was established near the site on May 4, 1868.

CALABASAS, PRESIDIO NEAR. Probably built in 1837. Located on the Manuel María Gándara grant near the mission *visita* of San Cayetano de Calabazas on the Santa Cruz River about nine miles north of Nogales. Erected by Gándara to protect his property against the Apache Indians. After the Gadsden Purchase the stone buildings, which were in good condition, were occupied by Major Enoch Steen and four companies of 1st U.S. Dragoons on November 27, 1856. They formed a part of what was first called Camp Calabazas then Camp Moore, probably for Captain Benjamin D. Moore, killed on December 6, 1846, in the Battle of San Pascual. Abandoned early in March, 1857, when Fort Buchanan was established. The old presidio was briefly occupied in 1862 by a Confederate force. Camp Mason (*q.v.*) was established nearby in 1865, and Camp Cameron, also, was in existence in this vicinity from October 1, 1866, to March 7, 1867.

CANBY. See Fort Defiance.

CRITTENDEN. Established May 4, 1868. Located half a mile northeast of the former Fort Buchanan and a quarter of a mile northwest of the source of the Sonoita River. Intended to control the Apache Indians and to protect the settlers in the general vicinity as well as to guard the Sonora frontier. Established by Captain Stephen G. Whipple, 32nd U.S. Infantry. Some of the buildings of Fort Buchanan were repaired for temporary use. Properly called Camp Crittenden, the post was never officially designated a fort. Named for Colonel Thomas L. Crittenden, 32nd U.S. Infantry, who had recommended the establishment of a post on the site. Abandoned on June 1, 1873, because the site was considered unhealthful. The military reservation was transferred to the Interior Department on July 22, 1884.

DEFIANCE. Established September 18, 1851. Located at the mouth of Cañon Bonito on the west side of Black Creek, thirty-five miles northwest of the town of Gallup, New Mexico, by present-day highway. The post was located near fertile valleys and good water. Intended as a base from which to control the Navaho Indians. Established by Major Electus Backus, 3rd U.S. Infantry, on a site selected by Lieutenant Colonel Edwin Vose Sumner, 1st U.S. Dragoons, commanding the Department of New Mexico. This was the first United States Army fort in what is now Arizona. Abandoned on April 25, 1861, when the garrison was withdrawn to Fort Fauntleroy (see Fort Wingate II), New Mexico. The post was reoccupied on July 25, 1863, by troops under the command of Colonel Kit Carson, 1st New Mexico Infantry. It served as a base for the Navaho campaign which led to the "Long Walk." The name was changed to Fort Canby in honor of Brigadier General Edward R. S. Canby, a former commander of the Department of New Mexico. Abandoned on October 20, 1864, at the conclusion of the Navaho campaign. Fort Defiance became the Navaho Indian Agency in 1868 and continues to serve as agency headquarters.

GOODWIN. Established June 18, 1864. Located south of the Gila River in the Tularosa Valley some seven miles west of the present town of Fort Thomas. (The original Camp Goodwin, located on the Gila thirty-three miles east of Fort Goodwin, was established on June 11, 1864. It was a temporary camp, occupied until a permanent site was selected.) Established in connection with a general campaign to subdue the Apache Indians and maintained to protect the settlements and routes of travel in the area. Established by Colonel Edwin A. Rigg, 1st California Infantry, by order of Brigadier General James H. Carleton, on a site previously selected by Major

Nelson H. Davis, assistant inspector general. Named in honor of John N. Goodwin, first territorial governor of Arizona. Originally called a fort, the post was later designated Camp Goodwin. The site was considered too malarial—indeed, the most unhealthful in the territory—and the post was abandoned on March 14, 1871. The post then served for a time as sub-agency for the San Carlos Apache Reservation. The military reservation was transferred to the Interior Department on July 22, 1884.

GRANT I. See Breckinridge.

GRANT II. Established December 19, 1872, in anticipation of the abandonment of Camp Grant (see Breckinridge). Located on a mesa at the head of Sulphur Spring (Grant) Creek Valley, about two miles from the western base of Mount Graham, some twenty miles southwest of the present town of Safford. The site was selected by Major William B. Royall, 5th U.S. Cavalry, who also established the post. The post was designed to control the Apache Indians and to protect the settlers in the area. Originally called Camp Grant, the post was designated a fort on April 5, 1879. Named for President Ulysses S. Grant. The garrison was withdrawn in 1898 to participate in the Spanish-American War, and the post was not regarrisoned. Abandoned as a military post on October 4, 1905, except for a caretaker. The post was transferred to the state of Arizona in 1912, and the buildings are now occupied by the state industrial school for boys.

HUACHUCA. Established February 12, 1877. Located at the mouth of Central (Post) Canyon toward the northeast end of the Huachuca Mountains, west of the San Pedro River and about fifteen miles north of the Mexican border. Intended to protect settlers and travelers from the Apache Indians. Established by Captain Samuel M. Whitside, 6th U.S. Cavalry, by order of Colonel August V. Kautz, 8th U.S. Infantry, commanding the department. The post, originally a camp, became permanent on January 21, 1878, and was designated a fort in 1882. It saw little activity after the capture of Geronimo until it became a base of supplies and patrols during the early years of the Mexican Revolution. On February 15, 1949, the post was transferred to the state of Arizona to be used by the National Guard and the state Fish and Game Commission. It was reactivated in 1951, deactivated in 1953, and again reactivated in February, 1954. It is still operative.

HUALPAI. Established May 9, 1869. Located on a mesa above Walnut Creek, one and one-half miles southeast of Aztec Pass and some forty miles northwest of Prescott. The post was located on the toll road between Prescott and Hardyville in the country of the Hualpai Indians. Established by Major William R. Price, 8th U.S. Cavalry. Originally called Camp Toll Gate, its name was changed to Camp Hualpai on August 1, 1870. The post was never officially designated a fort, although it was sometimes so called in official correspondence and reports. Abandoned on July 31, 1873. The reservation, although never officially declared, was transferred to the Interior Department on April 22, 1874.

LOWELL. Established May 20, 1862. Originally located in the city of Tucson, where it occupied several successive sites. Established by Lieutenant Colonel Joseph R. West, 1st California Infantry. The post was a supply depot for southern Arizona and was later a base of operations against hostile Apaches and a center for escort duties. On March 19, 1873, the post was moved to a site south of Rillito Creek, selected by Lieutenant Colonel Eugene A. Carr, 4th U.S. Cavalry. Originally called the Post of Tucson, on August 29, 1866, it became Camp Lowell, and on April 5, 1879, it was designated Fort Lowell. Named for Brigadier General Charles R. Lowell, who died on October 20, 1864, of wounds received at Cedar Creek, Virginia. Abandoned on September 15, 1864; reoccupied in May, 1865;

made a permanent post on August 29, 1866; and finally abandoned on April 10, 1891. The military reservation was transferred to the Interior Department on March 6, 1891. The old fort, now within the city limits of Tucson, has been partly restored.

McDOWELL. Established September 7, 1865. Located on the west bank of the Río Verde, seven miles above its junction with the Salt River. Intended to control the Yavapai Indians and various Apache groups and to protect the overland route. Established by Lieutenant Colonel Clarence E. Bennett, 1st California Cavalry. Originally called Camp Verde, it was soon renamed Camp McDowell. On April 5, 1879, it was designated a fort. Named in honor of Major General Irvin McDowell, commanding the department. Ordered abandoned on June 18, 1890. The last detachment of troops left the post on January 17, 1891. It was transferred to the Interior Department on October 4, 1890, and became the agency for the Yavapai and some of the Pima Indians.

MASON. Established August 21, 1865. Located at Calabasas on the Santa Cruz River, thirteen miles south of Tubac. It replaced the post at Tubac and was important because of its position on the main route of travel to Guaymas and other points in Sonora, Mexico. Established by Colonel Charles W. Lewis, 7th California Infantry, on a site selected by Brigadier General John S. Mason, commanding the District of Arizona, for whom the post was named. Although it was called a fort, it was never officially so designated. On September 6, 1866, it became Camp McKee. Abandoned on October 1, 1866, because of the prevalence of disease at the post. The garrison was transferred to Tubac.

MOJAVE. Established April 19, 1859. Located on the left bank of the Colorado River at Beal's Crossing near the head of the Mojave Valley opposite the present town of Needles, California. Intended to control the Mohave and Paiute Indians and to protect the emigrant route to California. The site was selected and the post established by Major William Hoffman, 6th U.S. Infantry. Originally called Camp Colorado by Major Hoffman, the post was designated Fort Mojave on April 28, 1859, by Captain Lewis A. Armistead, 6th U.S. Infantry, commander of the post, charged with erecting permanent quarters. Following the Civil War it was officially designated Camp Mojave; then, on April 5, 1879, it again became Fort Mojave. Abandoned on May 31, 1861, by order of Brigadier General Edwin Vose Sumner. The garrison was transferred to Los Angeles because of disaffection in southern California occasioned by the outbreak of the Civil War. Reoccupied on May 19, 1863, by order of Brigadier General George Wright. Finally abandoned in 1890. The military reservation was transferred to the Interior Department—its buildings to be used as an Indian school—on September 29, 1890. The school was discontinued by the Indian Service in 1935, and the buildings were demolished in 1942.

QUIBURI, PRESIDIO OF SANTA CRUZ DE. Established in 1775 or 1776. Located west of the San Pedro River near the Indian village of Quíburi and the present town of Fairbank, by order of Colonel Hugo Oconor. Established by the garrison transferred from the Presidio of Terrenate, Sonora, in an effort to bolster defenses against the Apache Indians. Abandoned in 1780 because of inability to cope with the Apaches and the continuous losses sustained at their hands.

STANFORD. See Breckinridge.

THOMAS. Established August 12, 1876. Located three-quarters of a mile south of the Gila River on the site of the present town of Geronimo. Established by Captain Clarence M. Bailey, 8th U.S. Infantry, on a site selected by Colonel August V. Kautz, 8th U.S. Infantry, commanding the department. In 1878 the post was moved

View of Fort McDowell, Arizona, about 1886, showing the
officers' headquarters, barracks, and parade grounds. The Río
Verde is in the distance at upper left.

Courtesy Arizona Pioneers' Historical Society Library

some five miles up the Gila to the site of the present town of Fort
Thomas. Established in connection with the removal of the Chiri-
cahua Apaches to the San Carlos Reservation and to replace Camp
Goodwin. First called New Post on the Gila, the name was changed to
Camp Thomas in September, 1876. The post was designated a fort in
1881. Named for Brigadier General Lorenzo Thomas, who died on
March 2, 1875. Abandoned on April 10, 1891. The military reserva-
tion was transferred to the Interior Department on December 3, 1892.

TUBAC, PRESIDIO OF SAN IGNACIO DE. Established in 1752. Located at the town of Tubac. Established by Diego Ortiz de Parilla, governor and captain general of the provinces of Sinaloa and Sonora, following the suppression of the Pima uprising of 1751. Designed to protect the missions, peaceful Indians, and settlers of the area. The presidio was relocated at Tucson in 1776, following the recommendation of the Marqués de Rubí, who inspected the presidio in 1767 and decided that the population of Tubac was sufficient to render the maintenance of a garrison there unnecessary. For a time after the removal of the troops, the town maintained a garrison of Pima Indians. Tubac is a Pima or Papago word. *Bac* means "house" or "ruin," but the meaning of the prefix *tu* seems to be unknown.

TUBAC. Established July 20, 1862. Located at the town of Tubac. Established primarily as a supply depot, the post was never officially designated a fort although it was sometimes so called in official documents. Established by order of Colonel Joseph R. West, 1st California Infantry. Abandoned by order of Brigadier General John S. Mason, in August, 1865, and the garrison withdrawn to establish Camp Mason. Reoccupied in October, 1866, when Camp McKee (Mason) was abandoned. Finally abandoned in 1868, and the garrison transferred to Camp Crittenden.

TUCSON, PRESIDIO OF SAN AGUSTÍN DE. Established in 1776. The garrison previously stationed at Tubac was removed to this post, marking the effective beginning of Tucson as a Spanish settlement. A small detachment, or mission guard, from the Presidio of Tubac had been maintained in the area previously. The name is also given as San Agustín de Tuquisón. Tucson is derived from the Papago Indian *Chuk Shon*, black base, and refers to the present Signal Mountain, which is darker at the base than at the summit. Following the Gadsden Purchase, Mexican troops remained at the presidio until

March 10, 1856. The presidio was then garrisoned briefly by four companies of 1st U.S. Dragoons, but they were soon withdrawn to occupy the presidio near Calabasas.

VERDE. Established in January, 1864. Originally located on the west bank of the Río Verde about thirty-five miles east of Prescott. Intended to provide protection for the newly opened Prescott mining district. Established by Lieutenant Colonel J. Francisco Chávez, 1st New Mexico Infantry. The post was originally an outpost of Fort Whipple. It was first occupied by regular troops in September, 1866. The site was considered unhealthful and unsuitable, and in the spring of 1871 the post was moved four miles south and about one mile west of the Verde, half a mile below the mouth of Beaver Creek. Originally called Camp Lincoln, for President Lincoln, its name was changed to Camp Verde on November 23, 1868, to avoid confusion with Camp Lincoln, Dakota Territory. On April 5, 1879, it was designated Fort Verde. Abandoned on April 10, 1890, because the Indian menace no longer existed. The military reservation was transferred to the Interior Department on October 15, 1890.

WHIPPLE. Established December 21, 1863. Originally located in the Chino Valley at Del Río Spring near the Verde, about twenty-four miles north of Prescott. On May 18, 1864, it was relocated on the left bank of Granite Creek, immediately northeast of Prescott, the newly established territorial capital. (The former site was then called Camp Clark, in honor of John A. Clark, Surveyor General, New Mexico Territory.) Established by Major Edward B. Willis, 1st California Infantry, by order of Brigadier General James H. Carleton. Intended to protect the newly opened gold-mining district. Named in honor of Major General Amiel W. Whipple, who died on May 7, 1863, of wounds received in the Battle of Chancellorsville. As a first lieutenant in the Corps of Topographical Engineers,

Whipple, in 1853, surveyed the route from Albuquerque through the country in which gold was later discovered. Whipple Depot was established adjacent to Fort Whipple when the post was relocated on Granite Creek and became a separate command on October 13, 1870. On April 5, 1879, Fort Whipple and Prescott Barracks were consolidated and the combined post was designated Whipple Barracks. The post was discontinued in March, 1898, except for a caretaker detachment, but was regarrisoned in 1902. The garrison was withdrawn on February 25, 1913, and the post again placed in the hands of a caretaker. In 1922 the military reservation was transferred to the Secretary of the Treasury to be used by the Public Health Service. It is now being used as a Veterans Administration hospital.

ARKANSAS

ARKANSAS POST. Established in 1686. Located originally on the north bank of the Arkansas River a short distance above its mouth. Because of flooding or for strategic reasons, the post was relocated on several occasions, remaining always on the north bank of the river but occupying sites from near the mouth to as much as fifty miles above the mouth of the river. The original French establishment was made by six men detailed for the purpose by Henry de Tonty. It developed into a settlement, a trading post, and, much of the time, was a garrisoned military post. In 1768, when the post was transferred to Spain, it was located some forty miles above the mouth of the Arkansas, on a deep bend of the river where the town of Arkansas Post is located today. At that time it consisted of a stockade and bastions, stood some two hundred yards from the river, and was garrisoned by two officers and thirty men. Under Spanish control the name of the military post was changed to Fort San Carlos. After the parish of San Estevan was established at the post, the fort was called—at least in the years 1797–98—the Fuerte de San Estevan de Arkanzas. The post served Spain as a center of contact with the Indians of the entire lower Arkansas valley.

Following the purchase of Louisiana by the United States, the post was officially transferred to First Lieutenant James B. Many, Regiment of Artillerists, on March 23, 1804. In 1805 a government Indian factory was established at the post; however, the trading facility was discontinued in 1810 because of the decline of business. In 1819, Arkansas Post became the first territorial capital of Arkansas and so remained for about two years. Fort Hindman was established at Arkansas Post by the Confederacy. It was taken by joint action of the Union army and navy on January 11, 1863. The town of Arkansas Post still exists.

ROOTS, LOGAN H. The establishment of the post was provided by an act of Congress dated April 23, 1892. Located on the left side of the Arkansas River, immediately above the town of Little Rock. Construction commenced in 1893, and the post was first garrisoned in 1896. It was designated Fort Logan H. Roots on April 22, 1897. Named for Captain Logan Holt Roots, commissary of subsistence, Volunteers, who died May 30, 1893. Construction of the post was discontinued in 1898 when the troops there stationed were ordered to Puerto Rico. A small garrison was maintained until World War I, when Camp Pike was established nearby. Since 1921 the facility has been a Veterans Administration hospital.

SAN CARLOS. See Arkansas Post.

SAN ESTEVAN DE ARKANZAS. See Arkansas Post.

SMITH. Established December 1, 1817. Located on Belle Point, a promontory on the right bank of the Poteau River near its junction with the Arkansas. Established as one of the cordon of military posts along the eastern edge of the Indian country. Intended to pro-

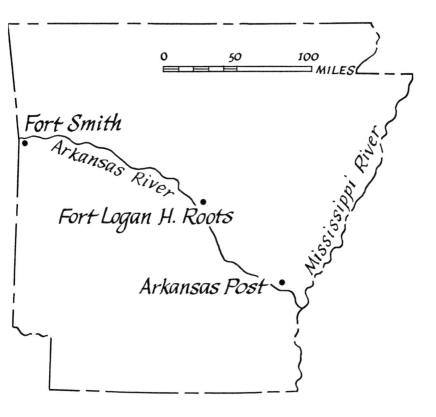

tect travelers and trading posts and to control the Indians, especially the Osages and Cherokees. Fort Smith was on land belonging to the Choctaw Nation in accordance with the 1820 Treaty of Doak's Stand. The Choctaw Strip, including the site of Fort Smith, was ceded to the United States on January 20, 1825. By an act of Congress in February, 1905, the state of Arkansas extended its boundaries westward to include the site of the fort. Established by Brevet Major

17

Stephen H. Long,[1] Topographical Engineers, and Captain William Bradford, Regiment of Riflemen, on a site selected by Major Long. First called Belle Point and Camp Smith, the post was designated a fort in 1818. Named in honor of Colonel Thomas A. Smith, Regiment of Riflemen, commanding the department, who had ordered its establishment. Abandoned April 9, 1824, except for a caretaker detachment, when the garrison was removed to Fort Gibson, Oklahoma.

The site was reoccupied by troops commanded by Second Lieutenant Gabriel J. Rains, 7th U.S. Infantry, on April 26, 1831, in connection with the removal of the Choctaw Indians from Mississippi. At this time it was considered that Fort Smith was located at the highest point safe for navigation on the Arkansas River. When reoccupied, the original post was in ruinous condition. Again abandoned on June 16, 1834, when the garrison was withdrawn to establish Fort Coffee, Oklahoma. Re-established on July 27, 1838, by Captain Benjamin L. E. Bonneville, 7th U.S. Infantry. The post was completely rebuilt immediately adjacent to the original site. The temporary camp occupied while the post was under construction was called Camp Thomas, for Major Charles Thomas, Quartermaster's Department, in charge of construction. Cantonment Belknap, named for Captain William G. Belknap, 3rd U.S. Infantry, was established nearby. The new post, occupied on May 15, 1846, included a stone fort, pentagonal in form.

Fort Smith was seized by troops of the state of Arkansas on April 24, 1861. Retaken by Union troops under Major General James G. Blunt, September 1, 1863. It was again evacuated in December, 1864, and reoccupied after the Civil War. The post was permanently abandoned on July 19, 1871, and the garrison transferred to Fort Gibson. The military reservation was transferred to the Interior Department on March 25, 1871. A portion of the post has been reconstructed and is now a National Historic Site.

[1] Long had been a second lieutenant in the Corps of Engineers, until he transferred to the Topographical Engineers with brevet rank.

CALIFORNIA

ALCATRAZ. Alcatraz Island was declared a military reservation by executive order on November 6, 1850. Located in San Francisco Bay, facing the Golden Gate, Alcatraz Island formed part of the defensive system designed to protect the entrance to the bay. Construction of fortifications on the island was commenced in 1853 under the supervision of First Lieutenant Zealous Bates Tower, Corps of Engineers. The island was first garrisoned on December 30, 1859. The fortifications consisted of batteries and a citadel. The official designation of the post was Alcatraz Island, although it was often referred to as Fort Alcatraz. Alcatraz Island became a United States military prison in 1907 and a federal prison for incorrigible civilians in 1934.

ANDERSON. Established in March, 1862. Located on the right bank of Redwood Creek in Humboldt County. Intended to protect the area between Redwood Creek and the Klamath River from Indian hostilities. Established by Captain Charles D. Douglas, 2nd California Infantry, by order of Colonel Francis J. Lippitt, 2nd California Infantry, commanding the District of Humboldt. Named for Colonel Allen L. Anderson, 8th California Infantry. The post was never officially designated a fort, although it was so called in the orders for its establishment and referred to as such in official correspondence. Abandoned late in 1862, the post was later used as a camp during the conduct of operations against the Indians in 1864. Permanently abandoned on August 9, 1866.

BAKER I. Established in March, 1862. Located some twenty-three miles east of the town of Hydesville on the west bank of the Van Dusen Fork of the Eel River in Humboldt County. Intended to protect the area between the Eel River and the Mad River from Indian hostilities. Established by Captain Thomas E. Ketcham, 3rd California Infantry, by order of Colonel Francis J. Lippitt. Named for

Colonel Edward D. Baker, 71st Pennsylvania Infantry, who was killed on October 21, 1861, in the Battle of Ball's Bluff, Virginia. Baker had resigned his seat in the United States Senate, where he represented California, to serve in the U.S. Army. The post was never officially designated a fort, although it was so called in the orders for its establishment and referred to as such in official correspondence. Lieutenant Colonel Stephen G. Whipple, 1st California Infantry, commanding the District of Humboldt, recommended the abandonment of the post on September 7, 1863, and its replacement by Camp Iaqua. It was abandoned before the end of the year.

BAKER II. The original military works on the site were erected during the Civil War. Located on the north side of the Golden Gate, opposite Fort Winfield Scott, on Lime Point. The post formed part of the defensive system for San Francisco Bay. The fortification was called Lime Point until April 29, 1897, when it was designated Fort Baker. Named for Colonel Edward D. Baker (see Fort Baker I). In the 1890's the post was rebuilt and the armament modernized. It was permanently garrisoned for the first time by a battery of artillery in June, 1897.

BIDWELL. Established in 1863. Located at the present town of Fort Bidwell, toward the northern end of Surprise Valley, in the northeastern corner of the state. Established to hold the Indians of the area in check. The post was strategically located to protect the roads leading into eastern Oregon and Idaho. Named for John Bidwell, a major in the California Volunteers during the Mexican War and a pioneer settler in California. Abandoned early in 1865. Re-established on July 17, 1865, by order of Major General Irvin McDowell, commanding the department, on a site selected by Major Robert S. Williamson, Corps of Engineers. The original post was called Camp Bidwell. When it was re-established, General McDowell referred to it as a fort, but it was officially designated Camp Bidwell

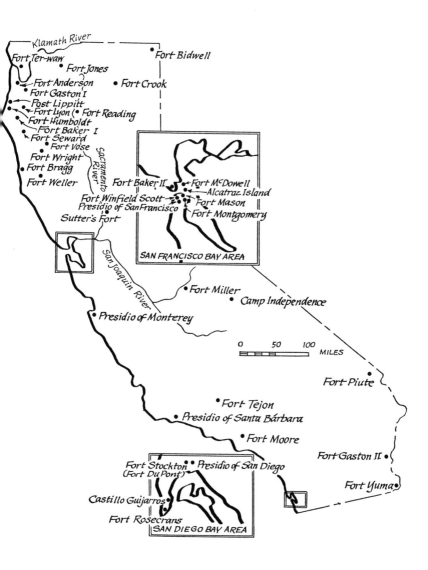

Klamath River
Fort Ter-waw
Fort Jones
Fort Bidwell
Fort Anderson
Fort Crook
Fort Gaston I
Post Lippitt
Fort Lyon • Fort Reading
Fort Humboldt
Fort Baker I
Fort Seward
Fort Vose
Fort Wright
Fort Bragg
Fort Weller
Fort Baker II
Fort McDowell
Alcatraz Island
Fort Winfield Scott
Fort Mason
Presidio of San Francisco
Fort Montgomery
Sutter's Fort
Sacramento River
San Joaquin River
SAN FRANCISCO BAY AREA
Fort Miller
Camp Independence
Presidio of Monterey

0   50   100   MILES

Fort Piute
Fort Tejon
Presidio of Santa Bárbara
Fort Moore
Fort Gaston II
Fort Stockton   Presidio of San Diego
(Fort Du Pont)
Fort Yuma
Castillo Guijarros
Fort Rosecrans
SAN DIEGO BAY AREA

21

until April 5, 1879, when it became Fort Bidwell. The military reservation was transferred to the Interior Department on November 22, 1890; however, the post was garrisoned until October 21, 1893. It then became a government Indian school and headquarters for the Fort Bidwell Indian Reservation.

BEALE. See Piute.

BLANCO. See Presidio of San Francisco.

BRAGG. Established June 11, 1857. Located to the north of the mouth of the Noyo River at the present town of Fort Bragg in Mendocino County. The post was established within the boundaries of the Mendocino Indian Reservation and was intended both to control and to protect the Indians of the area. Established by First Lieutenant Horatio Gates Gibson, 3rd U.S. Artillery. Named for Captain Braxton Bragg, 3rd U.S. Artillery, and later a general in the Confederate Army. Although there was some agitation to change the name, it was retained during the Civil War. Abandoned on October 19, 1864. The Mendocino Indian Reservation was discontinued in March, 1866, and the land opened to settlement a few years later.

CROOK. Established July 1, 1857. Located on the north bank of the Fall River, seven miles above its confluence with the Pit in Shasta County. Intended to protect the area from hostile Indians. Established by Captain John W. T. Gardiner, 1st U.S. Dragoons. Originally called Camp Hollenbush, for Assistant Surgeon Calvin G. Hollenbush, the post was designated Fort Crook in 1857. Named for First Lieutenant George Crook, 4th U.S. Infantry. The garrison was withdrawn in May, 1866, except for a small detachment from Fort Bidwell, of which Fort Crook now became a sub-post. Abandoned on July 1, 1869. On February 15, 1881, the military reservation, never formally declared, was restored to the public domain.

DU PONT. See Stockton.

22

GASTON I. Established December 4, 1858. Located in the Hoopa Valley on the west bank of the Trinity River, about fourteen miles above its juncture with the Klamath in Humboldt County. Designed to control and protect the Indians of the area, including those of the Hoopa Valley Reservation. Established by Captain Edmund Underwood, 4th U.S. Infantry. Named for Second Lieutenant William Gaston, 1st U.S. Dragoons, killed on May 17, 1858, during the expedition against the Spokane Indians. Originally called Fort Gaston, the post became a camp on January 1, 1867, and was again designated Fort Gaston on April 5, 1879. Abandoned on June 29, 1892. The military reservation was transferred to the Interior Department on February 11, 1892, for the use of the Indian Service.

GASTON II. Established in 1859. Located on the west bank of the Colorado River, about forty-five miles north of Fort Yuma by trail. Established by Captain Henry S. Burton, 3rd U.S. Artillery, to serve as a supply depot in connection with the establishment of Fort Mojave, Arizona. Intended as a temporary base only, the post was abandoned as soon as the stores were removed to Fort Mojave. It then served as an outpost of Fort Yuma and was garrisoned from time to time by small detachments as late as 1867. Presumably it was named for Second Lieutenant William Gaston (see Fort Gaston I).

GUIJARROS. In 1795, Punta de Guijarros (Ballast Point) was selected as the site for a fortification. Located on the east side of Point Loma near the entrance to San Diego Bay. The viceroy of New Spain, Antonio María de Bucareli y Ursúa, had expressed the wish that a fortification, similar to the Castillo de San Joaquín on San Francisco Bay, be erected at San Diego without cost to the crown. Timber was sent from Monterey, and Santa Barbara provided the axletrees and wheels for ten carts. Brick and tile were made at the presidio of San Diego and taken across the bay to the point by flatboat. In 1798 plans were made to build a road from the presidio to Point Guijarros. The fort was intended to mount ten guns. The post is referred to both as Castillo Guijarros and Fort Guijarros. Abandoned in 1838. By the time the United States occupied San Diego, the fortification had deteriorated considerably. The site was later occupied by Fort Rosecrans.

HUMBOLDT. Established January 30, 1853. Located on a bluff over-looking Humboldt Bay at Bucksport, now a part of Eureka. Established to protect the area from hostile Indians, it served also as a supply depot for the other northern California posts. Established by Captain Robert C. Buchanan, 4th U.S. Infantry. The garrison was withdrawn from Fort Humboldt in 1866 except for one company of artillery. The post then became a sub-depot, maintained primarily for the supply of Fort Gaston. On September 14, 1867, Brigadier General Irvin McDowell, commanding the department, stated that the company of artillery had been withdrawn and the post abandoned completely. The military reservation was transferred to the Interior Department on April 6, 1870.

INDEPENDENCE. Established on July 4, 1862. Located on the north side of Oak Creek, near its source in the Owens River Valley on the eastern slope of the Sierra Nevadas, about three miles west of the Owens River and two miles north of the town of Independence. Established by Lieutenant Colonel George S. Evans, 2nd California Cavalry. Intended to protect the settlers and the mining district from Indian depredations. The post was never officially designated a fort. Abandoned in 1864 and reoccupied in March, 1865. Finally abandoned on July 5, 1877. The military reservation was transferred to the Interior Department on July 22, 1884.

JONES. Established October 16, 1852. Located on the east side of Scott River at the present town of Fort Jones in Siskiyou County. The post may have been established by Second Lieutenant Joseph B. Collins, 4th U.S. Infantry. Intended to protect the gold-mining district from Indian depredations. Named for Colonel Roger Jones, adjutant general, U.S. Army, who died on July 15, 1852. Abandoned on June 25, 1858. The military reservation, although never officially declared, was transferred to the Interior Department on May 27, 1870.

LIPPITT. Established January 10, 1862. Located at Bucksport, now part of Eureka, on Humboldt Bay. Apparently, this was a temporary post established by Colonel Francis J. Lippitt, 2nd California Infantry, commanding the District of Humboldt, for whom the post was named, because of lack of facilities at Fort Humboldt to accommodate the enlarged command. The post consisted entirely of rented buildings and seems to have existed for not more than two months. It was never a fort.

LYON. Established in March, 1862. Located at Brehmer's Ranch on the right side of the Mad River about twenty miles east of Arcata. Intended to protect the area between the Mad River and Redwood Creek from Indian hostilities. Established by Captain Charles Heffernan, 2nd California Infantry, by order of Colonel Francis J. Lippitt, 2nd California Infantry. Named for Brigadier General Nathaniel Lyon, killed August 10, 1861, in the Battle of Wilson's Creek, Missouri. The post was never officially designated a fort, although it was so called in the orders for its establishment and referred to as such in official correspondence. Abandoned late in 1862.

McDOWELL. Reservation declared by executive order November 6, 1850; post established September 12, 1863. Located on Angel Island in San Francisco Bay. Fortification of Angel Island dates from the Civil War; it formed a part of the bay's defensive system. Camp Reynolds, named for Major General John F. Reynolds, killed on July 1, 1863, in the Battle of Gettysburg, was erected on the west side of the island in 1864 and served as post headquarters. Officially designated Angel Island until April 4, 1900, when it became Fort McDowell, for Major General Irvin McDowell. The island has at times served as prison camp, quarantine station, and immigration station. Since 1886, the site of a government-operated lighthouse. Discontinued as a military post in 1946, it is now a state park.

MASON. The sixty-eight-acre military reservation was set aside by executive order on November 6, 1850, but it was not occupied by troops until October 13, 1863. Located on San Francisco Bay, inside the Golden Gate, on Point San José. The site was originally occupied by a Spanish battery of six cannon, called Battery San José, established in 1797. The post, called simply Point San José, was not designated Fort Mason until November 25, 1882. Named for Colonel Richard Barnes Mason, 1st U.S. Dragoons, who was military governor of California, 1847–49. Fort Mason is the headquarters post for the San Francisco Port of Embarcation and serves as the post's passenger terminal.

MILLER. Established May 26, 1851. Located on the south side of the San Joaquin River, about 150 miles above Stockton, in the foothills of the Sierra Nevadas. The site is now covered by the waters of Millerton Lake. Established to protect the mining district, but especially to control the Indians between the Merced and Kern rivers. The first post on or near the site was Camp Barbour, established for the Indian commission appointed to negotiate treaties with the Indians, who were at that time in armed revolt. The camp, established April 14, 1851, by members of the Mariposa Battalion, a volunteer force, was named for George W. Barbour, one of the three commissioners. It is usually located on the site later occupied by Fort Miller, but it has also been placed on the south bank of the San Joaquin some ten miles below that site. The regular army post was established by Second Lieutenant Treadwell Moore, 2nd U.S. Infantry. Originally called Camp Miller, it was designated Fort Miller in 1852. Named for Major Albert S. Miller, 2nd U.S. Infantry. Abandoned in June, 1858, and reoccupied by order of Brigadier General George Wright, commanding the department, on August 22, 1863. Permanently abandoned on October 1, 1864, by order of Major General Irvin McDowell, except for one company of the 2nd California Cavalry, which occupied the post until December 1. The buildings were sold at auction by the government in 1866.

MONTEREY, PRESIDIO OF SAN CARLOS BORROMEO DE. Established June 3, 1770, at the same time that the Mission San Carlos Borromeo was founded. Located on Monterey Bay, adjacent to the town of Monterey. Established by Captain Gaspar de Portolá. In 1822 the Mexicans erected a fort or *castillo* about a mile northwest of the original presidio. The United States occupied Monterey on July 7, 1846. By order of Colonel Richard Barnes Mason, 1st U.S. Dragoons, commanding the department, a redoubt, in the form of a bastion, was built some seven hundred feet up the hill above the Mexican *castillo* in 1847. Construction of the redoubt was supervised by First Lieutenant Henry W. Halleck, Corps of Engineers. During the early period of United States occupancy, the post was known as "Post at Monterey" or "Monterey Redoubt." Evacuated in October, 1856. Although the military reservation was retained, the post was ungarrisoned throughout most of the second half of the nineteenth century. It was officially designated Presidio of Monterey in 1904.

MONTGOMERY. Established in July, 1846. Located at Yerba Buena (San Francisco). Established by Captain John Berrien Montgomery, commander of the U.S. sloop *Portsmouth*, immediately after the occupation of San Francisco Bay at the outset of the Mexican War, when it was rumored that a Mexican army was advancing to drive out the occupying force. On July 20, 1846, Captain Montgomery wrote, "We are progressing very well with the new fort . . . and

I have in view to erect a block house also, in a position to overlook the fort and command the town and hills in its rear." There are several references to Fort Montgomery in official correspondence of the period, but whether the fort, which was a temporary installation, was ever officially designated Fort Montgomery is not clear.

MOORE. Established January 12, 1847. Located on Fort Hill in Los Angeles. Erected for the purpose of maintaining control over Los Angeles, the principal center of population in California at the time of United States occupation. The site was selected and the plans prepared by First Lieutenant William H. Emory, Corps of Topographical Engineers, by order of Brigadier General Stephen Watts Kearny. The actual work of construction began on January 12, 1847, under Lieutenant Emory's direction. The plans were revised, and on April 23, 1847, a second fort was begun on the identical spot but twice as large as the original project. Construction of the second fort, an earthwork with embrasures for six cannon, was under the direction of Second Lieutenant John W. Davidson, 1st U.S. Dragoons. The post was designated Fort Moore on July 4, 1847, by Colonel John D. Stevenson, 1st New York Volunteers, commanding the southern district. Named for Captain Benjamin D. Moore, 1st U.S. Dragoons, killed in the Battle of San Pascual on December 6, 1846. The post was never completed. The garrison was withdrawn in 1848 and the post abandoned in 1849. The hill itself was removed in 1949.

PIUTE. Established in 1859. Located near Piute Springs in the Piute Mountains, approximately twenty-five miles west of Fort Mojave, Arizona. Established by Captain James H. Carleton, 1st U.S. Dragoons. Piute was one of a series of small posts erected to protect the route from San Bernardino across the Mojave Desert to Fort Mojave, a route used by both the military and travelers. The other posts along the route were designated either "camp" or "redoubt."

All were located near strategic water sources. During the Civil War the posts were garrisoned by detachments of California Volunteers, who, in addition to providing protection against the Indians, sought to intercept Confederate sympathizers attempting to make their way to Texas. The posts were evacuated at the close of the Civil War. Local demand for protection of the route, its importance enhanced by mining activity in western Arizona, led to the reoccupation of the posts in 1866. Captain Carleton called the post at Piute Springs, Fort Beale, for Lieutenant Edward F. Beale, U.S.N., who, in 1857–58, with his camel caravan, explored a route for a wagon road through the area. When the post was reoccupied in 1866, it was called Fort Piute. Abandoned, apparently, in 1868. Despite the fact that the post was called a fort, it was actually a sub-post, usually garrisoned by a detachment from Camp Cady, California.

POINT, FORT. See Winfield Scott.

READING. Established May 26, 1852. Located on the west side of Cow Creek, a tributary of the Sacramento River, a mile and a half above its mouth at the present town of Redding. Established to protect the mining district from Indian depredations. Established by First Lieutenant Nelson H. Davis, 2nd U.S. Infantry, by order of Colonel Ethan Allen Hitchcock, 2nd U.S. Infantry, commanding the department. Named for Major Pierson B. Reading, paymaster, California Volunteers, during the Mexican War, and a pioneer settler in California. The garrison was withdrawn on April 1, 1856, but the post was occasionally occupied until June 13, 1867. Completely abandoned on April 6, 1870. The buildings were sold, and on February 15, 1881, the military reservation was restored to the public domain.

ROSECRANS. The military reservation was established on February 26, 1852. The initial fortifications were located on Ballast Point at about the site of Castillo Guijarros. An earthwork, intended to protect the entrance to San Diego Bay, was commenced as early as May, 1873. The post was not designated Fort Rosecrans until 1899. Named for Brigadier General William S. Rosecrans, who died on March 11, 1898. The military reservation was transferred to the Navy Department on July 1, 1959.

SACRAMENTO. See Sutter's Fort.

SAN DIEGO, PRESIDIO OF. Established July 16, 1769, at the same time the Mission of San Diego was founded. Located on a hill overlooking San Diego Bay. Established by Captain Gaspar de Portolá. The establishment of the presidio and mission marked the beginning of Spanish colonization in Alta California. Initially the presidio was a mission guard, but it was elevated to the status of royal presidio on January 1, 1774. San Diego was occupied by United States forces in July, 1846. By this time the presidio was in an advanced state of dilapidation, and the mission became the principal United States military post and was occupied as such from 1849 until 1858.

SAN FRANCISCO, PRESIDIO OF. Established June 27, 1776. Located on the south side of the Golden Gate. The Spanish flag was raised over the presidio on September 17, 1776, by Lieutenant José Joaquín Moraga. The site had been selected by Juan Bautista de Anza on March 28, 1776. The presidio was the northernmost presidio established by Spain on the Pacific Coast. In 1793 cannon were brought from San Blas, New Spain, and, beginning in August, 1793, the Castillo de San Joaquín was erected on Fort Point on the south side of the Golden Gate. It was completed on December 9, 1794. The *castillo*, also called Fort Blanco, was razed when Fort Winfield Scott (*q.v.*) was constructed. Taken by the United States on July 9, 1846. First garrisoned by United States troops on March 7, 1847, under the command of Captain Francis J. Lippitt, 1st New York Volunteers. The presidio became a permanent United States military post in April, 1847. It was named "Presidio" by executive order on November 6, 1850, and "Presidio of San Francisco" by General Orders No. 3 on March 24, 1938. Now the oldest existing military post west of the Mississippi River by more than half a century, it is still operative.

SAN JOAQUÍN, CASTILLO DE. See Presidio of San Francisco.

SANTA BÁRBARA VIRGEN Y MARTIR, PRESIDIO DE. Established April 21, 1782. Located on a small bay about half a mile from the later mission and and near a large Indian town. Established by Captain José Francisco Ortega. Both Governor Felipe de Neve and Father Junípero Serra were present for the founding of the presidio. The United States flag was raised above the presidio on August 1, 1846, by Commodore Robert F. Stockton. A small garrison occupied the presidio briefly, then it ceased to be a military post.

SEWARD. Established September 1, 1861. Located on the Eel River at the present town of Fort Seward in Humboldt County. The site was selected and the post established by Major Charles S. Lovell, 10th U.S. Infantry. The post was established by order of Brigadier General Edwin Vose Sumner, commanding the department, who originally intended that it replace Fort Humboldt. Named for Secretary of State William H. Seward. The garrison was withdrawn to Fort Humboldt, probably in December, 1861, because of lack of provisions and forage at the post. Abandoned in April, 1862, by order of Colonel Francis J. Lippitt, 2nd California Infantry, commanding the District of Humboldt.

STOCKTON. Established in 1838. Located on Presidio Hill, overlooking the town and bay of San Diego. Built by the citizens of San Diego in preparation for an expected attack from Los Angeles during the course of the civil conflict between the forces supporting Juan Bautista Alvarado and those backing Carlos Carillo. Taken by the United States in July, 1846. The original fortifications consisted of an earthwork. They were briefly called Fort Du Pont, for Captain Samuel F. Du Pont of the U.S. sloop *Cyane*, and then Fort Stockton for Commodore Robert F. Stockton. The position was occupied until September, 1848, but was not thereafter maintained as a military post.

SUTTER'S FORT. Established as a private defensive and trading post by Johann August Sutter in 1841. Sutter named his establishment New Helvetia, although he sometimes referred to it as Fort Sacramento. Located near the junction of the American and Sacramento rivers and between the two streams. The fort was a formidable structure with adobe walls eighteen feet high and bastioned corners, armed with the ordnance from Fort Ross which Sutter had purchased from the Russian-American Company. The U.S. Army took possession of the fort on July 11, 1846. It was garrisoned by United States troops in 1846–47 and was referred to as both Sutter's Fort and Fort Sacramento.

TEJON. Established August 10, 1854. Located in the Cañada de las Uvas, about fifteen miles southwest of the Tejon (Sebastian) Indian Reservation, near the present town of Lebec. Intended to command the passes in the vicinity, to control the Indians, and to protect the friendly Indians, especially those on the reservation which had been established the previous year. In 1858 the post became a station on the Butterfield Overland route, the soldiers from the fort serving as military escorts through the pass. Established on a site selected by Lieutenant Edward F. Beale, U.S.N., who was named superintendent of Indian affairs in California in 1853. Established by First Lieutenant Thomas F. Castor, 1st U.S. Dragoons. Evacuated on June 15, 1861, by order of Brigadier General Edwin Vose Sumner. Reoccupied on August 17, 1863, by California volunteer troops by order of Brigadier General George Wright. Permanently abandoned on September 11, 1864, by order of Major General Irvin McDowell, at the time the Tejon Reservation was discontinued. The post then became part of the Rancho Tejón, a Mexican grant, purchased by Lieutenant Beale. Part of the site of the post is now a state historical monument and some of the buildings have been restored.

TER-WAW. Established October 12, 1857. Located on the north bank of the Klamath River, about six miles above its mouth, on the Klamath Indian Reservation and across the river from the agency. Intended to control and protect the Indians of the area. Established by First Lieutenant George Crook, 4th U.S. Infantry. Crook suggested the name Ter-waw, which is reported to be the Yurok Indian word for the locality, meaning "beautiful place." The garrison was withdrawn on June 11, 1861. Reoccupied on August 28, 1861. The post was flooded by the Klamath River four times during the winter of 1861–62, and seventeen of the twenty buildings were washed away. It was first ordered rebuilt, then abandoned, by order of Brigadier General George Wright, on June 11, 1862.

VOSE. Fort Vose does not appear on any of the official lists of the location and distribution of troops. It is probable that this is the same as the agency for the Nome Lackee Reservation, located some twenty miles southwest of the town of Tehama in Tehama County. Nome Lackee was first garrisoned on January 4, 1855, by troops commanded by Second Lieutenant John Edwards, 3rd U.S. Artillery. It was evacuated on April 21, 1858.

WELLER. Established January 3, 1859. Located on the Mendocino Indian Reservation near the headwaters of the Russian River in Redwood Valley. Established by Captain Edward Johnson, 6th U.S. Infantry. Constructed under the direction of First Lieutenant William P. Carlin, 6th U.S. Infantry. Named for John B. Weller, governor of California. The original plan had been to establish the post on the Nome Cult Indian Reservation, but transportation difficulties led to its location at this spot. Abandoned in September, 1859.

WINFIELD SCOTT. In 1854, Fort Point was graded to the water's edge, and the fort, somewhat similar to Fort Sumter in design, was commenced. Located on approximately the same site as the Castillo de San Joaquín, the fortress of the Presidio of San Francisco, at the southern anchorage of the present Golden Gate Bridge. The initial construction of the fort was under the supervision of First Lieutenant William H. C. Whiting, Corps of Engineers. The fort was first garrisoned in February, 1861, and construction was completed by November 30, 1861. The official designation of the post was Fort Point until 1882, when it was renamed in honor of Major General Winfield Scott. The fort was declared obsolete in 1905. It was seriously damaged in the San Francisco earthquake of 1906 and condemned as unsafe. It was abandoned for military purposes in 1914. The present Fort Winfield Scott is about half a mile south of the former fort.

WRIGHT. Established in December, 1858. Located near the center of Round Valley in Mendocino County. Established to control and protect the Indians of the Nome Cult Agency, later the Round Valley Indian Reservation. Originally established as a camp, called Nome Cult Indian Agency, by Second Lieutenant Edward Dillon, 6th U.S. Infantry. It was abandoned in September, 1861, then reoccupied on December 11, 1862, by Captain Charles D. Douglas, 2nd California Infantry, by order of Colonel Francis J. Lippitt, 2nd California Infantry. At that time the post was renamed Fort Wright, in honor of Brigadier General George Wright, commanding the department. Following the Civil War the post was designated Camp Wright. The garrison was withdrawn on June 17, 1875, because the Indians were no longer considered hostile. On July 26, 1876, the buildings and military reservation were transferred to the Interior Department for the use of the Indian Service.

YUMA. Established November 27, 1850. Originally located in the bottoms on the right side of the Colorado River about half a mile below the mouth of the Gila. In March, 1851, the post was moved to a low hill on the west bank of the Colorado, the site of the former Mission Puerto de la Purísima Concepción, opposite the present city of Yuma, Arizona. The same site had been the location of Camp Calhoun, named for John C. Calhoun, established on October 2, 1849, by First Lieutenant Cave J. Couts, 1st U. S. Dragoons, for the boundary survey party commanded by Second Lieutenant Amiel W. Whipple, Corps of Topographical Engineers. Fort Yuma was established to protect the southern emigrant route to California and to control the bands of warlike Yuma Indians in the vicinity. Later it served as a supply depot for the posts in Arizona. Established by Captain Samuel P. Heintzelman, 2nd U.S. Infantry. Originally called Camp Independence, its name was changed to Camp Yuma in March, 1851, when the post was moved to its permanent site. It became Fort Yuma in 1852. The post was virtually abandoned in June, 1851, because of the expense and difficulty of maintenance, then completely abandoned on December 6, 1851, because the provisions at the post were almost exhausted. Reoccupied by Captain Heintzelman on February 29, 1852. A quatermaster's depot was erected on the left bank of the Colorado River, below the mouth of the Gila, in 1864. The post was abandoned on May 16, 1883, after the expansion of the railways rendered it unnecessary as a depot of supplies. The military reservation was transferred to the Interior Department on July 22, 1884. Fort Yuma Indian School and the Mission of St. Thomas occupy the site today.

COLORADO

COLLINS. Established August 14, 1864. The first Camp Collins, established by the 1st Colorado Cavalry in the fall of 1863, was located near the town of Laporte on the South Platte River. It was destroyed by flooding on the night of June 9, 1864, necessitating its removal to higher ground. The permanent post was located on the

Cache la Poudre River at the present town of Fort Collins, which grew up around the post. Intended to protect the scattered settlers of the area and to guard the Overland Trail. Established by Captain William H. Evans, 11th Ohio Cavalry. The post, originally Camp Collins, apparently was first called Fort Collins on October 23, 1864. Named for Lieutenant Colonel William O. Collins, 11th Ohio Cavalry, commanding officer at Fort Laramie, Wyoming, and father of First Lieutenant Caspar W. Collins, for whom Fort Caspar, Wyoming, was named. Abandoned in the spring of 1867. The military reservation was transferred to the Interior Department on July 16, 1872, and thrown open to settlement.

CRAWFORD. Established July 21, 1880. Located on the left bank of the Uncompahgre River about four miles north of Los Pinos Indian Agency near the present town of Colona. Intended to control the Ute Indians after the White River massacre. Established by Colonel Ranald S. Mackenzie, 4th U.S. Cavalry. Constructed under the direction of First Lieutenant Calvin D. Cowles, 23rd U.S. Infantry. Originally a temporary supply camp, the post was first called "Cantonment on the Uncompahgre." On December 15, 1886, it was designated Fort Crawford, in honor of Captain Emmet Crawford, 3rd U.S. Cavalry, who died on January 11, 1886, of wounds received near Nácori, Mexico, while in pursuit of Geronimo. The last troops were withdrawn from the post on December 31, 1890. The military reservation was transferred to the Interior Department on December 30, 1890, and sold at public auction.

FAUNTLEROY. See Wise.

GARLAND. Established June 24, 1858. Located between Trinchera and Ute creeks in the San Luis Valley, near the mouth of Sangre de Cristo (La Veta) Pass[1] at the present town of Fort Garland. Built to

---

[1] The Sangre de Cristo Pass is essentially the same as La Veta Pass, crossed by U.S. Highway 160, but the approach to it was more commonly by way of the Huerfano River

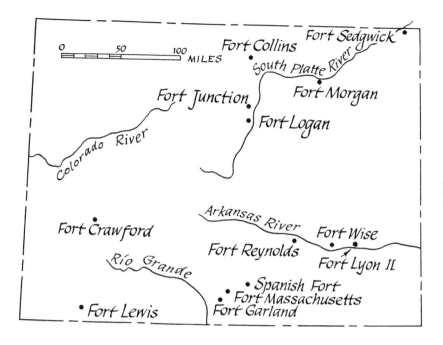

replace Fort Massachusetts (*q.v.*). Established by Captain Andrew W. Bowman, 3rd U.S. Infantry. Intended to curb the Utes and Jicarilla Apaches and to protect the settlers of the valley and to the south. The site for the post was chosen because of its proximity to an important Indian trail leading from the valley of the Río Grande to the valley of the Arkansas River. Named for Colonel John Garland, 8th U.S. Infantry, commanding the department. Abandoned on November 30, 1883, when the garrison was transferred to Fort Lewis. The post has been restored and is now a State Historical Monument.

JUNCTION. Built in July, 1864. Located at the junction of Boulder

than that taken by the present highway. The debouchment into the San Luis Valley is the same.

37

and St. Vrain rivers, from which circumstance the name was derived. Because of general Indian disorders, the Lower Boulder and St. Vrain Valley Home Guards were organized in the spring of 1864. The guards were authorized by the federal government, which provided them with arms and ammunition. Following the massacre of the Nathan W. Hungate family on June 11, 1864, the guards built the fort on a site chosen by Second Lieutenant Perry L. Smith, of the guards, as a place of refuge for the settlers during Indian attacks. Built of sod, the fort was 100 by 130 feet and was provided with two watch towers. After the cessation of Indian hostilities, the fort served as a stopping place for cowboys, travelers, and others for some years.

LEWIS. Established in July, 1880. The original site chosen for the post was at Pagosa Springs, and a camp was established there on October 15, 1878. However, on the recommendation of Lieutenant General Phil Sheridan, the post was relocated because of the White River Ute outbreak of 1879 and the threat of difficulties with other Ute tribes. The garrison was withdrawn from Pagosa Springs on October 8, 1879. The permanent post was located on the right side of La Plata River, west and a little south of the town of Durango, adjacent to the Southern Ute (Los Pinos) Reservation. Established by Lieutenant Colonel Robert E. A. Crofton, 13th U.S. Infantry, on a site selected by Colonel Thomas H. Ruger, 18th U.S. Infantry. The post provided protection for the Ute Indians against white encroachment on their reservation in accordance with the terms of the treaty of 1873, for the agency, for settlers in the area, and for railway construction.

Although the name Fort Lewis had been assigned as early as 1878, the post was called "Cantonment on La Plata" during the period of construction. Named for Lieutenant Colonel William H. Lewis, 19th U.S. Infantry, who died of wounds received in an engagement with Northern Cheyenne Indians at Punished Woman's Fork,

Kansas, on September 28, 1878. The post was abandoned in September, 1891, and the military reservation was transferred to the Interior Department for the use of the Indian Service on November 12, 1891. In 1910 the reservation and buildings were given to the state of Colorado and became a branch of the state agricultural college.

LOGAN. Established October 20, 1887. Congress, on February 17, 1887, approved the establishment of a military post near Denver if the state would provide 640 acres of land without cost to the United States. This was in line with the policy of reducing the number of small western posts and consolidating the troops in larger centers with adequate rail transportation facilities. The site, a barren knoll near the foothills of the Rockies on the outskirts of Denver, was selected by Lieutenant General Phil Sheridan and was donated by the state. The site was first occupied by Captain James H. Baldwin, 18th U.S. Infantry. Major George K. Brady, 18th U.S. Infantry, who was ordered to Denver with two companies, assumed command on October 25, 1887, and the erection of temporary quarters, called "Camp near the City of Denver," commenced the following day. In November, 1887, Captain Lafayette E. Campbell, assistant quartermaster, was ordered to Denver to supervise the construction of permanent quarters. Ground for the first permanent building, constructed by private contractor, was broken on July 25, 1888. For some time the post was called Fort Sheridan locally. However, it was officially a camp until it was designated Fort Logan on April 5, 1889. Named for Major General John A. Logan, who died on December 26, 1886. The post is still operative, but since 1939 it has been a sub-post of Lowry Air Force Base.

LYON I. See Wise.

LYON II. Established June 9, 1867. Located on the left bank of the Arkansas River about two and one-half miles below the mouth of the Purgatoire. Established by Captain William H. Penrose, 3rd U.S. Infantry, to replace the original Fort Lyon (see Fort Wise). Abandoned in October, 1889. The military reservation was transferred to the Interior Department on January 20, 1890. In 1934 the former post became a United States Veterans hospital.

MASSACHUSETTS. Established June 22, 1852, the first United States military post in the present state of Colorado. Located in a sheltered valley on Ute Creek about six miles north of the present town of Fort Garland and eighty-five miles north of Taos. The post was the northernmost in the Department of New Mexico. Established to provide protection for the settlers of the San Luis Valley and south against the Ute and Jicarilla Apache Indians, and to guard the approach to New Mexico by way of Sangre de Cristo (La Veta) Pass. Established by Major George A. H. Blake, 1st U.S. Dragoons, by order of Lieutenant Colonel Edwin Vose Sumner, 1st U.S. Dragoons, commanding the department. Sumner was a native of Boston, Massachusetts, which may account for the name of the post. The site proved to be swampy and unhealthful, and the post was abandoned on June 24, 1858, and replaced by Fort Garland (*q.v.*).

MORGAN. Established July 1, 1865. Located one mile south of the South Platte River, at the present town of Fort Morgan, on the Overland Trail at the point where the Denver branch left the main trail. The post provided protection for both emigrants and communications. First called Camp Tyler, then Camp Wardwell, and finally, in 1866, Fort Morgan. Named for Major Christopher A. Morgan, 1st Illinois Cavalry, who established the post and who died on January 20, 1866. The post was constructed of sod reinforced with logs. Abandoned on May 18, 1868, after the completion of the Union Pacific Railway to Denver rendered it unnecessary. The garrison was transferred to Fort Laramie, Wyoming, and the post buildings sold at auction.

REYNOLDS. Established July 3, 1867. Located on a plateau on the right side of the Arkansas River about two and one-half miles above the mouth of the Huerfano. Intended to protect the settlers of the area from hostile Indians. The post was established on a site previously selected by Colonel Randolph B. Marcy, inspector general, U.S. Army. Established by Captain Simon Snyder, 5th U.S. Infantry, with the garrison from the post of Pueblo, which was evacuated the previous day. Named for Major General John F. Reynolds, killed on July 1, 1863, at Gettysburg. Abandoned on July 15, 1872. The military reservation was transferred to the Interior Department on July 18, 1874.

SEDGWICK. Established May 17, 1864. Located on the right bank of the South Platte River a mile east of the mouth of Lodgepole Creek, near the present town of Julesburg. It was located near several fords across the South Platte, including one of the main branches of the Overland Trail and the Lodgepole Creek emigrant route. Intended to protect the routes of travel and the settlers of the area. Established by Colonel Christopher H. McNally, 3rd U.S. Volunteer Infantry, by order of Brigadier General Robert B. Mitchell, commanding the district. Originally called Camp Rankin, the post was designated Fort Sedgwick on September 27, 1865, in honor of Major General John Sedgwick, killed at Spotsylvania on May 9, 1864. Abandoned on May 31, 1871, by which time the Indians of the area were considered to be subjugated. The military reservation was transferred to the Interior Department on July 22, 1884.

SHERIDAN. See Logan.

UNCOMPAHGRE. See Crawford.

WISE. Established August 29, 1860. Located near Bent's New Fort on the left bank of the Arkansas River, near the "Big Timbers" and the present town of La Junta. Bent's Fort was leased by the government and used as a storage facility for the military post. Constructed under the direction of Major John Sedgwick, 1st U.S. Cavalry. First called Fort Fauntleroy, for Colonel Thomas T. Fauntleroy, 1st U. S. Dragoons, then Fort Wise, for Governor Henry A. Wise of Virginia. On June 25, 1862, the post was designated Fort Lyon in honor of Brigadier General Nathaniel Lyon, killed on August 10, 1861, in the Battle of Wilson's Creek, Missouri. Abandoned on June 9, 1867, because of flooding by the Arkansas River, and replaced by Fort Lyon II (*q.v.*). The military reservation was transferred to the Interior Department on July 22, 1884.

[NAME UNKNOWN.] A Spanish military post was established in 1819 close to Oak Creek, a confluent of the Huerfano River, twenty-five miles west of the present town of Walsenburg, on a hill overlooking Oak Creek and the valley down which the Taos Trail wound. The post was established by order of Governor Facundo Melgares of New Mexico and was intended to guard the Sangre de Cristo Pass against possible United States invasion. Abandoned some time in 1821, after the Adams-Onís Treaty fixed the international boundary along the Arkansas River. The post is sometimes referred to as Sangre de Cristo Fort although the Spanish designation, if there was one, appears to be unknown.

IDAHO

BOISE. Established July 4, 1863. Located on a small creek a mile and a quarter north of the Boise River, some forty-three miles from its confluence with the Snake, at the present town of Boise. Intended to control the Shoshoni Indians, to protect the emigrant route to Oregon, and to serve as a depot of supplies for the area. Established by Major Pinkney Lugenbeel, 19th U.S. Infantry, by order of Brigadier General Benjamin Alvord. On April 5, 1879, the designation of the post was changed to Boise Barracks. The garrison was with-

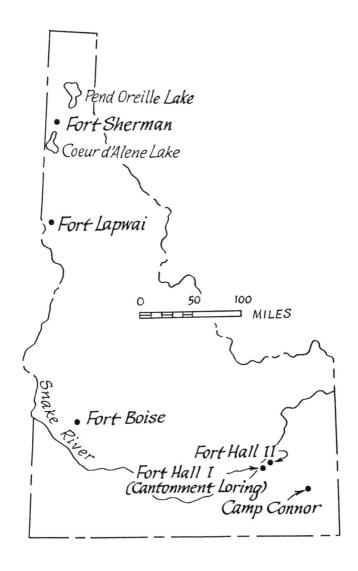

Pend Oreille Lake

• Fort Sherman

Coeur d'Alene Lake

• Fort Lapwai

0   50   100

MILES

Snake River

• Fort Boise

Fort Hall II

Fort Hall I
(Cantonment Loring)

Camp Connor

drawn in 1913 and the post placed in charge of a caretaker. The post has since been reactivated and discontinued on several occasions. It is now occupied by the Veterans Administration.

CONNOR. Established May 23, 1863. Located east of Soda Springs on the north bank of the Bear River. Established to protect the overland route and the settlement of Morrisites adjacent to the post. The Morrisites, a group of apostate Mormons, were escorted to Soda Springs to establish the settlement. It was hoped that they would block the further expansion of the Mormons as well as restrain the Bannock Indians. Established by Captain David Black, 3rd California Infantry, by order of Brigadier General Patrick Edward Connor, for whom the post was named. General Connor reached Soda Springs on May 17, 1863, and the site for both post and settlement was selected on May 20, following the arrival of the Morrisites. Properly called Camp Connor, the post was never officially designated a fort. On Febuary 24, 1865, General Connor ordered the abandonment of the post, the troops departing toward the end of April.

COEUR D'ALENE. See Sherman.

HALL I. Established August 5, 1849. Located about three miles above the Hudson's Bay Company's Fort Hall on the south side of the Snake River. Established by order of Secretary of War William L. Marcy, dated June 1, 1847. Intended to protect the Oregon Trail and to provide a stopping place for emigrants to rest, repair their wagons, and obtain supplies. Established by Lieutenant Colonel William W. Loring, Mounted Riflemen, in command of the Oregon expedition. Two companies of Mounted Riflemen were left to erect a permanent post. The post was called "Cantonment Loring," but it was frequently referred to as "Fort Hall" in official reports and correspondence. Colonel Persifor F. Smith, Mounted Riflemen, commanding the department, was of the opinion that the post was improperly located for the purpose of assisting emigrants. Abandoned on May 6, 1850, because of the scarcity of forage and provisions.

HALL II. Established May 27, 1870. Located east of the old Hudson's Bay Company post of the same name, between the Snake and Portneuf rivers, about eight miles south of the town of Blackfoot. Established at the request of the Interior Department to control the Shoshoni and Bannock Indians after they had been placed on reservations. Established by Captain James E. Putnam, 12th U.S. Infantry. The post was named for the original Fort Hall, a trading post established by Nathaniel Wyeth in 1834 and sold to the Hudson's Bay Company two years later. Abandoned on June 11, 1883, because the density of population in the area largely obviated the need for protection and the completion of the railways into the area made it possible to bring troops from Fort Douglas, Utah, if the need arose. The military reservation was transferred to the Interior Department on April 26, 1883, for the use of the Indian Service.

LAPWAI. Established August 6, 1862. Located on the left bank of the Lapwai River, a tributary of the Clearwater, three miles above its mouth. Intended to protect both the Indians and the whites from each other. At the time the post was established, miners were flocking into the area and were encroaching on the Nez Percé reservation. Established by Major Jacob S. Rinearson, 1st Oregon Cavalry, by order of Brigadier General Benjamin Alvord. Originally called Camp Lapwai, the post was designated Fort Lapwai in 1863. *Lapwai* is a Nez Percé Indian word meaning "place of the butterflies." The garrison was withdrawn in May, 1866, because the mustering out of volunteers left insufficient troops to garrison all of the posts in the department. Reoccupied on November 7, 1866; again evacuated in July, 1867, and reoccupied in November, 1867. Finally abandoned in 1884. The military reservation was transferred to the Interior Department on June 5, 1882, for the use of the Indian Service.

LORING, CANTONMENT. See Hall I.

SHERMAN. Established April 16, 1878. Located on the north shore of Lake Coeur d'Alene at the point where the Spokane River emerges from the lake. Established to protect the settlers of the area from hostile Indians. Established by Lieutenant Colonel Henry Clay Merriam, 2nd U.S. Infantry, by order of Brigadier General Oliver Otis Howard, commanding the department. Originally called Camp Coeur d'Alene, the post was designated Fort Coeur d'Alene in 1879, and Fort Sherman in 1887. Named for General William T. Sherman. Abandoned about September 1, 1900.

ILLINOIS

ARMSTRONG. Construction of the post commenced May 10, 1816. Located at the lower end of Rock Island, an island in the Mississippi River between the present towns of Davenport, Iowa, and Rock Island, Illinois. The post was one in the series established by the United States to stop British traders from operating in United States territory. A government Indian factory was opened at the post in the spring of 1822, not long before the factory system was abolished, and was discontinued on December 31, 1822. Established by Colonel Thomas A. Smith, Regiment of Riflemen. The Sac and Fox reservation was located in Iowa immediately west of the post, and much of the activity of the Black Hawk War was centered about the post. The post was named for a former secretary of war, John Armstrong. Abandoned on May 4, 1836. Rock Island Arsenal was established on the island on July 11, 1862. [See map of Iowa.]

IOWA

ATKINSON. Established May 31, 1840. Located on the left bank of the Turkey River above the present town of Fort Atkinson in Winneshiek County. Intended to protect the Winnebago Indians on whose

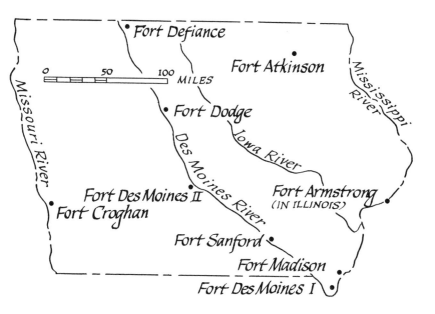

reservation it was located. Established by Captain Isaac Lynde, 5th U.S. Infantry, by order of Colonel Henry Atkinson, 6th U.S. Infantry, commanding the department. Originally a camp, the post was designated Fort Atkinson in 1841, in honor of Colonel Atkinson. In 1846 the garrison of the post went with Colonel Stephen Watts Kearny, 1st U.S. Dragoons, on the Santa Fe expedition, and the post was occupied by volunteer guards. Abandoned on February 24, 1849, because the removal of the Winnebagoes made the post unnecessary. The military reservation was turned over to the Interior Department by Congressional act on June 7, 1860.

BELLE VUE. See Madison.

CLARKE. See Dodge.

CROGHAN. Established May 31, 1842. Located on the left bank of the Missouri River a little below the mouth of the Boyer and above the present town of Council Bluffs. Established to prevent hostilities between the Potawatomi and Sioux Indians and to enforce regulations against the whisky traffic. Established by Captain John H. K. Burgwin, 1st U.S. Dragoons, and a contingent of dragoons from Fort Leavenworth, Kansas. Intended as a temporary post, it was first called Camp Fenwick, for Colonel John Roger Fenwick, 4th U.S. Artillery, then Fort Croghan, for Colonel George Croghan, one of the two inspector generals, U.S. Army. Flooding of the post in the spring of 1843 led to its abandonment on September 5, 1843. The garrison remained in the vicinity until October 6, then withdrew to Fort Leavenworth.

DEFIANCE. Erected in 1862. Located on the west fork of the Des Moines River at the town of Estherville. Following the Sioux uprising of August, 1862, in Minnesota, stockades were erected at various locations for the protection of Iowa. One of these, Fort Defiance, was established by Captain William H. Ingham, Northern Iowa Border Brigade. The name was later changed to Fort Ingham, for Governor Schuyler R. Ingham of Iowa. The post was occupied by Federal troops for a short time in 1863–64 by order of Brigadier General Benjamin Alvord. Other major posts, sometimes called forts but more often called stockades, were located at Chain Lakes, Cherokee, Correctionville, and Peterson. After this uprising the Indians ceased to play a significant part in Iowa military history.

DES MOINES I. Established May 19, 1834. Located above the mouth of the Des Moines River near the present town of Montrose. Intended to control the Sac and Fox Indians and to prevent white encroachment on their lands. The site was selected by First Lieutenant George H. Crosman, 6th U.S. Infantry, and the post was established by Lieutenant Colonel Stephen Watts Kearny, 1st U.S. Dragoons. The post, originally a camp, was designated a fort in 1835. The name was selected by Secretary of War Lewis Cass. It was intended to be a temporary post only and was abandoned gradually in 1836–37, the last troops leaving on June 1, 1837.

DES MOINES II. Established May 20, 1843. Located at the junction of the Des Moines and Racoon rivers. Intended to provide protection for the Sac and Fox Indians. Established by Captain James Allen, 1st U. S. Dragoons. Captain Allen named the post Fort Racoon, but the War Department would not sanction the name. The post was designated Fort Des Moines by Major General Winfield Scott. Evacuation of the post began early in 1846 as the Dragoons escorted the Sac and Fox Indians to their new homes in Missouri. The post was abandoned on March 10, 1846, and the government property was sold to the settlers in the area, the town of Des Moines developing at the site.

DODGE. Established August 2, 1850. Located opposite the mouth of Lizard Creek on the east bank of the Des Moines River, at the present town of Fort Dodge. Established by Captain Samuel Woods, 6th U.S. Infantry. First designated Fort Clarke, for Colonel Newman S. Clarke, 6th U.S. Infantry, the name was changed to Fort Dodge, for Colonel Henry Dodge, 1st U.S. Dragoons, on June 25, 1851. Abandoned on June 1, 1853. William Williams, former post sutler, purchased the barracks and fort site in 1854 and laid out the town of Fort Dodge.

INGHAM. See Defiance.

MADISON. Established in the autumn of 1808. Located on the west bank of the Mississippi River on the site of the present town of Fort Madison. Established to control the Sac and Fox Indians and to serve as a government Indian factory. Established by First Lieutenant Alpha Kingsley, 1st U.S. Infantry. Named for Secretary of State James Madison. The post was sometimes referred to as Fort Belle

Vue. The Indians considered the erection of the post a violation of their treaty rights and were troublesome throughout its existence. The post was abandoned while under Indian attack on the night of September 3, 1813, and was burned by the departing garrison.

RACOON. See Des Moines II.

SANFORD. Established on October 3, 1842. Located on the left bank of the Des Moines River near the present town of Ottumwa. Established by Captain James Allen, 1st U.S. Dragoons. Troops were sent from Fort Atkinson to expel squatters from the Sac and Fox lands. By permission of John Sanford of the American Fur Company, the troops were quartered in eight log cabins belonging to the company. Quarters for officers and stables were erected by the troops. Captain Allen called the post Fort Sanford in recognition of the courtesy shown to the military. The War Department, however, because of the temporary nature of the post, rejected the name. Officially the post was designated Sac and Fox Agency. Abandoned on May 17, 1843.

KANSAS

ATKINSON. Established August 8, 1850. Located about two miles west of the present Dodge City, on the left side of the Arkansas River. Intended to control the Indians and protect the Santa Fe Trail. Established by Lieutenant Colonel Edwin Vose Sumner, 1st U.S. Dragoons. The post was called Camp Mackay, in honor of Lieutenant Colonel Aeneas Mackay, deputy quartermaster general, who died on May 23, 1850. The post was constructed, apparently, under the supervision of Captain William Hoffman, 6th U.S. Infantry. It was rebuilt, commencing in June, 1851, on or adjacent to the original site, and was called New Post or Fort Sumner until June 25, 1851, when it was designated Fort Atkinson, in honor of Colonel Henry Atkinson, 6th U.S. Infantry, who died on June 14, 1842.

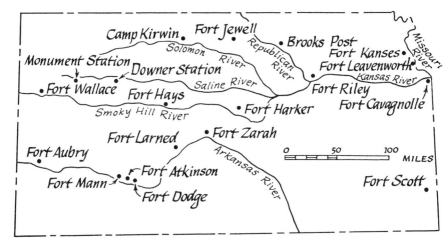

Because the post was constructed of sod, it was popularly known as Fort Sod or Fort Sodom. This fort was abandoned on September 22, 1853, reoccupied in June, 1854, and permanently abandoned on October 2, 1854, because of the high cost of supplying it and the lack of suitable buildings. The site was occupied as a camp from time to time until the establishment of Fort Dodge in 1865.

AUBRY. Established early in September, 1865. Located in the present Hamilton County at the head of Spring Creek about two and one-half miles north of the Arkansas River and about midway between the present towns of Kendall and Syracuse. The site was originally recommended by Francis X. Aubry, trader and explorer, who was killed in Santa Fe on August 18, 1854, and for whom the post was named. The post, intended to be temporary, was designed to protect the mountain branch of the Santa Fe Trail and the Aubry Cutoff during the Indian troubles of 1865–66. Established by Captain Adolph

Whitman, 48th Wisconsin Infantry. Abandoned on April 15, 1866, after the Indian troubles had subsided.

BROOKS. Constructed in August or September, 1864. Located on the north bank of the Republican River in the present Cloud County. Erected by the Shirley (now Cloud) County Militia. The post, a log blockhouse, served as headquarters for defense against hostile Indians.

CAVAGNOLLE. Established in 1744 or 1745. Located below the mouth of the Kansas River, possibly on the present site of Kansas City, Kansas. Erected by the Sieur Deruisseau, who, in 1744, was granted a monopoly to trade with the Indians along the Missouri. The post was connected with the French plans to open trade with Santa Fe. It consisted of a circular palisade, enclosing a few cabins. In 1758 it was garrisoned by one officer and seven or eight soldiers. The French and Indian War seriously affected the Indian trade and the post was abandoned prior to 1760.

DODGE. Established April 10, 1865. Located on the left bank of the Arkansas River on the Santa Fe Trail a few miles east of the present Dodge City. The site lay near the intersection of the "wet" and "dry" routes of the Santa Fe Trail and between two points where the Indians frequently crossed the Arkansas—the Cimarron Crossing, about twenty-five miles to the west, and the Mulberry Creek Crossing, some fifteen miles to the east. The post was designed to protect the Santa Fe Trail and to serve as a base of operations against hostile Indians. Established by Captain Henry Pierce, 11th Kansas Cavalry, by order of Major General Grenville M. Dodge, commanding the department. Although there seems to be some doubt, the post was probably named for Colonel Henry Dodge, 1st U.S. Dragoons. Abandoned on October 2, 1882. The military reservation was transferred to the Interior Department on January 12,

1885. The remaining buildings of the post now form part of the state soldiers' home.

DOWNER. Established as a stage station in 1865, it served as a military post from May 30, 1867, to May 28, 1868. Located on Downer Creek on the Smoky Hill route to Colorado, about fifty miles west of Fort Hayes. Intended to protect the stage route, it was also used by Lieutenant Colonel George A. Custer, 7th U.S. Cavalry, during his operations against the Indians in 1867. More properly called Downer's Station, the post name was derived from the creek, which was named for James P. Downer, a Civil War veteran and a member of the party which surveyed the Smoky Hill route. Downer is usually referred to as a major, but he did not hold such rank in either the regular or volunteer service.

ELLSWORTH. See Harker.

FLETCHER. See Hays.

HARKER. Established in August, 1864. Originally located on the left bank of the Smoky Hill River at the point where the Santa Fe stage route crossed the river, about three miles east of the present town of Ellsworth. In January, 1867, the post was moved one mile to the northeast to the site of the present town of Kanapolis. The post was used as a base for the distribution of supplies to posts farther west and for operations against hostile Indians in 1868–69. The original post was established by troops of the 7th Iowa Cavalry, under the command of Second Lieutenant Allen Ellsworth, by order of Major General Samuel R. Curtis, commanding the department, to protect the more remote frontier settlements. Later it served to protect the construction crews of the Kansas Pacific Railway. Originally called Fort Ellsworth, for Lieutenant Ellsworth, it was designated Fort Harker on November 11, 1866, for Brigadier General Charles G. Harker, killed on June 27, 1864, in the Battle of Kenesaw Mountain.

The usefulness of the post ended when the railroad reached Denver, and it was abandoned in April, 1872. The military reservation was transferred to the Interior Department on July 12, 1880.

HAYS. Established October 11, 1865. Originally located on Big Creek, some fifteen miles southeast of its later site. On June 5, 1867, a flood destroyed the post, which was then relocated on higher ground south of Big Creek and half a mile south of the present town of Hays. Established primarily to protect employees of the Kansas Pacific Railway from hostile Indians. The post was first designated Fort Fletcher, in honor of Governor Thomas C. Fletcher of Missouri. On November 11, 1866, the name was changed to Fort Hays, for Brigadier General Alexander Hays, killed on May 5, 1864, in the Battle of the Wilderness. The new post was established on June 22, 1867, on a site selected by Major Alfred Gibbs, 7th U.S. Cavalry. Abandoned in November, 1889, largely as a result of the termination of Indian hostilities. The military reservation was transferred to the Interior Department on November 6, 1889, and to the state by a Congressional act of March 28, 1900. Part of the site is now the campus of Fort Hays State College.

JEWELL. Built on May 13 and 14, 1870. Located at the town of Jewell in north central Kansas. The post was erected by the home guard, William D. Street, captain, because of a rumor that the Cheyenne Indians were on the warpath. It consisted of a sod enclosure fifty yards square with walls four feet thick and seven feet high. A militia company organized by all of the settlers along Buffalo Creek garrisoned the post, and the settlers remained in it until June 28, 1870, by which time the Indian scare had abated. At that time a company of the 3rd U.S. Artillery took over and remained in the fort until fall.

KANSES. There are very few references to this post which may be the same as Fort Cavagnolle (*q.v.*), although the presumed locations differ. Located on the right bank of the Missouri River about thirty-five miles above the mouth of the Kansas in the present Atchison County. The ruins of the post were noted by Lewis and Clark in 1804. The fort, a military and trading post erected by the French, was located about a mile from the Kansa Indian village usually referred to as Fort Village. The garrison, under a commandant, was under the jurisdiction of the governor of Louisiana. The post was still in existence in 1757, but was probably abandoned shortly thereafter.

KIRWIN. Established July 10, 1865. Located near the confluence of Bow Creek and the North Solomon River in the present Phillips County. Established by Lieutenant Colonel John S. Kirwin, 12th Tennessee Cavalry, and a company of Tennessee volunteers who were sent as an escort for a survey party and to scout the country for hostile Indians. The post was a summer encampment only, not a fort. Abandoned on September 3, 1865.

LARNED. Established October 22, 1859. Originally located some three miles east of its permanent site, which was on the right side of the Pawnee River, about eight miles above its junction with the Arkansas. Established by First Lieutenant David Bell, 1st U.S. Cavalry. Designed for protection of the Santa Fe Trail and to provide a more centralized point for the distribution of annuities, as provided by treaty, to the Indians. First called "Camp on Pawnee Fork," the name was changed to Camp Alert on February 1, 1860, then to Fort Larned, for Colonel Benjamin F. Larned, paymaster general, U.S. Army, on May 29, 1860. For several years the agency for the Cheyenne and Arapaho Indians was located at the post. The agency was discontinued in 1868. Abandoned on July 19, 1878, except for a small detachment which remained to protect the quartermaster supplies until they could be removed. The military reservation was transferred to the Interior Department on March 26, 1883. The post, now privately owned, is well preserved.

LEAVENWORTH. Established May 8, 1827. Located on the right bank of the Missouri River, some twenty-three miles above the mouth of the Kansas River. Intended originally for the protection of the Santa Fe Trail. Established by Colonel Henry Leavenworth, 3rd U.S. Infantry, for whom the post was named. Originally called Cantonment Leavenworth, it was designated Fort Leavenworth on February 8, 1832. The post was evacuated in May, 1829, and was occupied by Kickapoo Indians until it was regarrisoned in the fall of 1829. Until well into the 1870's, the post served as a chief unit in the system of frontier defense, and in the 1850's and 1860's it was the general depot from which supplies were sent to all military posts of the Rocky Mountain area. The post is still operative, the oldest post established by the United States west of the Mississippi River which is still in existence.

MACKAY. See Atkinson.

MANN. Established, probably, in April, 1847. Located on the north bank of the Arkansas River, about eight miles west of the present Dodge City and twenty-five miles below the Cimarron Crossing of the Santa Fe Trail. Established because the government needed a post about equidistant from Fort Leavenworth and Santa Fe for the repair of wagons and the replacement of animals. Erected by Captain Daniel P. Mann, master teamster, for whom the post was named, and a corps of forty teamsters, by order of Captain William M. D. McKissack, assistant quartermaster. Although this was not a regular military post, it was defensible and was occupied by U.S. Army troops from time to time. It was repaired and enlarged in 1848. Abandoned in 1850 when Fort Atkinson was established.

MONUMENT. Established in November, 1865. Located in Gove County on the route of the Kansas Pacific Railway, between Forts Hays and Wallace, near some monument-shaped rocks which gave the post its name. It was originally a station on the stage and mail route, a detachment of troops being sent by order of Major General Grenville M. Dodge to protect the station from Indian depredations. The post was also referred to as Fort Pyramid, but in official documents it is designated Monument Station. The garrison was withdrawn in June, 1868.

PYRAMID. See Monument Station.

RILEY. Established May 17, 1853. Located on the north bank of the Kansas River at the junction of the Republican and Smoky Hill rivers. Established by Captain Charles S. Lovell, 6th U.S. Infantry, on a site recommended by Colonel Thomas T. Fauntleroy, 1st U.S. Dragoons. Colonel Fauntleroy was of the opinion that the post would improve the efficiency of the service and reduce expenditures. He suggested that its establishment would permit the abandonment of Forts Leavenworth, Scott, Atkinson, Kearny, and Laramie. The post was first called Camp Center because of its proximity to the geographical center of the United States. On June 27, 1853, it was designated Fort Riley, in honor of Colonel Bennett Riley, 1st U.S. Infantry, who died on June 9, 1853. Construction of the permanent cavalry post was commenced in 1855 under the direction of Captain Edmund A. Ogden, 8th U.S. Infantry. The post is still operative.

SCOTT. Established May 30, 1842. Located on the Marmaton River, a confluent of the Osage, about eight miles west of the Missouri line. Designed to protect the military road between Fort Gibson, Oklahoma, and Fort Leavenworth. The site was recommended in 1837 by a board which included Colonel Stephen Watts Kearny and Captain Nathan Boone, both 1st U.S. Dragoons, and selected on April 9, 1842, by Captain Benjamin D. Moore, 1st U.S. Dragoons, and Jacob Rhett Motte, assistant surgeon. Sergeant John Harrison, with a force of 1st U.S. Dragoons, was left at the site to begin work on the post.

Captain Moore with the garrison from the abandoned Fort Wayne, Oklahoma, arrived to assume command on May 30, 1842, which is considered the official date of establishment.

First called Camp Scott, for Major General Winfield Scott, the post was designated Fort Scott when the erection of permanent buildings began in 1843. The post was virtually abandoned in April, 1853, when the garrison was transferred to Fort Riley and other western posts. The buildings were sold at public auction on May 16, 1855. The government did not own the land. Troops were sent to the town of Fort Scott on various occasions during the troubled period prior to the outbreak of the Civil War, but the post itself was not re-established until March 29, 1862, when it was occupied by a force of the 2nd Ohio Cavalry, commanded by Colonel Charles Doubleday. Blockhouses, lunettes, and other fortifications were erected at strategic locations about the town. Fort Scott also served as a military supply depot for the area. It was again abandoned in October, 1865, and reoccupied in October, 1869, to serve as headquarters for troops operating in southeastern Kansas. Finally abandoned in 1873. Several of the buildings still stand.

SUMNER. See Atkinson.

WALLACE. Established in September, 1865. Located at the junction of Pond Creek and the south fork of the Smoky Hill River, about two miles southeast of the present town of Wallace, and close to what was then Pond Creek Station on the Butterfield Overland route to Denver. Intended to control the Indians of the area, protect the stage route, and provide escort service. Originally called Camp Pond Creek, on April 18, 1866, the post was designated Fort Wallace, in honor of Brigadier General William H. L. Wallace, who died on April 10, 1862, of wounds received in the Battle of Shiloh. Established by order of Major General Grenville M. Dodge. First garrisoned by regular troops under the command of Captain Edward

The parade grounds at Fort Riley, Kansas, about 1897.
The post, established in 1853, is still operative.

Pennell Collection, University of Kansas Library

Ball, 2nd U.S. Cavalry, in March, 1866. Abandoned on May 31, 1882, although some troops were still at the post as late as September. The military reservation was transferred to the Interior Department on July 22, 1884.

ZARAH. Established September 6, 1864. Located east of Walnut Creek, about three miles from its confluence with the Arkansas River, three miles east of the present town of Great Bend. Primarily used to guard the Santa Fe Trail, providing escorts both east and west. Established by Major General Samuel R. Curtis, commanding the department, and named for his son, Major Henry Zarah Curtis, assistant adjutant general, Volunteers, killed on October 5, 1863, in Quantrell's Baxter Springs massacre. The lessening of the Indian menace and the decreasing traffic along the Santa Fe Trail led to the abandonment of the post on December 4, 1869. The military reservation was transferred to the Interior Department on March 25, 1871.

LOUISIANA

ADAES, PRESIDIO DE NUESTRA SEÑORA DEL PILÁR DE LOS. Established November 1, 1721. Located at the present town of Robeline, about fifteen miles southwest of French Natchitoches but on territory considered a part of Texas by Spain. It was located half a league beyond the old mission of San Miguel de los Adaes, which was refounded on September 29, 1721. Established as a part of the Spanish effort to block French encroachment on Spanish territory and to protect the three Franciscan missions founded in the vicinity. Established by the Marqués de San Miguel de Aguayo. The name was derived from the Adai Indians, members of the Caddo confederation. The rotting of the logs of which the buildings and stockade were constructed necessitated the rebuilding of the post in 1726. Abandoned in 1772 on the recommendation of the Marqués de Rubí, who had examined the post in 1767.

BOURBON. Established in 1792. Located on the right bank of the Mississippi River, below New Orleans and opposite Fort San Felipe (Plaquemines), about one mile above the later Fort Jackson. Intended to protect the approaches to New Orleans. Erected by order of the Baron de Carondelet, governor of Louisiana. The fort was totally ruined by a hurricane in August, 1795, and subsequently rebuilt. Apparently the post had been abandoned prior to the purchase of Louisiana. No mention is made of its transfer to the United States. The site has been washed away so that nothing remains of the fort.

CLAIBORNE. See St. Jean Baptiste.

JACKSON. The site was first occupied in 1814, during the War of 1812, but construction of the fort was commenced not earlier than 1822 when an appropriation was made for collecting materials for a "Fort Opposite St. Philip." Located on the right bank of the Mississippi River, sixty-five miles below New Orleans and immediately opposite Fort San Felipe (Plaquemines). The post was first included in the official list of location and distribution of troops in 1831. Named for President Andrew Jackson. The fort was kept in a state of repair and additions were made to it from time to time, but it was not regularly garrisoned after May 11, 1835. Although it was located some distance above the mouth of the Mississippi, it was part of the system of seacoast defenses and served to guard the approaches to New Orleans. The Louisiana state militia seized the fort on January 11, 1861. It was recaptured by a Union naval force, commanded by Captain David D. Porter, on April 28, 1862. After 1870 the post was in the hands of an ordnance sergeant, again not regularly garrisoned. Abandoned in 1920.

JESUP. Established in May, 1822. Located on the crest of a high ridge on the watershed between the Red and Sabine rivers on the San Antonio Trace, some twenty-two miles southwest of Natchito-

ches and east of the present town of Many. Designed to protect the Louisiana-Texas frontier and to serve as a part of the system for Indian control. Established by Lieutenant Colonel Zachary Taylor, 1st U.S. Infantry. Constructed under the supervision of Captain George Birch, 7th U.S. Infantry. The post was called Cantonment

Jesup until 1832 when it was designated a fort. Named for Brigadier General Thomas Sydney Jesup, quartermaster general, U.S. Army. The garrison of the post was withdrawn in July, 1845, and transferred to Texas, immediately following the annexation of that area, except for one officer, First Lieutenant Zebulon M. P. Inge, 2nd U.S. Dragoons, who was left in charge. Permanently abandoned in February, 1846. The post buildings were sold at public auction on April 23, 1850. The military reservation was transferred to the Interior Department on March 25, 1871.

LIVINGSTON. Located on Grand Terre Island at the mouth of Barataria Bay. The island had been occupied for military purposes at least as early as 1814. In 1822 an appropriation was made for the collection of materials for a fort at Grand Terre, although there is no indication that work on a post was undertaken at this time. In 1834 the island was sold to the state of Louisiana by Étienne de Gruy and his wife, and the state deeded it to the federal government that same year. It is believed that work on the fort was started as early as 1835, but it was not completed until 1861. It was not regularly garrisoned but was kept in a state of repair. Seized by the Louisiana militia at the outbreak of the Civil War, but evacuated by Confederate forces on April 27, 1862. Occupied by Federal troops on October 26, 1863. Named for Robert Livingston, one of the negotiators of the Louisiana Purchase. Following the close of the Civil War, the fort was no longer garrisoned. It was turned over to the Quartermaster's Department in 1888 and placed in charge of a lighthouse keeper. After the hurricane of 1893 partly destroyed the fort, it was not rebuilt, but the reservation was retained.

MIRÓ. Established in 1785. Located on the Ouachita River at Prairie des Canots, the present site of the town of Monroe. Established by Juan Filhiol. The original post was called Ouachita Post. Erection of the fort was commenced on September 8, 1790. At that time it was named Fort Miró for Estevan Miró governor of Louisiana (1785–91). The fort was officially transferred to Captain Daniel Bissell, 1st U.S. Infantry, on April 17, 1804. Under the United States it was first garrisoned by a force commanded by First Lieutenant Joseph Bowman, 2nd U.S. Infantry. Because Fort Miró itself was considered the private property of the former civil commandant, the United States post was located some four hundred yards below the Spanish fort. It consisted of log structures enclosed in a slight stockade. The name of the settlement was changed to Monroe in May, 1819.

St. Jean Baptiste. Established in 1715. Located on the left bank of the Cane River. In 1721 it was moved to Natchitoches, to a site on a low hill close to and about thirty feet above the banks of the Cane River. The post was intended to counter Spanish activity along the Spanish-French frontier. It was transferred to the United States on April 20, 1804, and occupied by a force under the command of Captain Edward D. Turner, 1st U.S. Infantry. The United States used the post to guard the frontier between Louisiana and Spanish Texas and to control the Indians of the area. A government Indian factory was established at Natchitoches in 1805. Under the United States the post was named Fort Claiborne, for W. C. C. Claiborne, governor of Louisiana Territory. (It is also said that it was named for Captain Ferdinand L. Claiborne, 1st U.S. Infantry, but this seems doubtful.) Abandoned in June, 1819.

San Luis de Naches. Established in 1767. Located on the right bank of the Mississippi River opposite Natchez, Mississippi. Because a British force had occupied Natchez, Governor Juan de Ullóa sent Captain Pedro Piernas in September, 1767, to erect a fort to counter the British threat. The fort was evacuated in 1768, following the British withdrawal from Natchez.

Selden. Established in November, 1820. Located on the crest of a high bluff rising above old Bayou Pierre, some two miles above Grand Ecore. Established by Lieutenant Colonel Zachary Taylor, 8th U.S. Infantry. Established to protect the Louisiana-Texas frontier. First called Camp Ripley, for Brigadier General Eleazar W. Ripley, then designated Fort Selden, for Captain Joseph Selden, Corps of Artillery. Abandoned in 1822.

MINNESOTA

BEAUHARNOIS. Established September 18, 1727. Located on the western shore of Lake Pepin. Designed to protect the French trade with the Sioux Indians, to serve as a point of departure for expeditions in search of a route to the Pacific, and to detach the Sioux Indians from their alliance with the Fox Indians. Established by René Boucher, Sieur de la Perrière. Named for Charles de la Boische, Marquis de Beauharnois, governor of New France. Abandoned in October, 1728, because of the hostile attitude of the Sioux. Reoccupied in 1732 and rebuilt on higher ground near the original site. Again rebuilt in 1750. Abandoned in 1756 when the garrison was withdrawn for use against the British during the French and Indian War.

FORTIFICATIONS OF THE SIOUX UPRISING OF 1862. Following the Sioux uprising, which began in August, 1862, fortified positions were established in many places in southern Minnesota. Most were either in or near towns and were established by residents or by various Minnesota or Wisconsin volunteer units. Many were referred to, at least occasionally, as forts.

GAINS. See Ripley.

RIDGELY. Established April 29, 1853. Located some three-quarters of a mile to the north of the Minnesota River at the mouth of the Rock River, about twenty miles above New Ulm, near the ordinary

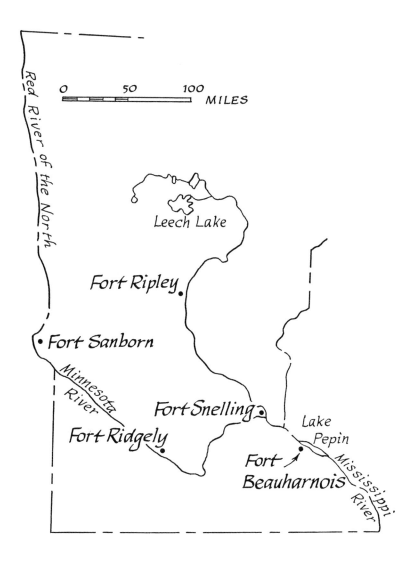

head of navigation on the Minnesota River. Probably established by Captain Samuel Woods, 6th U.S. Infantry. The first garrison of the post was commanded by Captain James Monroe, 6th U.S. Infantry. Intended to protect the frontier against the Sioux Indians. Named for three officers from Maryland, all of whom died or were killed during the Mexican War: First Lieutenant Henderson Ridgely, 4th U.S. Infantry; First Lieutenant Randolph Ridgely, 3rd U.S. Artillery; and Captain Thomas P. Ridgely, 2nd U.S. Artillery. Abandoned on May 22, 1867. The military reservation was transferred to the Interior Department on July 1, 1870.

RIPLEY. Established April 13, 1849. Located on the right bank of the Mississippi River, seven miles below the mouth of the Crow Wing and opposite the mouth of the Nokay. The military reservation, declared on September 15, 1849, by President Zachary Taylor, was on the east side of the Mississippi, except for one square mile which contained the site of the post. The site is included in the military reservation comprising the present Camp Ripley. Established to control and protect the Winnebago Indians after they were moved to a reservation west of the Mississippi, as provided by treaty, and to provide protection to the area of settlement from the Sioux and Chippewa Indians.

The site was chosen by Colonel George M. Brooke, 5th U.S. Infantry, in November, 1848. Construction was commenced under the direction of Captain Napoleon J. T. Dana, 7th U.S. Infantry, by civilian workers brought in for the purpose. Some troops from Fort Snelling were stationed at the site for about a month in 1848 to protect the workers. Captain John B. Todd, 6th U.S. Infantry, arrived at the post on April 13, 1849, with the first garrison. The post was first designated Fort Gaines, in honor of Brigadier General Edmund P. Gaines. The name was changed to Fort Ripley on November 4, 1850, because the name Fort Gaines had been assigned to a "permanent fortification" on Mobile Bay. Named for Brigadier General Eleazar W. Ripley, a distinguished officer of the War of 1812. Evacuated on July 8, 1857, but reoccupied on September 12, 1857, in anticipation of an outbreak of Indian hostilities. Finally abandoned on July 11, 1877, after a fire on January 14, 1877, destroyed the officers' and laundresses' quarters and the post storehouse. Military reservation transferred to the Interior Department on July 2, 1880, and restored to the public domain.

ST. ANTHONY. See Snelling.

SANBORN. Established in 1862. Located on the right side of the Red River some fifty miles below Fort Abercrombie, North Dakota, at the town of Georgetown. Established to provide protection against the Sioux Indians. Established by a Captain Luez, 4th Minnesota Infantry. The post consisted of the barracks erected by the Minnesota Stage Company. Named by Captain Luez in honor of Colonel John B. Sanborn, 4th Minnesota Infantry. Pressure of Indian hostilities forced the abandonment of the post on March 21, 1863.

SNELLING. Established August 24, 1819. Located at the confluence of the Minnesota and Mississippi rivers, on a tract of land purchased from the Sioux Indians by First Lieutenant Zebulon M. Pike, 1st U.S. Infantry, in the winter of 1805–1806, but not paid for until 1819. The post was established to control the Indians, encourage settlement, and prevent British encroachment on United States territory. The original post was established by Lieutenant Colonel Henry Leavenworth, 5th U.S. Infantry, on the south side of the Minnesota River. It was called both Cantonment New Hope and Cantonment Leavenworth. High water the following spring caused the removal of the camp on May 5, 1820, to a point on the right bank of the Mississippi, about one and one-half miles above the later site of the fort. The new camp was called Camp Coldwater. In August, 1820, Colonel Joshua Snelling, 5th U.S. Infantry, arrived and chose the permanent site. Actual work of construction commenced on September 10, 1820.

The permanent post was first called Fort St. Anthony, for the nearby St. Anthony Falls, at Snelling's suggestion. The post was designated Fort Snelling on January 7, 1825, at the suggestion of Brigadier General Winfield Scott, who had inspected the post in the spring of 1824. On June 6, 1857, the reservation and post were sold, largely through the efforts of Secretary of War John Floyd. The reservation was turned over to the purchasers on July 19, 1857, but on July 31, 1857, the post itself was reserved by Floyd for the use of troops and maintenance until further orders. The garrison was withdrawn on June 1, 1858. The post was reoccupied in 1861 as a training center during the Civil War and was continued as a permanent post after the war ended, though subject to litigation for many years thereafter. Fort Snelling became a major post when the era of smaller frontier posts ended. It was expanded considerably in size beginning in the 1880's. Abandoned as a military post on October 14, 1946, and transferred to the Veterans Administration.

MISSOURI

BELLEFONTAINE. Established in July, 1805. Located on the right bank of the Missouri River, about four miles above its mouth, near the mouth of Coldwater Creek. Bellefontaine was the first fort established by the United States west of the Mississippi River. It consisted of a military post and a government Indian factory, established by Brigadier General James Wilkinson at the direction of the War Department. The site was selected by General Wilkinson on July 23, 1805, and troops encamped nearby before the end of the month. Erected under the direction of Lieutenant Colonel Jacob Kingsbury, 1st U.S. Infantry. Colonel Thomas Hunt, 1st U.S. Infantry, was the first commander of the post and Rudolph Tillier the first and only

Early view of Fort Snelling, Minnesota, from an oil painting
by Seth Eastman which hangs in the Capitol, Washington, D. C.
Like many of the early forts, Snelling was located in a strong
defensive position and built with an eye to defense.

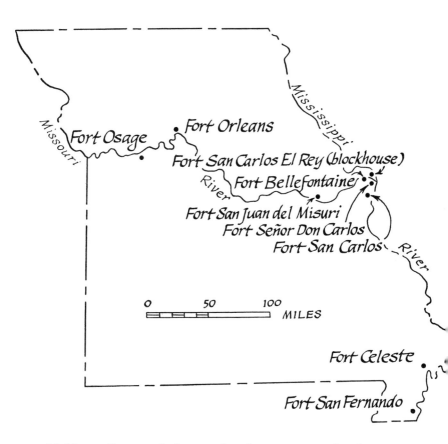

chief factor. Because of a large spring of pure water nearby, the post was named Bellefontaine. Originally it was located directly on the river, but flooding and erosion of the river banks led to its removal to higher ground, the top of Belle Mont, in 1810. The factory was discontinued in the fall of 1808 when Fort Osage (*q.v.*) was established, but the military post was maintained until the establishment of Jefferson Barracks south of St. Louis. It was abandoned on July 10, 1826, but the buildings were retained for storage purposes until 1834.

BLOCKHOUSES, FORTS: WAR OF 1812. On June 6, 1812, two weeks before the declaration of war, there were only 241 soldiers of the regular army west of the Mississippi River in the Missouri area, 134 at Fort Bellefontaine, 63 at Fort Osage, and 44 at Fort Madison, Iowa. Just before and during the war, a number of defensive posts were prepared in Missouri in anticipation of British-inspired Indian hostilities. Some were erected by the settlers, some by the Missouri Rangers, and some, apparently, with the assistance of the U.S. Army. All were called forts, although some were simply fortified homes and others were blockhouses, while some were more elaborate, being provided with stockades, blockhouses, and even moats. These forts were established from the present Ralls County in the north to the mouth of the Missouri River in the south and in the Boone's Lick country in the west. Apparently there were none south of the Missouri River except in the Boone's Lick area. Regular troops were stationed at times in some of these posts while the Missouri Rangers occupied others. In all probability there were posts other than those listed.

Best's Fort. Located on the left side of the Loutre River near the Missouri.

Boone's Fort. Probably located on Femme Osage Creek about six miles above its mouth. This, the fort of Daniel Morgan Boone, was the largest and strongest of the forts in the St. Charles district.

Buffalo Fort. Erected in 1812 by the Missouri Rangers. Located on Buffalo Creek, about two miles south of the town of Louisiana.

Callaway's Fort. Located near the old French village of La Charette, the present Marthasville. It was probably erected by Second Lieutenant James Callaway of the Missouri Rangers.

Cap-au-Gris. Located on the Mississippi River, some eight miles or more above the mouth of the Cuivre. It took its name from Cap-au-Gris in Illinois, almost directly opposite. The post was erected by the Missouri Rangers. A company of the Rangers, under the command of Captain David Musick, was stationed there until April, 1813, when it left to establish Fort Lookout. The post was occupied, although irregularly, until 1815.

Castlio's Fort. Located southwest of St. Charles, not far from Howell's Fort.

Clark's Fort. Located about three and one-half miles east and a little to the south of the town of Troy, at the residence of Major Christopher Clark.

Clemson. Located on Loutre Island at the junction of the Loutre and Missouri rivers. Named for Captain Eli B. Clemson, 1st U.S. Infantry. There is nothing to indicate that the fort was erected by the regular army.

Cooper's Fort. Probably erected in 1812 by the Missouri Rangers. Located on the left side of the Missouri River opposite Arrow Rock, about two miles from the Boone's Lick salt works, at the residence of Captain Benjamin Cooper, Missouri Rangers. It was the largest and most important of the Boone's Lick forts.

Côte sans Dessein. The village of Côte sans Dessein was located on the left side of the Missouri River near the present town of Tebbetts, down river from the Boone's Lick district. On the hill from which the town took its name were two forts, Roi's (Roy's) Fort and Thibault's (Tibeau's, Tebo's) Fort, with a powder magazine located between them. Jean Baptiste Roi was the founder of the village and Thibault was one of the settlers. The village has long since disappeared.

Cox's Fort. Located above Arrow Rock on the right side of the

Missouri River, almost opposite Cooper's Fort, at the settlement known as Cox's Bottom. Jesse Cox was the founder of the settlement.

Cuivre. Probably the same as Fort Howard (*q.v.*).

Hannah Cole's Fort. Erected late in 1814. Located on a river bluff in what is now east Booneville. Hannah Cole, a widow with nine children, was Booneville's first settler.

Head's Fort. Located on Big Moniteau Creek a few miles above the town of Rocheport. Named for Moses Head.

Hempstead. Located on the bluff about a mile north of the present town of New Franklin. The fort was first called McLain's Fort. It was renamed in honor of Edward Hempstead, Missouri's first territorial delegate to Congress.

Howard. Erected in 1812. Located on the left bank of the Cuivre River near its mouth, not far from the town of Old Monroe. Built by Captain Nathan Boone's Mounted Rangers. This was one of the largest and most important of the forts in Missouri. Named for Benjamin Howard, first territorial governor of Missouri.

Howell's Fort. Located on Howell's Prairie between the La Charette road and Dardenne Creek, southwest of St. Charles. François Howell settled in the area about 1797 and the prairie took its name from him.

Kennedy's Fort. Located on the right side of the Perrugue River near its source, southeast of the present Wright City. Probably established in 1812 by the Missouri Rangers.

Kinkead. Located about a mile north of the Missouri River and about a mile above the town of Old Franklin. Named for David Kinkead.

Kountz' Fort. Probably erected in 1812. Located on the Boone's Lick road, about eight miles west of St. Charles. The fort was a log structure erected by John and Nicholas Kountz. Following the end of the war it became a tavern.

Lookout. Established April 11, 1813. Located a short distance below the village of Portage des Sioux on the right bank of the Mississippi River. The site was selected by Colonel Daniel Bissell, 5th U.S. Infantry, on April 8, 1813, and the post was established three days later by Captain David Musick of the Missouri Rangers, with troops from the post at Cap-au-Gris, which may not have been occupied after that date. The post consisted of a blockhouse with a battery on an island in the river a mile below the blockhouse.

McLain's Fort. See Hempstead.

McMahan's Fort. Located on the right bank of the Missouri River some miles above Cox's Fort, not far from the present town of Glasgow.

Mason. Established in March, 1812. Located on the right bank of the Mississippi River in Ralls County, near the present town of Hannibal. It was garrisoned, at least for a time, by regular troops from Fort Bellefontaine. Intended to provide defense against the movement of hostile Indians down the Mississippi. Abandoned on May 1, 1814.

Pond Fort. Probably erected in 1812 by the Missouri Rangers. Located on Dardenne Prairie, southwest of the present town of Wentzville. The name was derived from a small pond located north of the fort. The fort consisted of a group of temporary residences built in the form of a hollow square and continued to be occupied for some time after the end of the war.

Quick's Fort. Located on the left side of Loutre River not far from its mouth. Probably the fort of Jacob Quick, a settler in the area.

Roi's Fort. See Côte sans Dessein.

Stephen Cole's Fort. Erected in 1812. Located some two miles east of Booneville. Stephen Cole, Hannah Cole's brother-in-law, was among the first settlers in the area. Hannah Cole's Fort (*q.v.*) replaced this fort late in 1814 when it was decided that a stronger fort was necessary.

Stout's Fort. Probably erected in 1812 by the Missouri Rangers. Located on what is called the Fort Branch, about a mile south of the town of Auburn in Lincoln County.

Talbot's Fort. Located on Loutre Island in the Missouri River at the mouth of Loutre River. Fort Clemson was on the same island.

Thibault's Fort. See Côte sans Dessein.

White's Fort. Located either on Dog Prairie or Big Prairie in the St. Charles district.

Wood's Fort. Located at the present town of Troy. Zachary Taylor, then a captain in the 7th U.S. Infantry, was supposedly stationed at the fort. The name is sometimes given as Wood Fort.

Zumwalt's Fort. Located near the present town of O'Fallon in the St. Charles district. A cabin built by Jacob Zumwalt in 1798 was incorporated in the fort which was erected in 1812.

CELESTE. Established in 1789. Located at New Madrid. In July, 1789, Pierre Foucher was ordered to New Madrid by Governor Estevan Miró, with instructions to build a fort and to take civil and military command of the district. The fort was named for Governor Miró's wife. The original fort was located too close to the river and was partly destroyed when the bank was washed away. It was rebuilt, farther from the river, prior to 1796. The new structure was an irregular square with blockhouses at the four corners, palisades, and a moat, and mounted eight small cannon. The garrison in 1796 consisted of twenty-four soldiers of the regular army, and the fort was the residence of the military commandant of the Illinois (Upper Louisiana) district. The post was transferred to Captain Daniel Bissell, 1st U.S. Infantry, on March 18, 1804. It was garrisoned for a time by United States troops.

CLARK. See Osage.

ORLEANS. Construction of the post was commenced on November 15, 1723. The exact location has been questioned. It was on the left bank of the Missouri River, somewhere in the vicinity of the mouth of the Wakenda or the Grand River. Established by Étienne Véniard, Sieur de Bourgmond, to block anticipated Spanish encroachment, keep peace among the Indians, and protect the mines in the vicinity. Named for the Duke of Orleans. There seems to be no basis for the tradition that the post was wiped out and the garrison massacred by the Indians. Pierre Margry states that it was suppressed by the Company of the Indies in 1726. It seems, however, that Governor Périer issued an order to abandon the post in October, 1727, because it was not profitable as a center of trade and too many Frenchmen were being killed in the vicinity. It was probably evacuated peaceably in 1728 or early in 1729. Baron Marc de Villiers du Terrage is of the opinion that the post was re-established at a later date but the evidence is not convincing.

OSAGE. Established in the fall of 1808. Located on the right side of the Missouri River about forty miles below the mouth of the Kansas River, northeast of the present town of Sibley, on a hill overlooking the river. The site, the strategic nature of which had been recognized by the Lewis and Clark expedition in 1804, was chosen by Brigadier General William Clark of the Upper Louisiana militia. The post was both a military establishment and a government Indian factory. Captain Eli B. Clemson, 1st U.S. Infantry, commanded the garrison which established the post and George C. Sibley was the factor. Sources vary concerning the date on which construction began. It seems probable that the troops arrived at the site on October 2, 1808, and that construction began almost at once. However, it is also said that Clark arrived at the site on September 4—Clemson and Sibley already being there—and that actual construction began on September 9. The post was intended to aid in the control of the Osage, Kansa, and Iowa Indians. When established, it was to keep a watchful eye on the river, allowing only licensed traders to ascend, and to observe the movements of the Indians.

Originally called Fort Clark, for General Clark, it was designated Fort Osage on November 10, 1808. It was also referred to as Fort Sibley, Clark's Fort, and Fiery Prairie Fort. Evacuated in June, 1813, as a result of the War of 1812. During the period in which it was not occupied, a factory was maintained for the Osage Indians at Arrow Rock and one for the Sac and Fox on Little Moniteau Creek. Sibley returned to the post late in the fall of 1815 to put it in order. Regarrisoned in July, 1816. Except for a guard of seven men to protect the factory, the garrison was removed in 1819 to establish Camp Missouri (see Fort Atkinson, Nebraska). The post was regarrisoned in 1820 by order of Secretary of War John C. Calhoun. The Indian factory was discontinued on November 5, 1822, and the post was not regularly garrisoned thereafter. It was apparently abandoned entirely in 1827 when Fort Leavenworth, Kansas, was established.

EL PRÍNCIPE DE ASTURIAS, SEÑOR DON CARLOS. Established in 1767. Antonio de Ullóa, the first Spanish governor of Louisiana, sent an expedition headed by Francisco Rui y Morales, captain of the Company of Louisiana, up the Mississippi River to build forts on either side of the mouth of the Missouri. The fort on the north side of the river, which was to be the larger and more important of the two, was designated San Carlos el Rey, Don Carlos Tercero, by Ullóa. When Rui arrived at the Missouri, he found it impossible to erect a fort on the north side because of the swampy nature of the ground and the danger of periodic floods. The fort, which was built on the south side, consisted of a palisaded square, eighty feet on a side, including bastions. A blockhouse, constructed of logs, eighteen feet on each side and seven feet high, was constructed on the north side of the river. It was dutifully named San Carlos el Rey, Don Carlos Tercero. The garrison for the blockhouse usually consisted of a corporal and four men. The fort is sometimes referred to simply as "Fort Charles" or "Fort Prince Charles" and the blockhouse as "Fort San Carlos del Misuri." In April, 1779, Spain became involved in the American Revolution as an ally of France. The following year a British expeditionary force, composed primarily of Indians, was sent against St. Louis. In preparation for the attack the fort was abandoned and destroyed in April, 1780, and the garrison transferred to St. Louis. (See San Carlos.)

SAN CARLOS. Established April 17, 1780. Located on rising ground immediately west of the town of St. Louis. The post was erected to protect St. Louis from an expected attack by British and Indian forces during the American Revolution. Established by Lieutenant Governor Fernando de Leyba, commandant at St. Louis, and captain of the infantry regiment of Louisiana. The fortification consisted of a tower built of stone and mounted five cannon. Some accounts say that the tower had a stone foundation and a wooden superstructure; however, in 1792, it was reported that the tower had not rotted because it was made of stone. Leyba intended to erect four towers, one on each side of the town, but all available funds, which had been raised by the residents of St. Louis, were expended in building the first. The British force attacked on May 26, 1780, and was repulsed. In official correspondence the fortification is usually referred to as the "Tower of San Carlos."

In 1792 Baron de Carondelet, governor of Louisiana, instructed Zenón Trudeau, lieutenant governor for Upper Louisiana, to incorporate the tower in a fort which he referred to as the fort of San Luis de Ylinoa. The new construction, to consist of a stockade and banquette, was to cost no more than two thousand pesos. The fort mounted eight cannon. Authorization for the construction of barracks within the fort at an additional cost of one thousand pesos was granted later. St. Louis, together with its fortifications, was transferred to Captain Amos Stoddard, Corps of Artillerists, on March 9, 1804. United States troops were stationed at Fort San Carlos until Fort Bellefontaine was occupied in 1805.

SAN FERNANDO. A fort by this name is said to have been established during the Spanish period. It was located in what is now Pemiscot County in the "Boot Heel" of Missouri, in the area later called Little Prairie. The site of the fort has been washed away by the Mississippi River.

SAN JUAN DEL MISURI. Established about 1796. Located on the north side of the Missouri River at La Charette, the present Marthasville. Probably established by Antoine Gaultier, a lieutenant of militia. Little is known of this post. It was probably a small log structure designed to protect the settlers who were just beginning to move into the area. It had disappeared entirely by 1804.

SAN LUIS DE YLINOA. See San Carlos.

SAN LUIS DEL MISURI. See San Carlos.

SIBLEY. See Osage.

MONTANA

Assiniboine. Established May 9, 1879. Located on the left bank of
Beaver Creek, about four miles above its juncture with the Milk
River, some ten miles southwest of the town of Havre. Established to
prevent the return of Sitting Bull and his Sioux warriors from
Canada and to control the Indians of the area, particularly the Black-
feet. Established by Colonel Thomas H. Ruger, 18th U.S. Infantry.
Named for the Assiniboine Indians. Abandoned early in 1911.

Benton. Originally an American Fur Company post established in
1845. It was relocated in 1846 (some sources say 1847) and rebuilt
in 1850. It was christened Fort Benton on December 25, 1850, although it had already been listed by that name in the company's
books as early as 1848. Named in honor of Senator Thomas Hart
Benton of Missouri. In its permanent location it was situated at the
head of steam navigation, on the left bank of the Missouri River, at
the present town of Fort Benton. It was leased by the United States
government and was first occupied by troops on October 11, 1869.
Troops were quartered in the buildings of the old fur company fort
until 1874 after which quarters were rented in the town to house
them. As a military post Fort Benton was used to receive and forward freight from and to Forts Shaw and Ellis. Abandoned on
May 31, 1881, and the troops transferred to Fort Shaw. The military reservation was transferred to the Interior Department on
January 5, 1883.

Custer. Established July 4, 1877. Located on the bluff above the
confluence of the Big Horn and Little Big Horn rivers. Intended to
control the Sioux and other Indians of the area. Established by Lieutenant Colonel George P. Buell, 11th U.S. Infantry. Originally
called Big Horn Post or Big Horn Barracks, it was officially designated Fort Custer on November 8, 1877. Named for Lieutenant
Colonel George A. Custer, 7th U.S. Cavalry, killed in the Battle of

the Little Big Horn on June 25, 1876. Abandoned on April 17, 1898.

ELIZABETH MEAGHER. Established in May, 1867. Located eight miles east of the town of Bozeman at the mouth of Rock Creek. Established by Brigadier General Thomas Thoroughman and Colonel Walter W. De Lacy of the Montana volunteer militia. A picket-post was also erected on the approaches to Bridger Pass. The settlers of the Gallatin Valley were fearful that the area was about to be invaded by large bands of hostile Crow and Sioux Indians, following the murder of John Bozeman in April, 1867. The posts were designed to block the passes through the mountains into the valley.[1] The fort probably consisted of a stockade. Named for the wife of Thomas F. Meagher, secretary and former acting governor of the territory.

ELLIS. Established August 27, 1867. Located on the left bank of the East Gallatin River, three miles west of the town of Bozeman. Established by Captain Robert S. LaMotte, 13th U.S. Infantry, by order of Brigadier General Alfred H. Terry, commanding the department, to protect the settlers and miners of the area from hostile Indians. The post was strategically located to command Bozeman, Bridger, and Flathead Passes, and to block raids across them. Named for Colonel Augustus Van Horn Ellis, 124th New York Infantry, killed on July 2, 1863, in the Battle of Gettysburg. Abandoned in 1886 as no longer useful. The military reservation was transferred to the Interior Department on July 26, 1886.

FIZZLE. Erected in 1877. Located where the Lolo Trail enters the Bitterroot Valley, about five miles west of the town of Lolo. Two companies of the 7th U.S. Infantry, commanded by Captain Charles C. Rawn, were engaged in the construction of Fort Missoula. When news of Chief Joseph and his fleeing Nez Percé reached Captain

[1] There was at least one additional post, a stockade called Fort Howie, east of Bozeman Pass on the Yellowstone River near the mouth of Shield's River.

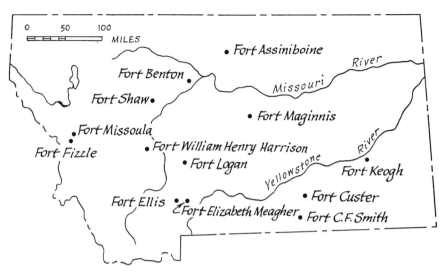

Rawn, he, with his small command and a force of citizen vounteers, hastily constructed entrenchments and barricades in the hope of blocking Chief Joseph's advance. The Indians reached the position on July 28, 1877, in such numbers that any attempt to halt them was impossible. After this the temporary fortification was popularly known as Fort Fizzle.

HARRISON, WILLIAM HENRY. Established in 1892. A Congressional act of May 12, 1892, provided for the establishment of a new post at Helena. It was a part of the program for the abandonment of smaller posts and the concentration of troops in a few larger establishments. It was named, on December 13, 1892, for the former President and grandfather of Benjamin Harrison, who then occupied the presidency, by Secretary of War Stephen B. Elkins. The post was first garrisoned on September 23, 1895, with troops from Fort Assiniboine. The garrison was withdrawn in 1913 and the post placed in charge of a caretaker. It has since been occupied on various occasions and the military reservation has been retained. It is now a Veterans Administration Hospital.

KEOGH. Established in August, 1876. Located on the right bank of the Yellowstone River, just west of Miles City and two miles above the mouth of the Tongue River. Established by Colonel Nelson A. Miles, 5th U.S. Infantry, by order of Brigadier General Alfred H. Terry, commanding the department. Intended to serve as a base of supply and operations against the Sioux Indians. Construction of permanent buildings commenced in 1877. Originally called "New Post on the Yellowstone," "Cantonment on Tongue River," and "Tongue River Barracks," the post was designated Fort Keogh on November 8, 1878, in honor of Captain Myles W. Keogh, 7th U.S. Cavalry, killed in the Battle of the Little Big Horn on June 25, 1876. The post was one of several established during this period for the purpose of subduing the Indians of the northern plains and securing permanent control over them. Fort Keogh remained an army post until 1900. From 1900 until 1908 it was an army remount station. In 1908 it was converted into a livestock experiment station. During World War I it was used as a quartermaster's depot. The military reservation was transferred to the Interior Department in 1924.

LOGAN. Established November 30, 1869. Located in a valley half a mile west of the Smith River, some seventeen miles northwest of the present White Sulphur Springs. Established to protect Diamond City and other mining camps in the vicinity, as well as the Fort Benton freight route, from hostile Indians, especially the Blackfeet. Established by a company of the 2nd U.S. Cavalry at the urgent request of the settlers, by order of Major General Winfield Scott Hancock. Until May 1, 1870, the post was a sub-post of Fort Ellis. It was first called Camp Baker, for Major Eugene Mortimer Baker, 2nd U.S. Cavalry, commanding Fort Ellis. On December 30, 1878, it was designated Fort Logan, in honor of Captain William Logan, 7th U.S. Infantry, killed in the Battle of Big Hole on August 9, 1877. Abandoned on October 27, 1880, and the military reservation sold at auction on June 4, 1881.

MAGINNIS. Established August 22, 1880. Located about twenty miles northeast of the town of Lewiston on Ford's Creek, a tributary of the Musselshell River, near the eastern edge of Judith Basin. Established by Captain Daingerfield Parker, 3rd U.S. Infantry, to protect settlers, cattlemen, and transportation routes from the Indians. The post was named for Major Martin Maginnis, 11th Minnesota Infantry, who was Montana's territorial delegate to Congress. Abandoned on July 20, 1890, except for two men who remained to protect the public property. The military reservation was transferred to the Interior Department on August 14, 1890.

MISSOULA. Established June 25, 1877. Located on the right side of the Bitterroot River at the mouth of Grant Creek, about four miles southwest of the town of Missoula. Established at the urgent request of the settlers of the Missoula Valley who feared that efforts to remove the Salish Indians from the Bitterroot Valley to the Jocko Reservation might cause an uprising. The site was selected by Lieutenant Colonel Charles C. Gilbert, 7th U.S. Infantry, and Second Lieutenant Charles A. Worden, 7th U.S. Infantry, acting engineer officer for the Department of Dakota. Lieutenant Colonel Wesley Merritt, 9th U.S. Cavalry, recommended the establishment of the post on February 8, 1876. Established by Captain Charles C. Rawn, 7th U.S. Infantry. Originally called "Post at Missoula," it was designated Fort Missoula on November 8, 1877. The post was not garrisoned from 1898 to 1901, but has since been reactivated and discontinued several times. The military reservation has been retained.

SHAW. Established June 30, 1867. Located on the right bank of the Sun River, some twenty-five miles above its junction with the Missouri (fifteen in a direct line), and about five miles above the point where the Fort Benton–Helena stage road crossed the Sun River. Established to protect the route between Fort Benton and Helena and to prevent the movement of hostile Indians into the settled area to the south. Four companies, under the command of Major William Clinton, 13th U.S. Infantry, selected the site on June 30, 1867, and went into camp. First called Camp Reynolds, the post was designated Fort Shaw on August 1, 1867, in honor of Colonel Robert G. Shaw, 54th Massachusetts Infantry, killed before Fort Wagner in 1863. Abandoned on July 21, 1891. The military reservation was transferred to the Interior Department on April 30, 1892. The former post served as an Indian school from 1892 until 1910.

SMITH, C. F. Established August 12, 1866. Located on a bluff on the right side of the Big Horn River, some eight miles above the mouth of Rotten Grass Creek, on what is now the Crow Indian Reservation and what was then the eastern edge of Crow Indian land. The post was the northernmost of the three established to protect the Bozeman Trail from the Sioux Indians. Established by Captain Nathaniel C. Kinney, 18th U.S. Infantry, by order of Colonel Henry B. Carrington, 18th U.S. Infantry. Originally designated Fort Ransom, probably for Brigadier General Thomas E. G. Ransom, who died on October 29, 1864. The name of the post was soon changed to Fort C. F. Smith, in honor of Major General Charles Ferguson Smith, who died on April 25, 1862. Abandoned on July 29, 1868, as a result of the Fort Laramie treaty of April 29, 1868, with the Sioux. It was August before all of the stores could be removed. (See note, p. 183.)

NEBRASKA

ATKINSON. Established September 29, 1819. Located at Council Bluffs on the right bank of the Missouri River some nine miles north of the later Omaha, near the present town of Fort Calhoun. Estab-

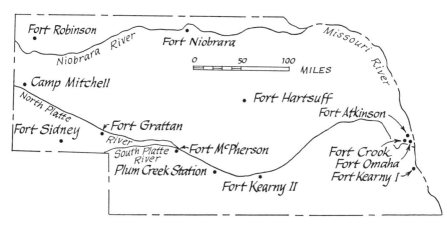

lished by Colonel Henry Atkinson, 6th U.S. Infantry, with a rifle regiment and five companies of the 6th U.S. Infantry. At the time it was established it was the government's westernmost outpost. It was originally called Camp Missouri, then Cantonment Missouri. Because of flooding, the post was moved on June 12, 1820, to the top of Council Bluffs, more than one mile from the original site, and the name changed to Cantonment Council Bluffs. The post was designated Fort Atkinson by the explicit order of Secretary of War John C. Calhoun to Colonel Atkinson, dated January 5, 1821. Abandoned on June 6, 1827, on the recommendation of Colonel George Croghan, inspector general, U.S. Army, who held that the post served no useful purpose, was unhealthful, and was too far from the starting point of the Santa Fe Trail. The garrison was transferred to Jefferson Barracks, Missouri, and the post itself was superseded by Fort Leavenworth, Kansas.

CHILDS. See Kearny II.

COTTONWOOD. See McPherson.

CROOK. Established in 1891. Located about eight miles south of Omaha. The post was authorized by an act of Congress dated July 25, 1888. It was intended to replace Fort Omaha and to provide a large military post farther removed from the city. Except for fencing the reservation, no construction work was undertaken prior to 1891. Originally referred to as the New Post of Fort Omaha, it was designated Fort Crook on March 3, 1891, in honor of Major General George Crook, who died on March 21, 1890. The post was first garrisoned in 1895. It is now Offutt Air Force Base.

GRATTAN. Established September 8, 1855. Located at the mouth of Ash Hollow south of the North Platte River on the Oregon Trail. Erected by Colonel William S. Harney, 2nd U.S. Dragoons, immediately after his engagement with the Sioux in the so-called Battle of Blue Water. Named for Brevet Second Lieutenant John L. Grattan, 6th U.S. Infantry, killed by the Oglala Sioux near Fort Laramie, Wyoming, on August 19, 1854. The fort was an earthwork, about one hundred feet across, with two bastions. According to Colonel Harney, the post was intended to provide protection for emigrant trains and the monthly mail passing between Forts Kearny and Laramie. Abandoned on October 1, 1855.

HARTSUFF. Established September 5, 1874. Located on the left side of the North Loup River near the present town of Burwell. Established to quiet the fears of the settlers of the Loup Valley who were concerned about the Brulé and Oglala Sioux. Established by Captain Samuel Munson, 9th U.S. Infantry, on a site selected by Brigadier General Edward O. C. Ord, commanding the department. Originally called "Post on North Loup," it was designated Fort Hartsuff in November, 1874, in honor of Major General George Lucas Hartsuff, who died on May 16, 1874. Abandoned on May 1, 1881, as it was considered unnecessary after Fort Niobrara was established. The post buildings were sold on July 20, 1881, and the military reservation was transferred to the Interior Department on July 22, 1884.

KEARNY I. Established in May, 1846. Located on the right bank of the Missouri River, some fifty miles below Omaha, at the mouth of Table Creek, where Nebraska City now stands. Colonel Stephen Watts Kearny, 1st U.S. Dragoons, and Colonel George M. Brooke, 5th U.S. Infantry, selected the site on May 23, 1846. (Kearny and Captain Nathan Boone, 1st U.S. Dragoons, had recommended that a post be established on the site in 1838.) Established by Major Clifton Wharton, 1st U.S. Dragoons. Wharton returned to Fort Leavenworth, Kansas, shortly after the post was established, and the only significant building erected, a blockhouse, was constructed under the direction of First Lieutenant William E. Prince, 1st U.S. Infantry, who succeeded Wharton in command. Abandoned in June or July, 1846, and reoccupied on September 15, 1847. The post was intended to protect the Oregon Trail but was too far removed from the general route of travel. Named for Colonel Kearny. Permanently abandoned in May, 1848, and replaced by Fort Kearny II.

KEARNY II. Established in June, 1848. Located on the right side of the Platte River, about eight miles southeast of the present town of Kearney. The site, chosen by First Lieutenant Daniel P. Woodbury, Corps of Engineers, in the fall of 1847, was purchased from the Pawnee Indians for $2,000 in trade goods. Established by two companies of Mounted Riflemen. Constructed under the direction of Lieutenant Colonel Ludwell E. Powell, Missouri Mounted Volunteers. First called "Post at Grand Island," it was soon referred to, although never so designated officially, as Fort Childs, in honor of Major Thomas Childs, 1st U.S. Artillery. It was designated Fort Kearny on December 30, 1848. The post was frequently referred to as New Fort Kearny to distinguish it from its predecessor. It was one of the most important posts on the Oregon Trail, providing protec-

tion for emigrants and serving as a depot for munitions for use between Forts Leavenworth and Laramie. It served also to protect the
peaceable Indians from hostile Indians and outlaws. Abandoned
on May 17, 1871, as no longer necessary. The military reservation
was transferred to the Interior Department on December 2, 1876.

McKEAN. See McPherson.

McPHERSON. Established September 27, 1863. Located on the right
bank of the South Platte River, two miles west of Cottonwood
Springs, eight miles above the confluence of the North and South
Platte. Established to protect travelers from Indian attack and to
prevent the Indians from crossing the South Platte at a point which
they had long used as a ford. Established by Major George M.
O'Brien, 7th Iowa Cavalry. Originally called Cantonment McKean,
for Major Thomas McKean, 38th Pennsylvania Militia, commanding officer for the territory. The post was designated Post of Cottonwood in February, 1864; Fort Cottonwood on May 18, 1864; then,
on January 20, 1866, it was named Fort McPherson, in honor of
Brigadier General James B. McPherson, killed near Atlanta on July
22, 1864. The burial ground at the post was declared a national
cemetery in 1873 and is still maintained as such. Abandoned on
March 29, 1880, except for a small detachment which remained
until June 20, 1880, to dispose of post property. The post buildings
were sold on May 23, 1881, and the military reservation was transferred to the Interior Department on January 5, 1887.

MITCHELL. Established in August, 1864. Located on the left bank
of the North Platte River above Scott's Bluff, some twelve miles east
of the Wyoming line. Intended to protect the area against hostile
Indians. Established by Captain Jacob S. Shuman, 11th Ohio Cavalry, by order of Brigadier General Robert B. Mitchell, commanding the District of Nebraska. Originally called Camp Shuman, the
name was changed (prior to August 31, 1864) to Camp Mitchell by

Captain Shuman. The post was never officially designated a fort. Abandoned in 1867.

NIOBRARA. Established April 22, 1880. Located on the right bank of the Niobrara River near the mouth of the Minnechaduze, a few miles east of the present town of Valentine. Established to provide the settlers and cattlemen of the area with protection against the Sioux Indians, who were by this time a broken people but were still feared, and to control the Indians at the Spotted Tail Agency. Established by Major John Jacques Upham, 5th U.S. Cavalry. Abandoned on October 22, 1906. The military reservation is now a National Wildlife Refuge.

OMAHA. Established December 5, 1868. Located on the right bank of the Missouri River above Omaha, although within the present city limits. Established by Captain William Sinclair, 3rd U.S. Artillery. The post was originally called Camp Sherman, in honor of Lieutenant General William Tecumseh Sherman. In 1869 the name was changed to Omaha Barracks, and on December 30, 1878, the post was designated Fort Omaha. The garrison was withdrawn in 1895 when the post was replaced by Fort Crook. Two officers and thirty-five men remained at the post until September, 1896, to dispose of removable public property. Efforts to sell the post were given up when it proved impossible to get what was considered a reasonable price for the property. The post has been reactivated and discontinued several times and the military reservation has been retained.

PLUM CREEK. Established in 1864 as a sub-post of Fort McPherson. Located south of the Platte River at Plum Creek. Established as an intermediate station between Forts Kearny II and McPherson and supplied from Fort Kearny. Intended to protect the emigrant route and the mails. This was one of several posts along the Oregon Trail, usually, and more properly, referred to as stations and actually serving as such for the stage route. Abandoned in 1866.

ROBINSON. Established March 8, 1874. Located north of the White River, near the confluence of Soldier Creek, west of the present town of Crawford, at the Red Cloud Agency headquarters. Established by order of Lieutenant General Phil Sheridan during the difficulty with the Sioux Indians over the Black Hills region. The post was also a center for the control of the Indians at the Red Cloud and Pine Ridge agencies. Erected under the direction of Colonel John E. Smith, 14th U.S. Infantry. First called Camp Red Cloud Agency, the post became Camp Robinson on March 29, 1874, and was designated Fort Robinson in January, 1878. Named for First Lieutenant Levi H. Robinson, 14th U.S. Infantry, killed by Indians in Wyoming on February 9, 1874. The post was used as a training center for dogs of the K–9 Corps during World War II and later as a quartermaster's depot. Abandoned in 1948. The Fort Robinson State Park and Museum are located on the post reservation.

SIDNEY. Established November 19, 1867. Located at the present town of Sidney, in the Lodgepole Creek Valley. Established to protect the construction crews of the Union Pacific Railway. Originally an outpost of Fort Sedgwick, Colorado, it became a separate post in 1870. Until 1879 it was called Sidney Barracks, then it was designated Fort Sidney. Abandoned on May 24, 1894. The military reservation was transferred to the Interior Department on November 14, 1894.

NEVADA

BAKER. In 1855 the Mormon Church established an Indian mission in Las Vegas (the Meadows) Valley where there was grass and a good spring. An adobe fort was erected to protect the little settlement, which was abandoned in 1858. In December, 1861, Colonel James H. Carleton, 1st California Infantry, commanding the District of Southern California, issued instructions for the occupation of the old Mormon fort to protect the route from southern California

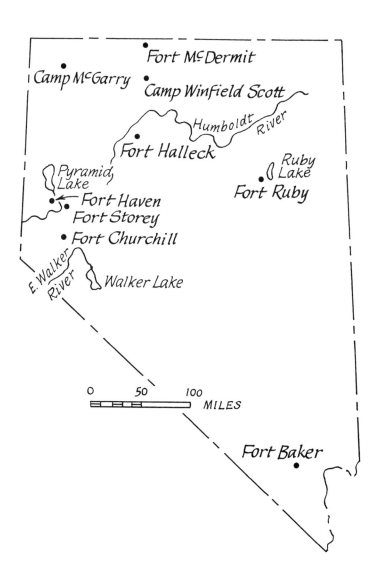

Fort McDermit

Camp McGarry

Camp Winfield Scott

Humboldt River

Fort Halleck

Pyramid Lake

Ruby Lake

Fort Ruby

Fort Haven
Fort Storey

Fort Churchill

E. Walker River

Walker Lake

0   50   100
MILES

Fort Baker

91

to Salt Lake City in anticipation of the reoccupation of Fort Crittenden. The post was designated Fort Baker in honor of Colonel Edward D. Baker, 71st Pennsylvania Infantry, killed on October 21, 1861, in the Battle of Ball's Bluff, Virginia. Apparently the post was never established. Part of the Mormon fort still stands.

CARLIN. A military reservation was created near the town of Carlin by executive order on November 9, 1874. It was transferred to the Interior Department as no longer useful for military purposes on March 20, 1888. Only in the report of the abandonment of the reservation is reference made to Fort Carlin, which actually never existed.

CHURCHILL. Established July 20, 1860, on the north side of the Carson River, some thirty miles below Carson City, near the present town of Weeks. Established because of the Paiute Indian uprising in western Nevada. The post was located between the Pyramid Lake and Walker River Indian reservations, and served to maintain order on both. Established by Captain Joseph Stewart, 3rd U.S. Artillery. Briefly called Post on Carson River then, on August 28, 1860, designated Fort Churchill for Colonel Sylvester Churchill, inspector general, U.S. Army. Also frequently referred to as Churchill Barracks, although never so designated officially. Abandoned September 29, 1869, by order of Major General George H. Thomas, commanding the division, because it was no longer considered necessary for control of the Indians. Transferred to the Interior Department June 15, 1871. No formal military reservation had been declared. The buildings were sold at auction. The site is now a state historical monument.

HALLECK. Established July 26, 1867. Located southwest of Humboldt Wells on the right bank of Cottonwood Creek at the base of the northern slope of the Humboldt Mountains, some twelve miles south of the Humboldt River. Established to protect the settlers in the Humboldt River area and the route of the Central Pacific Railway.

Established by Captain Samuel P. Smith, 8th U.S. Cavalry. Named for Major General Henry W. Halleck. The post was a camp until April 5, 1879, when it was designated a fort. Abandoned on December 1, 1886. The military reservation was transferred to the Interior Department on October 11, 1886.

HAVEN. Established in June, 1860. Located on the Truckee River near Pyramid Lake. The post was a temporary earthwork erected during the war with the Paiute Indians. Erected by troops commanded by Captain Joseph Stewart, 3rd U.S. Artillery. It was abandoned in mid-July when Fort Churchill was established.

McDERMIT. Established August 14, 1865. Located near the mouth of a canyon in the Santa Rosa Mountains on the right bank of the east branch of the Quinn River, just south of the Oregon line at the present town of McDermitt. Established by units of the 2nd California Cavalry. Intended to control the Paiute Indians, to protect the routes of travel in the area, and, later, to protect the Indian agency established nearby. First called Quinn River Station, Camp No. 35; then, still in August, 1865, Camp McDermit. The post was designated a fort on April 5, 1879. Named for Lieutenant Colonel Charles McDermit, 2nd California Cavalry, commanding the District of Nevada, who was killed by Indians in the Quinn Valley on August 8, 1865. The name was often spelled "McDermitt," even in official documents. Abandoned on December 1, 1888. On July 24, 1889, the military reservation was transferred to the Interior Department to be used as a reservation and school for the Indians. The buildings of the fort serve as headquarters for the Fort McDermit Indian Agency.

McGARRY. Established September 9, 1867. Located near Summit Lake in the High Rock Canyon country of western Humboldt County, on the Applegate Cutoff to Oregon. Established to protect the emigrant route from hostile Indians. Established by Major Albert G. Brackett, 1st U.S. Cavalry. The post was a camp and was never officially designated a fort. Named for Colonel Edward McGarry, 2nd California Cavalry, and later lieutenant colonel, 32nd U.S. Infantry. Abandoned in 1868 by order of Brigadier General Edward O. C. Ord, commanding the department, and the garrison transferred to Camp Winfield Scott. A detachment remained at the post until the public property could be disposed of, the last troops leaving on December 18, 1868. The military reservation was transferred to the Interior Department on March 25, 1871.

RUBY. Established September 1, 1862. Located on the western side of the Ruby Valley near the south end of Ruby Lake. Established by Colonel Patrick E. Connor, 3rd California Infantry, by order of Brigadier General George Wright, commanding the department. The first garrison was under the command of Major Patrick A. Gallagher, 3rd California Infantry, who supervised the erection of the post. Established to protect the Indians of the area and to guard the Overland Mail and the emigrant route. The post later became a relay station on the transcontinental telegraph. Originally called Fort Ruby, it was designated a camp at the close of the Civil War. The order to evacuate the post was issued on March 10, 1869, when the completion of the Central Pacific Railway destroyed its usefulness. Abandoned on September 20, 1869. Some of the buildings of the post are still standing.

STOREY. Established on June 3, 1860. Located south of Pyramid Lake. The post consisted of a temporary breastwork erected by the Washoe Regiment (Volunteers) during the war with the Paiute Indians. Named for Captain Edward Faris Storey of the Virginia Rifles, who died on June 7, 1860, of wounds received in the fighting with the Paiutes.

WINFIELD SCOTT. Established December 12, 1866. Located about forty-five miles north of Winnemucca at the foot of the Santa Rosa Mountains near the head of Paradise Valley. Established by order

94

of Major General Henry W. Halleck, commanding the department, to keep the Indians of the area under control. The post was a camp and was never officially designated a fort. Named for Major General Winfield Scott. Abandoned on February 19, 1871, as no longer necessary.

NEW MEXICO

BASCOM. Established August 15, 1863. Located on the right bank of the Canadian River, about eight miles north of the present town of Tucumcari on land leased for the purpose. Established to protect the travel routes across central New Mexico, including the Fort Smith–Santa Fe Trail, to discourage incursions by the Kiowa and Comanche Indians, and to encourage settlement down the Canadian Valley. Established by Captain Peter W. L. Plympton, 7th U.S. Infantry, by order of Brigadier General James H. Carleton, commanding the department. The post was first called Camp Easton for Major Langdon C. Easton, Quartermaster's Department. In January, 1864, it was designated Fort Bascom in honor of Captain George N. Bascom, 16th U.S. Infantry, killed on February 21, 1862, in the Battle of Valverde. Abandoned in December, 1870, and the property returned to the lessor in January, 1871.

BAYARD. Established August 21, 1866. Located ten miles east of the present town of Silver City, near the base of the Santa Rita Mountains. Established by First Lieutenant James M. Kerr, 125th U.S. Infantry, on a site chosen by Major Nelson H. Davis, assistant inspector general, to protect the Pinos Altos mining district, particularly against the Warm Spring Apaches. Brigadier General James H. Carleton believed that gold seekers venturing into Indian country should be protected so that they might exploit the mineral wealth for the good of the country. Named for Brigadier General George D. Bayard, who died on December 14, 1862, of wounds received at Fredericksburg. Abandoned as a military post in 1900. On January 2, 1900, all buildings were transferred to the Surgeon General for the establishment of a general hospital. It remains today a Veterans Administration hospital.

BURGWIN. Established August 14, 1852. Located on the Río Grande del Rancho, a confluent of the Río Grande, near the mouth of the Rito de la Olla, about ten miles south of Taos. The post was planned by and built under the direction of Second Lieutenant Robert Ransom, 1st U.S. Dragoons. It was named Cantonment Burgwin, in honor of Captain John H. K. Burgwin, 1st U.S. Dragoons, who died on February 7, 1847, of wounds received in the Taos uprising. It was never officially designated a fort. The post was also referred to as Fort Fernando de Taos. Established to protect the Taos Valley from depredations by the Jicarilla Apache and Ute Indians. Abandoned on May 18, 1860. The post has been reconstructed and is now known as the Fort Burgwin Research Center.

BUTLER. The War Department directed the establishment of Fort Butler on March 12, 1860. Plans were made, a military reservation, located on the Canadian River, was approved by the secretary of war on March 22, 1861, and troops to establish the post were assigned. Events connected with the coming of the Civil War blocked the actual establishment. After Fort Bascom was established in 1862, there was no need for Fort Butler. Although the post never existed, it sometimes appears on maps, located on the Gallinas River near Santa Rosa, or on the left bank of the Canadian River about twelve miles above Fort Bascom. The military reservation was transferred to the Interior Department on July 22, 1884.

CONRAD. Established September 8, 1851. Located on the right side of the Río Grande, twenty-four miles south of Socorro at the foot of Valverde Mesa. Established by Major Marshall S. Howe, 2nd U.S. Dragoons, by order of Lieutenant Colonel Edwin Vose Sumner,

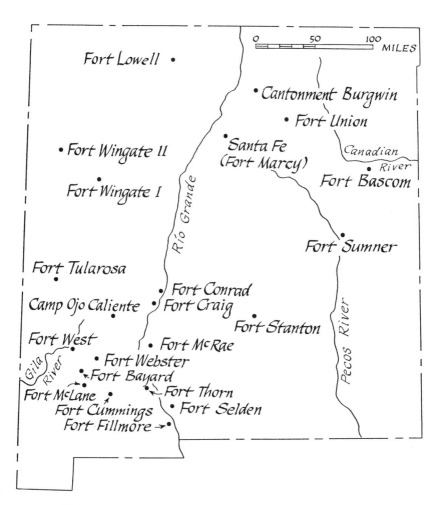

Fort Lowell •

0   50   100
                    MILES

• Cantonment Burgwin

• Fort Union

•Santa Fe
(Fort Marcy)

Canadian
      River

• Fort Wingate II

Fort Bascom

Fort Wingate I

Río Grande

Fort Sumner

Fort Tularosa

• Fort Conrad
• Fort Craig

Camp Ojo Caliente

Fort Stanton

Fort West

• Fort McRae

Gila River

• Fort Webster

Pecos River

Fort Bayard

Fort McLane

Fort Thorn

Fort Cummings

• Fort Selden

Fort Fillmore →

1st U.S. Dragoons, commanding the department. Named for Secretary of War Charles M. Conrad. The post formed part of the defensive system to restrain hostile Indians and protect the north-south route along the Río Grande. Abandoned on March 31, 1854, on the recommendation of Colonel Joseph K. F. Mansfield, Inspector General's Department, and replaced by Fort Craig. The site was then used to grow forage for Fort Craig and was called Hay Camp.

CRAIG. Established April 1, 1854, when Fort Conrad was abandoned, the buildings having been in the process of construction for some months before. Located on the tableland to the right of the Río Grande, about four miles below the present town of San Marcial and about nine miles below the abandoned Fort Conrad, near the northern end of the *Jornada del Muerto*. Intended to provide protection from roving bands of Apaches and to guard the north-south route along the Río Grande. Established by Captain Daniel T. Chandler, 3rd U.S. Infantry. Named for Captain Louis S. Craig, 3rd U.S. Infantry, murdered in California by deserters on June 6, 1852. Abandoned in 1885. The military reservation was transferred to the Interior Department on March 3, 1885.

CUMMINGS. Established October 2, 1863, at Cook's Springs in the Cook's Range, fifty-three miles west of the Río Grande, on the Mesilla-Tucson road. Established by Captain Valentine Dresher, 1st California Infantry, by order of Brigadier General James H. Carleton, to restrain the Apaches. Carleton said that except for Apache Pass, Arizona, the post guarded the most dangerous point on the southern route to California. Named for Major Joseph Cummings, 1st New Mexico Cavalry, killed by Navahos near Cañon Bonito August 18, 1863. Evacuated in August, 1873. Reoccupied in 1880. Evacuated August 14, 1884, except for small detachment remaining to protect the buildings. Reoccupied in 1886 because of Apache hostilities. Finally abandoned October 3, 1886. Military reservation transferred to the Interior Department October 20, 1891.

FAUNTLEROY. See Wingate II.

FERNANDO DE TAOS. See Burgwin.

FILLMORE. Established September 23, 1851. Located on the left bank of the Río Grande, about six miles south of Mesilla. At that time the Río Grande ran between Fort Fillmore and Mesilla but has since changed its course. Established by Lieutenant Colonel Dixon S. Miles, 3rd U.S. Infantry, with troops from the Post of El Paso (see Fort Bliss), Texas. Established by order of Lieutenant Colonel Edwin Vose Sumner, 1st U.S. Dragoons. The post formed part of the system of frontier defense for the control of marauding Indians. Named for President Millard Fillmore. Abandoned on July 26, 1861, by Union troops and occupied by Confederate troops from Texas. Abandoned by Confederate troops on July 8, 1862, because of the approach of Union forces from California. The United States flag was raised over the post in August, 1862, by Lieutenant Colonel Edward E. Eyre, 1st California Cavalry, but the troops were withdrawn by order of Colonel Joseph R. West, 1st California Infantry, dated October 10, 1862, and moved to Mesilla. The post was not again permanently garrisoned.

FLOYD. See McLane.

LOWELL. Established November 6, 1866. Located on the Chama River southwest of the town of Tierra Amarilla. Established by order of Brigadier General John Pope. Intended to protect the area against Ute Indian depredations. Originally called Camp Plummer, probably for Captain Augustus H. Plummer, 37th U.S. Infantry. The post was designated Fort Lowell on July 13, 1868, in honor of Brigadier General Charles R. Lowell, who died on October 20, 1864, of wounds received at Cedar Creek, Virginia. Abandoned on July 27, 1869, because the army considered the Utes to be entirely pacified. In 1872 the agency for certain Ute and Apache tribes was transferred from Abiquiu to the buildings of former Fort Lowell.

The agency was consolidated with the Pueblo agency in 1878, and the last rations were isued at Tierra Amarilla in December, 1881.

LYON. See Wingate II.

McLANE. Established September 16, 1860. Located fifteen miles south of the Santa Rita copper mines at Apache Tejo, south of the present town of Hurley. Established by Major Isaac Lynde, 7th U.S. Infantry. First called Fort Floyd, for Secretary of War John B. Floyd, Major Lynde proposed that it be named Fort Webster, to avoid confusion with Camp Floyd, Utah. Instead, on January 18, 1861, it was officially designated Fort McLane. Named for Captain George McLane, Mounted Riflemen, killed in action with the Navahos on October 13, 1860. Abandoned on July 3, 1861. Because of the outbreak of the Civil War and the threatened Confederate invasion of New Mexico, the garrison was transferred to strengthen Fort Fillmore. In 1862 troops of the California Column reoccupied the post and it was garrisoned, at least intermittently, until the close of the war, when it was permanently abandoned.

McRAE. Established April 3, 1863. Located near Ojo del Muerto, about five miles west of the *Jornada del Muerto* and three miles east of the Río Grande. Intended to protect travelers along the *Jornada del Muerto* and stop Indian depredations in the general area. Established by Captain Henry A. Greene, 1st California Infantry. Named for Captain Alexander McRae, 3rd U.S. Cavalry, killed on February 21, 1862, in the Battle of Valverde. Abandoned on October 30, 1876, except for a small detachment which remained to dispose of post property. The military reservation was transferred to the Interior Department on July 22, 1884.

MARCY. Established in 1846, construction commencing on August 23. Barracks, corrals, and other facilities were located adjacent to

Soldiers' quarters, Fort Marcy, New Mexico.

National Archives

Company officers' quarters, Fort Marcy, New Mexico. This fort is an example of a post that has genuine fortifications associated with it. Gun carriages, with ammunition boxes at the front and rear, are shown in the foreground.

National Archives

the Palace of the Governors, as they had been in the Spanish and Mexican periods. An earthwork of irregular shape and a blockhouse were constructed on an elevation about six hundred yards northeast of and from sixty to one hundred feet above the central plaza in Santa Fe.

Established by Brigadier General Stephen Watts Kearny. The site was chosen by First Lieutenant William H. Emory, Corps of Topographical Engineers, and First Lieutenant Jeremy F. Gilmer, Corps of Engineers. The construction was under the direction of Lieutenant Gilmer. Named for Secretary of War William L. Marcy. The fort was deactivated and the garrison withdrawn on August 23, 1867. From 1867 until 1875 the military establishment in Santa Fe was designated the Post at Santa Fe, New Mexico. During this period Santa Fe contained quarters for officers and troops, and facilities for the storage of supplies. For a part of the time it was headquarters for the Military District of New Mexico. In 1875 Fort Marcy was reactivated. It was ordered abandoned as a military post in the spring of 1891, and the military reservation, except for the post cemetery, was transferred to the Interior Department on October 7, 1891, to be sold at public auction. The order was rescinded on November 21, 1891, and the post was reoccupied. Permanently abandoned on October 10, 1894. The military reservation was transferred to the Interior Department on June 28, 1895.

OJO CALIENTE. Established in 1859. Located on the right bank of the Alamosa River, near the foothills of the San Mateo Mountains, some eighteeen miles north of the present town of Winston. Established as an advanced picket post of Fort Craig and designed to aid in the control of the Navaho Indians. It was a camp and was never officially designated a fort. The post was abandoned during the Civil War. In the late 1860's it became agency headquarters for the Warm Spring Apache Reservation. Troops were stationed there from late in 1877 until 1882 because of difficulties with the Apaches. There seems to be no record of the post after that date.

SANTA FE, PRESIDIO OF. Santa Fe was founded, probably in the spring of 1610, by Pedro de Peralta, governor and captain-general of New Mexico. Except for the period of the Pueblo Revolt, 1680–93, it was a garrisoned town under both Spain and Mexico. Initially the entire pueblo constituted a fortification, described by Diego de Vargas in 1692 as having neither windows nor doors facing outward and only one entrance, and being protected by trenches and towers with embrasures. After the reconquest Santa Fe was provided with a presidio, El Real Presidio de Nuestra Señora de los Remedios y la Exaltación de la Santa Cruz. The government palace was a defensible structure. The central plaza, on which the plaza fronted, served also as a *plaza de armas*. A *castrense*, or military chapel, consecrated to María Santísima de la Luz, was erected on the south side of the plaza during the years 1717–22. Barracks and other facilities for the garrison were located north of the palace and at one time, according to an old but undated plan, were fortified. The same site continued to be occupied throughout the Spanish and Mexican periods by barracks and later constituted a part of the United States military establishment in Santa Fe. Santa Fe, then, inasmuch as it was a permanently garrisoned town, was a presidio from the time it was founded until it was occupied by the United States on August 18, 1846.

SELDEN. Established May 8, 1865. Located at the southern end of the *Jornada del Muerto*, about one and one-half miles east of the Río Grande, some twelve miles above the town of Doña Ana. Established to protect the north-south route along the Río Grande and the settlers of the Mesilla Valley. The site was chosen by Major Nelson H. Davis, assistant inspector general, in April, and the order to establish the post was issued by Brigadier General James H. Carleton on April 25, 1865. Colonel John C. McFerran, quartermaster, Department of New Mexico, was in charge of construction. Named for Colonel Henry R. Selden, 1st New Mexico Infantry, who died on February 2, 1865. When the Santa Fe Railway was built down the Río Grande to meet the Southern Pacific, the need for the post ended and it was not garrisoned from 1877 to 1882. In 1882, during the Geronimo raids, it was regarrisoned by order of Brigadier General Nelson A. Miles. Permanently abandoned in April, 1889. The military reservation was transferred to the Interior Department on March 30, 1892.

STANTON. Established May 4, 1855. Originally located on the Río Bonito March 19, 1855, by Colonel John Garland, 8th U.S. Infantry, commanding the department, two miles south of its later site. Intended to control the Mescalero Apaches. A camp, called Camp Garland, was established near the original site by Lieutenant Colonel Dixon S. Miles, 3rd U.S. Infantry. He was joined there by an additional force under Captain James H. Carleton, 1st U.S. Dragoons. Two blockhouses were erected pending construction of the permanent post. On May 8 Captain Isaac V. D. Reeve, 8th U.S. Infantry, assumed command of the post and supervised the initial construction. Named for Captain Henry W. Stanton, 1st U.S. Dragoons, killed by Apaches near the site of the post on January 19, 1855. Evacuated August 2, 1861, because of the invasion of New Mexico by Confederate troops from Texas, and fired by Federal troops, but not entirely destroyed. Temporarily held by the Confederates, then reoccupied by Colonel Kit Carson, 1st New Mexico Infantry, in October or November, 1862, by order of Brigadier General James H. Carleton. Post rebuilt in 1868 and later removed to present position and substantial buildings erected. Abandoned as a military post August 17, 1896, and transferred to the Interior Department. Buildings remanded to the Public Health Service April

27, 1899, to be used as a U.S. Marine hospital. In June, 1953, the federal government closed the hospital as an economy measure. The New Mexico Public Welfare Department then operated it as a tuberculosis sanatorium.

SUMNER. Established in 1862. Located in the Bosque Redondo on the east bank of the Pecos River south of the present town of Fort Sumner. The site was selected by Captain Joseph Updegraff, 5th U.S. Infantry, in accordance with plans of Brigadier General James H. Carleton for confining the Navaho Indians. A licensed Indian trading post had occupied the site since 1851. The post was constructed by troops of the California Column. Named for Major General Edwin Vose Sumner, former commander of the department. It was to Fort Sumner that Colonel Kit Carson, 1st New Mexico Infantry, brought the Navahos, some 7,000 strong, when he dislodged them from Cañon de Chelly. Several hundred Apaches were held there at the same time. When the Indians were permitted to leave, the post was abandoned and put up for auction in 1868. It was purchased by Lucien B. Maxwell. The military reservation, except for the cemetery, was transferred to the Interior Department on March 25, 1871.

THORN. Established December 24, 1853. Located on the right bank of the Río Grande at Santa Barbara, now Hatch. Established by Captain Israel B. Richardson, 3rd U.S. Infantry. Garrisoned by troops from the abandoned Fort Webster. The post guarded the El Paso–Santa Fe route along the west bank of the Río Grande and the San Diego road where it turned west from the river against Apaches and outlaws. Named for First Lieutenant Herman Thorn, 2nd U.S. Infantry, who drowned in the Colorado River on October 16, 1849. The post occupied an unhealthful site on the edge of an extensive marsh and was abandoned in March, 1859. The public property, including doors and window casings, was taken to Fort Fillmore, but the hospital and one storeroom were left intact for the use of travelers. Occupied by Confederate troops, 1861–62. The Union flag was raised over the post on July 5, 1862, by troops of the California Column, commanded by Lieutenant Colonel Edward E. Eyre, 1st California Cavalry, but it was not again premanently garrisoned.

TULAROSA. Established April 30, 1872. Located in the present Catron County. The original site was on the left bank of Tularosa Creek, about fifteen miles north of the town of Reserve. Established to protect the agency for the newly opened Apache reservation. Established by Captain Frederick W. Coleman, 15th U.S. Infantry. Before the post was completed, the Indian Bureau decided to move the agency headquarters. The post was moved to Horse Creek, about eighteen miles east of the original site. Abandoned on November 26, 1874, when the Indians were removed to Ojo Caliente, Arizona.

UNION. Established July 26, 1851. Troops were already encamped on the site. Located about twenty-four miles northeast of Las Vegas on the Mountain Branch of the Santa Fe Trail on the west side of the valley of Wolf Creek, an affluent of the Mora River. Established by Lieutenant Colonel Edwin Vose Sumner, 1st U.S. Dragoons, commanding the department. Sumner intended the post to replace Santa Fe as departmental headquarters, because he considered Santa Fe to be a "sink of vice and extravagance." Established to act as a deterrent to the Jicarilla Apache and Ute Indians, to protect the Santa Fe Trail, and to serve as a depot of supplies. The original buildings, which were built of logs, were considered to be too close to the mesa forming the western rim of the valley to be militarily secure. Hence, Colonel Edward R. S. Canby, 19th U.S. Infantry, ordered the erection of a new post, located on the valley floor, about a mile from the original site and east of Wolf Creek, in anticipation of a Confederate attack.

Construction of the second fort began in August, 1861. It was an earthwork in the form of an eight-pointed star with quarters in the demilunes. Need for additional facilities, coupled with the deterioration of the earthwork and the dampness of the quarters, led Brigadier General James H. Carleton to order the construction of a new post.

The third and final site of Fort Union was almost immediately north of the star-fort. Construction of the new post, which was built of adobe and brick, began in 1863, but none of the buildings were completed until 1866. The ordnance depot (arsenal) occupied the site of the original post. For many years Fort Union served as the general depot of supplies for New Mexico. The construction of railroads into the area lessened its importance, and the arsenal was discontinued in 1882. The fort was abandoned on February 21, 1891, except for a caretaker detail. On April 1, 1894, the military reservation was relinquished, the land and buildings reverting to the owners of the original land grant. The site is now a national monument.

WEBSTER. Fort Webster, apparently, occupied at least three separate locations. (See Fort McLane for a fourth possible site.) On January 23, 1851, the advance party of the United States–Mexican Boundary Commission arrived at the Santa Rita copper mines and found them abandoned. The main body of the commission moved from El Paso del Norte (Ciudad Juárez) in April and occupied the old private Mexican fort which had been erected in 1804 by Francisco Manuel Elguea to protect the mines. The commission was escorted by one company of infantry, commanded by Captain Louis S. Craig, 3rd U.S. Infantry. The post was called Cantonment Dawson by the commission. When the commission moved on in October, 1851, the post was occupied by the army and garrisoned by one company of the 3rd U.S. Infantry and one company of the 2nd U.S.

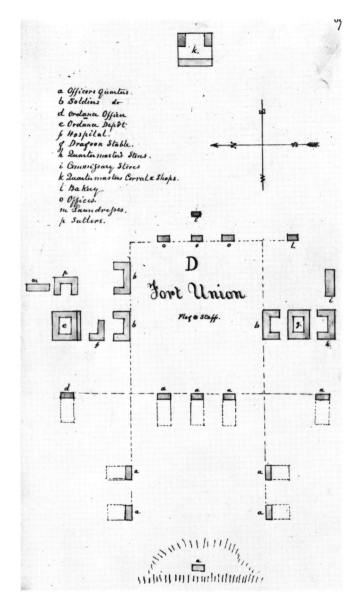

Plan of Fort Union, New Mexico, an example of the large, long-lived, multi-purpose post, but largely lacking in fortifications.

From MANSFIELD ON THE CONDITION OF WESTERN FORTS, 1853–54.

Dragoons. At this time the post was named Fort Webster in honor of Secretary of State Daniel Webster.

On September 9, 1852, the post was moved to the Río Mimbres, about fourteen miles northeast of the copper mines, where a new post was constructed under the command of Major Gouverneur Morris, 3rd U.S. Infantry, but the old name was retained. The new post did not have the desired effect in restraining the Indians. Colonel Joseph K. F. Mansfield, Inspector General's Department, who inspected the post in October, 1853, thought that it was too small and that it should be on the Gila River, where it would be on the emigrant route. It was abandoned on December 20, 1853, and the garrison was removed to Fort Thorn.

In June, 1859, Colonel Benjamin L. E. Bonneville, 3rd U.S. Infantry, ordered Second Lieutenant Henry C. McNeill of the Mounted Riflemen and twenty men to the copper mines to guard them against Indians. Bonneville intended to establish a permanent two-company post between Black and Burro Mountains, but this was not done, probably because Navaho and Kiowa hostilities made it impossible to spare the troops. In his report of 1866, Brigadier General John Pope, commanding the department, announced that he had established a new post near the headwaters of the Mimbres for defense against the Apaches. This post appears on Colton's 1877 map of Arizona and New Mexico territories on the west bank of the Mimbres, about fifteen miles north of Santa Rita. Apparently it was a temporary post, garrisoned during Indian hostilities. Still another Fort Webster is said to have existed briefly at the village of Mowry (Mimbres Station of the Butterfield mail route). It is reported that when the Overland mail route was abandoned at the outset of the Civil War, the station was converted into a fort called Fort Webster under the command of a Major Mowry, who resigned to join the Confederacy. If such a post existed, it was not an army post.

WEST. Established February 24, 1863. Located on the east side of the Gila River in the Pinos Altos Mountains, north of the present Silver City. Established by Captain William McCleave, 1st California Cavalry, by order of Brigadier General James H. Carleton. Intended to protect the Pinos Altos mining district from the Apache Indians. Named for Brigadier General Joseph Rodman West. Abandoned on January 8, 1864.

WINGATE I. Established October 22, 1862. Located at El Gallo, the great spring at the present San Rafael. The site was selected by Brigadier General Edward R. S. Canby in the summer of 1862. The post was established by Lieutenant Colonel J. Francisco Chávez, 1st New Mexico Infantry, by order of Brigadier General James H. Carleton, in preparation of Colonel Kit Carson's campaign against the Navahos the following year. Named for Captain Benjamin Wingate, 5th U.S. Infantry, who died on June 1, 1862, of wounds received in the Battle of Valverde. Abandoned in 1868 and the garrison transferred to Fort Wingate II.

WINGATE II. Established August 31, 1860. Located at Ojo del Oso at the north end of the Zuñi Range near the headwaters of the Río Puerco of the West. Established by Captain William Chapman, 5th U.S. Infantry. Named for Colonel Thomas T. Fauntleroy, 1st U.S. Dragoons. When Fauntleroy resigned to join the Confederacy, the post was renamed Fort Lyon, on September 25, 1861, for Brigadier General Nathaniel Lyon, killed on August 10, 1861, in the Battle of Wilson's Creek, Missouri. The garrison was withdrawn on September 10, 1861, because of the invasion of New Mexico by Confederate forces from Texas. A mail station was maintained at the post, and throughout the Civil War it was referred to as Fort Fauntleroy in official despatches. Reoccupied in June, 1868, by troops returning the Navahos from their imprisonment at Fort Sumner and by the garrison transferred from Fort Wingate I. At the time of reoccupation the post was designated Fort Wingate. Evacuated in 1911 except for a small detachment which remained until March 19, 1912, when the post was placed in charge of a caretaker. In 1918 the reservation was taken over by the Ordnance Department for the storage of high explosives and was designated the Wingate Ordnance Depot. In 1925 part of the reservation and buildings were transferred to the Indian Service to be used as a school for the Navahos. In August, 1960, the name of the military post was changed to Fort Wingate Ordnance Depot.

NORTH DAKOTA

ABERCROMBIE. Established August 28, 1857. Located on the left bank of the Red River of the North at Graham's Point, twelve miles north of the confluence of the Bois de Sioux and Otter Tail rivers. Intended to protect the settlers of the Red River Valley from the Sioux Indians. Established by Lieutenant Colonel John J. Abercrombie, 2nd U.S. Infantry, for whom the post was named. It was later the terminus of the military mail routes from Fort Stevenson via Fort Totten and from Fort Wadsworth via Fort Ransom, and an important post in the control of the Sioux Indians. Evacuated on July 25, 1859, but reoccupied in July, 1860, and rebuilt. Finally abandoned on October 23, 1878, and the buildings sold to settlers in the area. By this date the danger of Indian hostilities in the area was considered to have ended. The military reservation was transferred to the Interior Department on July 14, 1880.

BERTHOLD. Originally erected as a trading post, Fort Atkinson, in 1858–59. Located on the left bank of the Missouri River on a bend below the mouth of the Little Missouri. The site is now covered by the waters of the Garrison Reservoir. The post was purchased by the American Fur Company in 1862 and renamed Fort Berthold, the previous trading post of that name having been abandoned. It was probably named for Bartholomew Berthold, although it may possibly have been for his son Pierre. On August 29, 1864, Brigadier General Alfred Sully left Captain Abraham B. Moreland with his company of the 6th Iowa Cavalry to protect the trading post against the Sioux Indians. On September 3, 1864, the troops occupied the fort, having previously encamped outside the stockade. Because of some disagreement with the company's agent, log buildings were erected outside the stockade and the troops moved into them in April, 1865. Fort Berthold was never owned by the government, and, apparently, no rent was ever paid for its use by the military. The post was evacuated on June 14, 1867, when Fort Stevenson was established. In 1868, Fort Berthold became the agency headquarters for the Arikara, Gros Ventre (Hidatsa), and Mandan Indians and so remained until 1874. The fort continued to operate as a trading post also until 1874.

BUFORD. Established June 15, 1866. Located on the left bank of the Missouri River, just below the confluence of the Yellowstone and some two and one-half miles below the American Fur Company's Fort Union. The post was intended to protect the emigrant route from Minnesota to Montana as well as navigation along the Missouri River, principally from the Sioux. Established by Captain William G. Rankin, 31st U. S. Infantry, on a site chosen by Major General Alfred H. Terry. In 1867 Fort Union was dismantled and the materials used in the enlargement of Fort Buford. Named for Major General John Buford, who died on December 16, 1863. The post, situated in the heart of the buffalo country, was particularly offensive to the Sioux. However, once the power of the Sioux had been broken and the railways constructed, it no longer served a useful purpose. It was abandoned on October 1, 1895, and the garrison transferred to Fort Assiniboine, Montana. A small contingent remained at the post until November 7, 1895, to dispose of public

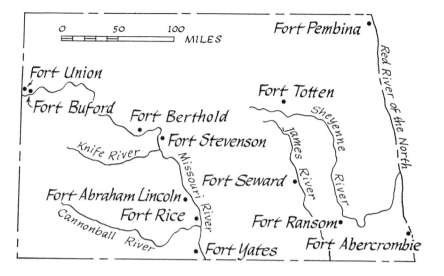

property. The buildings of the post were sold at public auction, and the military reservation was transferred to the Interior Department on October 31, 1895.

CROSS. See Seward.

HAYS. Major General John Pope, commanding the department, directed the establishment of a post on Devils (Minnewaukan) Lake in the spring of 1864. By order of Secretary of War Edwin M. Stanton, issued May 12, 1864, the post, previously referred to as "Post on Devils Lake," was named Fort Hays. The post, as it happened, was not established, but Fort Totten (*q.v.*) was founded nearby a few years later.

LINCOLN, ABRAHAM. Established June 14, 1872. Located on the right bank of the Missouri River at the mouth of the Heart River, three miles south of the town of Bismarck. Established to protect the engineers and workers engaged in the construction of the Northern Pacific Railway. Established by Lieutenant Colonel Daniel Huston, 6th U.S. Infantry. The post was first named Fort McKean for Colonel Henry Boyd McKean, 81st Pennsylvania Infantry, killed in the Battle of Cold Harbor on June 3, 1864. On November 19, 1872, it was designated Fort Abraham Lincoln, in honor of the martyred president. The original post was located on the bluffs overlooking the river. In 1873 it became a nine-company cavalry and infantry post with the infantry stationed on the level river plain near the mouth of the Heart River, the two together comprising Fort Abraham Lincoln. Abandoned on July 22, 1891, as no longer necessary. (Fort Lincoln, on the east side of the river, was authorized on March 2, 1895, and was first occupied in 1903.) The military reservation was transferred to the Interior Department on October 15, 1891. The area is now a state park and the post has been partly restored.

MCKEAN. See Abraham Lincoln.

PEMBINA. Established July 8, 1870. Located a mile and a half south of the town of Pembina on the left bank of the Red River of the North, just above the mouth of the Pembina River. The Minnesota legislature petitioned Congress for the establishment of a post at Pembina because of the unrest in the Red River Valley and the danger of depredations by the Sioux Indians, who had been driven into Canada some years before. Major General Winfield Scott Hancock recommended the establishment of the post on December 8, 1869. The post served also to check illicit trade between the United States and Canada. Established by Captain Loyd Wheaton, 20th U.S. Infantry. Originally called Fort Thomas, for Major General George H. Thomas, who died on March 28, 1870. The post was designated Fort Pembina on September 6, 1870. A large part of the post was destroyed by fire on May 27, 1895, leading to its abandonment on August 15, 1895. The military reservation was transferred to the Interior Department on December 2, 1895, and sold at public auction.

RANSOM. Established June 18, 1867. Located on the right side of the Sheyenne River, about seventy-five miles above its junction with the Red River of the North, at Grizzly Bear Hill. Established on a site chosen by Brigadier General Alfred H. Terry. Erected under the direction of Captain George H. Crosman, 10th U.S. Infantry. Designed to keep the Sioux in check and to protect the emigrant trail from Minnesota to Montana. Named for Brigadier General Thomas E. G. Ransom, who died on October 29, 1864. Abandoned on July 31, 1872, when Fort Seward was established. The military reservation was transferred to the Interior Department on July 22, 1884.

RICE. Established July 7, 1864. Located on a high point on the right bank of the Missouri River opposite the mouth of Long Lake Creek and immediately below the present town of Fort Rice. Established by Brigadier General Alfred Sully during his punitive expedition against the Sioux. Intended to control the Sioux, protect the emigrant route from Minnesota to Montana, and to protect navigation on the Missouri River. Erected under the direction of Colonel Daniel J. Dill, 30th Wisconsin Infantry. The original post consisted of rude huts made of cottonwood logs with earth roofs, but it was rebuilt in more substantial form in 1868. By order of Secretary of War Edwin M. Stanton, issued May 12, 1864, the post was named for Brigadier General James Clay Rice, killed in the Battle of Laurel Hill, Virginia, on May 10, 1864. After the establishment of Fort Yates, Fort Rice was no longer considered necessary, and it was abandoned on November 25, 1878, and dismantled. A small detachment remained until February 6, 1879, to dispose of public property. The military reservation was transferred to the Interior Department July 22, 1884. Part of the site is now a state park.

SEWARD. Established May 27, 1872. Located on the right bank of the James River a little above the present Jamestown. Established to protect the construction of the Northern Pacific Railroad, and located at the point where the railroad crossed the James River. Established by Captain John C. Bates, 20th U.S. Infantry. The post was first called Camp Sykes, for Colonel George Sykes, 20th U.S. Infantry. It was designated Fort Cross on September 7, 1872. The name was changed to Fort Seward in 1873 in honor of former Secretary of State William H. Seward, who died on October 10, 1872. Abandoned on September 30, 1877. The military reservation was transferred to the Interior Department on July 14, 1880.

STEVENSON. Established June 14, 1867. Located on the left bank of the Missouri River above the mouth of the Knife River at the mouth of Douglas Creek and about one-quarter mile from the river. The site, some twelve miles below Fort Berthold, was selected by Brigadier General Alfred Sully in 1864. It is now covered by the waters of Garrison Reservoir. Established by Major Joseph N. G. Whistler, 31st U.S. Infantry, with troops from Fort Berthold, which it replaced. The post served as a base of supplies for Fort Totten and as a link in the chain of posts along the proposed emigrant route from Minnesota to Montana. It protected navigation along the Missouri as well as the Indians of the Fort Berthold Agency, and aided in the control of the Sioux. Named for Brigadier General Thomas G. Stevenson, by order of Secretary of War Edwin M. Stanton, dated April 12, 1864. General Stevenson was killed on May 10, 1864, in the Battle of Spotsylvania. The building of the railroads and the waning power of the Sioux eventually rendered the post unnecessary. It was abandoned on July 22, 1883, except for a small detachment which remained until August 31 to dispose of public property. The garrison was transferred to Fort Buford. The post was turned over to the Fort Berthold Indian Agency on August 7, 1883, and was used as an Indian school until 1894. The military reservation was transferred to the Interior Department on February 13, 1895.

THOMAS. See Pembina.

TOTTEN. Established July 17, 1867. Located on the south side of Devils (Minnewaukan) Lake, about five hundred yards from the lake shore, on a site chosen by Brigadier General Alfred H. Terry. Established as a step toward placing the Indians of the region on reservations. The post served also as one of the chain of posts to protect the emigrant route from Minnesota to Montana. Established by Captain Samuel A. Wainwright, 31st U.S. Infantry. The post lay within the limits of Devils Lake, or Fort Totten, Indian Reservation when it was established on January 11, 1870. The original, hastily constructed buildings were replaced by permanent buildings in 1869–70. The rolling plains, timbered hills, and lake made this one of the most attractive posts on the plains. Named for Brigadier General Joseph Gilbert Totten, chief engineer of the U.S. Army, who died on April 22, 1864. Abandoned in 1890, the last of the garrison leaving the post on December 31. The post and reservation were transferred to the Interior Department on October 4, 1890, and became the headquarters for the Fort Totten Indian Agency and industrial school. It is now a sub-agency of the Turtle Mountain Indian Agency.

UNION. Originally established in 1828 as a trading post by the American Fur Company. Located on the left bank of the Missouri River, three miles above the mouth of the Yellowstone. On August 18, 1864, Brigadier General Alfred Sully occupied the post, leaving one company of the 30th Wisconsin Infantry to protect the traders and the public property stored there for the post to be established nearby (see Fort Buford). The evacuation of Fort Union by the military was completed on August 31, 1865. In 1867, Fort Union was purchased by the government, dismantled, and its materials used in the enlargement of Fort Buford.

YATES. Established December 23, 1874. Located on the right bank of the Missouri River at the present town of Fort Yates, about ten miles above the South Dakota line. Established as headquarters for the Standing Rock Sioux Indian Agency and originally called Standing Rock Agency. It was designated Fort Yates on December 30, 1878. Named for Captain George W. Yates, 7th U.S. Cavalry, killed on June 25, 1876, in the Battle of the Little Big Horn. Abandoned on September 11, 1903, as a military post. It remains the headquarters for the Standing Rock Reservation.

OKLAHOMA

ARBUCKLE I. Established June 24, 1834. Located on the Arkansas River near the mouth of the Cimarron. Established by Captain George Birch, 7th U.S. Infantry, with two companies from Fort Gibson. The post consisted of a blockhouse, stockade, and some cabins. It was intended to impress the Indians with the military might of the United States. Although it was substantially built, it was probably intended as a temporary post and should not be called a fort even though it is frequently referred to as Old Fort Arbuckle. Named for Colonel Matthew Arbuckle, 7th U.S. Infantry. Abandoned on November 11, 1834.

ARBUCKLE II. Established August 22, 1850. Originally located a few miles west of Mustang Creek and a mile south of the Canadian River. Established by Captain Randolph B. Marcy, 5th U.S. Infantry. Intended to safeguard travel along the emigrant route to New Mexico and California and to protect the relocated Chickasaw Indians from the plains Indians. Called Camp Arbuckle for Colonel Matthew Arbuckle, 7th U.S. Infantry, commanding the department. The site was not considered satisfactory by the War Department and

Fort Union, North Dakota, from a drawing made by Alexander Murray, April 10, 1845. Like Sutter's Fort in California, Fort Union was a private defensive post taken over by the army and garrisoned briefly.

Courtesy Library of Congress

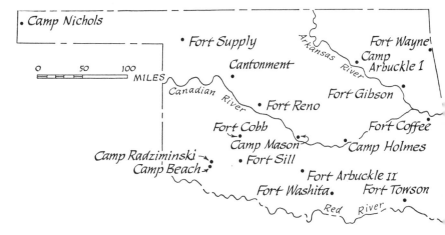

the post was relocated by Captain Marcy on April 19, 1851. The
new location was on the right side of Wild Horse Creek, about five
miles from the Washita River, on the site of a Kickapoo Indian village from which the Indians, a year or two earlier, had moved to
Mexico. Marcy first called the post, in its new location, "Fort Near
the Crossing of the Washita River." On June 25, 1851, it was designated Fort Arbuckle for Colonel Arbuckle, who died on June
11, 1851.

The post was virtually abandoned on February 13, 1858, when all
but five of the garrison, who remained to guard the post property,
were sent to Utah in connection with the Mormon campaign (Utah
War). The threat of a Comanche uprising led to the reoccupation of
the post by volunteers in June of the same year. Regular troops arrived to garrison the post on June 29, 1858. Evacuated on May 5,
1861, and occupied the following day by Texas troops in the name
of the Confederacy. Reoccupied by two companies of Federal troops
from Fort Gibson on November 18, 1866. Permanently abandoned
on June 24, 1870. The land reverted to the Chickasaw Nation on

117

July 9, 1870, in accordance with the terms of the treaty of April 28, 1866.

BEACH. Established August 13, 1874. Located on Otter Creek, a confluent of the North Fork of the Red River, near the present town of Tipton. The post was a supply camp, protected by a redoubt, used to forward supplies to troops from Fort Sill in the field. Construction of the post was under the direction of Captain Warren C. Beach, 11th U.S. Infantry, for whom it was named. Although it was only a camp, it was sometimes called Fort Beach or Fort Otter. It may have been built on one of the sites previously occupied by Camp Radziminski (*q.v.*).

BLUNT. See Gibson.

CANTONMENT. Established March 6, 1879. Located on the North Canadian River, near the present town of Canton, some sixty miles northwest of Fort Reno and the old Darlington (Cheyenne-Arapaho) Agency. Established by Lieutenant Colonel Richard I. Dodge, 23rd U.S. Infantry, after the raid of the Northern Cheyenne Indians in 1878 led the people of Kansas to demand that a post be established to control the Cheyenne and Arapaho. The post was referred to as "Cantonment," "New Cantonment," or "Cantonment on the North Fork of the Canadian River," the latter being the most common. It was never officially designated a fort. After the Northern Cheyenne were permitted to return to their former homeland, the need for the post decreased and orders to abandon it were issued on June 14, 1882, the garrison going to Fort Sully. On September 7, 1882, the post was transferred to the Interior Department which contracted with the Mennonites to maintain a school there for the plains Indians. As late as 1885, after the school had opened, a company of infantry was stationed at Cantonment temporarily because of trouble which arose over the fencing of Cheyenne and Arapaho lands. In

1898 the government took over the supervision of the school which continued to function until 1949.

COBB. Established October 1, 1859. Located on the east side of Pond (Cobb) Creek, where it empties into the Washita River, near the present town of Fort Cobb and three miles west of what was then the Wichita Indian Agency. The post was established by two companies of the 1st U.S. Cavalry and one company of the 1st U.S. Infantry, commanded by Major William H. Emory, 1st U.S. Cavalry. Established to protect the agency for the newly established reservation for the Penateka Comanches, Wacoes, Caddoes, and Tonkawas, after they had been removed from Texas. Named for Secretary of the Treasury Howell Cobb of Georgia. Abandoned on May 3, 1861, because of the outbreak of the Civil War, and occupied by Confederate troops from Texas on May 5. On the night of October 23, 1862, Osage, Shawnee, Delaware, and Caddo Indians attacked the post, killed most of the small Confederate garrison, and set fire to the buildings. They then turned on the Tonkawas, who had co-operated fully with the Confederates, and whom they accused of cannibalism. The outbreak ended in the near extermination of the Tonkawas and the destruction of Fort Cobb. In 1868 the Kiowa and Comanche Indians from the vicinity of Fort Larned, Kansas, were moved, with Colonel William B. Hazen, 38th U.S. Infantry, as agent, to Fort Cobb. Troops from Fort Arbuckle, sent to protect the agency, repaired a few of the ruined buildings. Major General Phil Sheridan occupied the post in December, 1868, at the start of his campaign against the plains Indians, but soon decided to establish a new post (Sill). Abandoned on January 6, 1869, except for one company of the 6th U.S. Infantry, which remained until March 12, 1869, when the Kiowa and Comanche Agency was transferred to Fort Sill.

COFFEE. Established April 22, 1834. Located on a bluff on the right side of the Arkansas River at a spot called Swallow Rock, near the present town of Spiro. Established by Captain John Stewart, 7th U.S. Infantry. Intended to stop whisky shipments up the Arkansas River into Indian territory and to protect the newly relocated Choctaw and Chickasaw Indians. Named for Brigadier General John Coffee, Tennessee Mounted Vounteers. General Coffee, a nephew of President Andrew Jackson, had gained considerable fame for his campaign against the Creek Indians in 1812–13. Abandoned on October 19, 1838, when Stewart and his troops were ordered to Arkansas to protect the people of that state from fancied danger from the Cherokee Indians. The post was turned over to the Choctaw Nation in 1843, and the Choctaw Council established there the Fort Coffee Academy for boys, which was operated under the direction of Methodist missionaries. The school was closed after the outbreak of the Civil War, and the buildings were occupied by a Confederate force. About the beginning of October, 1863, Fort Coffee was captured and burned by Federal troops.

GIBSON. Established April 20, 1824. Located on the left bank of the Neosho (Grand) River, three miles above its confluence with the Arkansas. Erected by troops from Fort Smith, Arkansas, which was abandoned at this time, under the command of Colonel Matthew Arbuckle, 7th U.S. Infantry. Construction was under the direction of First Lieutenant Pierce M. Butler, 7th U.S. Infantry. The immediate cause for the establishment of the post was the massacre of a party of white trappers on the Blue River in November, 1823. It was intended to restrain the Osage Indians, to end their fighting with the Cherokees, and to protect white hunters in the area. Named for Colonel George Gibson, commissary general, U.S. Army, the post was first designated Cantonment Gibson, then, in 1832, Fort Gibson. Evacuated in May, 1836, when the entire garrison was ordered to the Texas border.

The post was reoccupied in January, 1837, when the rumored

Mexican invasion of the Republic of Texas failed to materialize. Ordered abandoned on June 8, 1857, and substantially evacuated by June 22, 1857. The last troops left the post in September, 1857. The land and buildings were turned over to the Cherokee Nation. Occupied by Confederate troops early in the Civil War. Retaken by a force of Union troops, including Cherokee volunteers, commanded by Colonel William A. Phillips, 3rd Indian Home Guards, on April 5, 1863. A fortification was erected on the hill above the old post and named Fort Blunt, for Major General James G. Blunt, then commanding the District of Kansas. The buildings of the old post were repaired, new buildings were erected, and extensive earthworks constructed.

The name "Fort Gibson" was restored on December 31, 1863. The post was reoccupied by regular army troops on February 17, 1866. Broken up as a military post on September 30, 1871, but retained as a quartermaster's depot. Reoccupied on July 31, 1872. Finally abandoned on September 22, 1890. The military reservation, except for the national cemetery, was transferred to the Interior Department on February 7, 1891. The site was occupied as "Camp at Fort Gibson" from April 6, 1897, to November, 1897, and again from April 7, 1901, to November 19, 1901. Many of the post buildings were torn down and others were converted into private dwellings.

HOLMES. Established June 21, 1834. Located on the east bank of the Little River, about a mile and a half above its confluence with the Canadian, near the present town of Bilby. Established by Second Lieutenant Theophilus Hunter Holmes, 7th U.S. Infantry, by order of Colonel Henry Leavenworth, 3rd U.S. Infantry. The post marked the terminus of the military road constructed, at Colonel Leavenworth's order, from Fort Gibson to the Canadian River. It was strategically located near the crossing of the Canadian on the Old Osage

Trail. The post was first called Camp Canadian, then Camp Holmes, for Lieutenant Holmes. Apparently, it was never officially designated a fort. The site was considered unhealthful, and the post was abandoned after it had been occupied for about a year. Edwards Trading Post was established nearby and is sometimes confused with Camp Holmes.

MASON. Established in June, 1835. Located on the north bank of the Canadian River near the present town of Lexington. Established by Major Richard B. Mason, 1st U.S. Dragoons, primarily to provide a meeting place for the great Indian council held by Governor Montfort Stokes in August, 1835. The post was never officially designated a fort. After the conclusion of the council, Auguste Chouteau established a trading post on or near the site, which continued to be known as Fort Mason.

NICHOLS. Established June 1, 1865. Located on a high knoll near Cold Springs on the Cimarron branch of the Santa Fe Trail, about four miles east of the present New Mexico line and twenty-three miles west of the present Boise City. The site was also known as Cedar Bluffs, and the springs as Upper Cimarron Springs. It was about 140 miles from Fort Union, or nearly halfway from Fort Union to the Cimarron crossing, a distance of about three hundred miles. Established by Colonel Kit Carson, 1st New Mexico Infantry, by order of Brigadier General James H. Carleton, dated May 7, 1865. Intended to protect travel along the Santa Fe Trail and to exert a peaceful influence over the Kiowa, Comanche, and Cheyenne Indians. Probably named for Captain Charles P. Nichols, 1st California Cavalry. The post was a camp and was never officially designated a fort. Abandoned on or about September 22, 1865.

OTTER. See Beach.

RADZIMINSKI. Established September 23, 1858. Originally located on the left bank of Otter Creek near the present town of Tipton. In November the camp was moved several miles upstream, and in March, 1859, it was moved to the right bank of Otter Creek, four miles northwest of the present town of Mountain Park. Established by Captain Earl Van Dorn, 2nd U.S. Cavalry, as a base of operations against the Kiowa and Comanche Indians. Named for First Lieutenant Charles Radziminski, 2nd U.S. Cavalry, who died of tuberculosis on August 18, 1858. The post was a camp and was never officially designated a fort. No permanent buildings were erected. Abandoned on December 6, 1859. The post was immediately occupied by Texas Rangers, who remained there for about a year, patrolling the border and skirmishing with Indians.

RENO. Established in July, 1874. Located on the right side of the North Canadian River a few miles above the present town of El Reno. The site was selected by John D. Miles, Cheyenne Indian agent, and Captain Theodore J. Wint, 4th U.S. Cavalry. Established after the Cheyenne uprising of 1874, to protect the Darlington (Cheyenne-Arapaho) Indian Agency, which was located on the opposite side of the North Canadian. The military reservation was declared on July 17, 1874, but during the first year thereafter, the troops were engaged in putting down the Cheyenne and were quartered in or near the Darlington Agency. The original garrison was under the command of Lieutenant Colonel Thomas H. Neill, 6th U.S. Cavalry. The first buildings of the post were not erected until 1875. The post was named for Major General Jesse L. Reno, killed on September 14, 1862, in the Battle of South Mountain. Abandoned as a military post on February 24, 1908, except for a small detachment which remained until May 25 to dispose of public property. The post then became an army remount station. In 1938 it became the Reno Quartermaster's Depot. In 1949 the military reservation became the Fort Reno Livestock Research Station.

SILL. Established January 7, 1869. Located at the junction of Cache and Medicine Bluff creeks, near the eastern base of the Wichita Mountains. The site had been examined the previous summer by Colonel Benjamin Grierson, 10th U.S. Cavalry. The final reconnaissance of the site was made on December 27–29, 1868, by Colonel Grierson, Colonel William B. Hazen, 38th U.S. Infantry, and Major George A. Forsyth, 9th U.S. Cavalry, who recommended immediate occupation. Construction of the post commenced on January 8, 1869. Established by Major General Phil Sheridan to serve as a base of operations against the Cheyenne and Kiowa Indians and to replace Fort Cobb (*q.v.*) as agency headquarters. Colonel Grierson was in charge of initial construction. Originally called Camp Wichita, the post was designated Fort Sill on July 2, 1869. Named in honor of Brigadier General Joshua W. Sill, killed on December 31, 1862, in the Battle of Stone River, Tennessee. The post became the center for the control of the southern plains Indians, and the headquarters for the agency for the Comanche, Kiowa, Kiowa-Apache, Waco, Wichita, Kichai, and Caddo Indians. After 1876 the garrison more often found it necessary to protect than subdue the Indians. The post is still operative.

SUPPLY. Established November 18, 1868. Located on a low, sandy bottom between the North Canadian River and Wolf Creek, near their junction, and close to the present town of Fort Supply. Established by Captain John H. Page, 3rd U.S. Infantry, by order of Lieutenant Colonel Alfred Sully, 3rd U.S. Infantry, in connection with Major General Phil Sheridan's winter campaign against the Cheyenne, Kiowa, and other plains Indians. Originally called Camp Supply, the post was designated a fort in 1878. Abandoned on February 25, 1895. The military reservation was transferred to the Interior Department on November 14, 1894. The reservation was turned over to Oklahoma Territory, and in 1903 the territory auth-

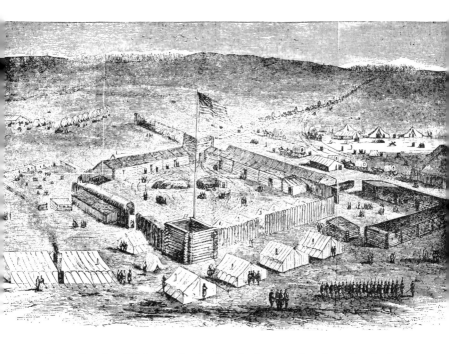

Camp Supply, Oklahoma, in the days before statehood, as sketched
by A. R. Waud for *Harper's Weekly*, February 27, 1869.
One of the posts provided with both stockade and blockhouses,
Camp Supply was officially designated a fort in 1878.

Courtesy University of Oklahoma Library

orized the establishment of the Western State Hospital for the mentally ill on the site.

TOWSON. Established in May, 1824. Originally located on the east bank of Gates Creek, about six miles north of the Red River. Established by Major Alexander Cummings, 7th U.S. Infantry, with troops from Fort Jesup, Louisiana. Intended to control the activity of outlaws and Indian bands along the Red River—at that time the frontier between the United States and Mexico—and to serve as a center for the control and protection of the Choctaw and Chickasaw Indians. Named Cantonment Towson in honor of Colonel Nathan Towson, paymaster general, U.S. Army. Abandoned in June, 1829. Most of the post buildings were burned soon thereafter.

The post was re-established on April 26, 1831, by Major Stephen Watts Kearny, 3rd U.S. Infantry. The new post was located about six miles north of the Red River, immediately south of Gates Creek, near the present town of Fort Towson. Intended to provide protection for the Choctaw Nation and to guard the Red River frontier. The new post was first called Camp Phoenix, then, on November 20, 1831, Cantonment Towson, and finally, on February 8, 1832, Fort Towson. Orders to abandon the post were issued on April 7, 1854, the last troops leaving on June 8. The Choctaws took possession of the post, which became the capital of the Choctaw Nation, and, briefly, served as headquarters for the Choctaw Agency. The post was occupied by Confederate troops during the Civil War and served as headquarters for the Confederate Indian Territory Department during much of the war. The Confederate Cherokee general, Stand Watie, surrendered there in June, 1865. The post was not again occupied by the military.

WASHITA. Established April 23, 1842. Located a mile and a half east of the False Washita River, about thirty miles above its junction with the Red. (This was near the spot where Colonel Henry Dodge,

1st U.S. Dragoons, had established Camp Washita during his expedition of 1834.) The site was selected by Colonel Zachary Taylor, 1st U.S. Infantry, commanding the department, in 1841, in response to the pleas of the Chickasaw Indians for protection from marauding Texans and hostile Indians. Established by Captain George A. H. Blake, 2nd U.S. Dragoons. The post had deteriorated considerably by the early 1850's, and it was substantially rebuilt and improved in 1855–56. Evacuated on February 17, 1858. Abandoned on April 16, 1861, and occupied by Confederate troops from Texas on the following day. Toward the close of the Civil War, the headquarters for the Indian Territory Department of the Confederacy was moved to the post. On the night of August 1, 1865, incendiaries fired and destroyed the buildings. The post was not again occupied by the U.S. Army. On July 1, 1870, the military reservation, which had never been formally declared, was turned over to the Interior Department for the use of the Chickasaw Nation.

WAYNE. Established October 29, 1838. Originally located south of the Illinois River, just to the west of the Arkansas line, on the site of the present town of Watts. Established by Captain John Stewart, 7th U.S. Infantry, with troops from the abandoned Fort Coffee. The site was unhealthful, and a number of men soon died, including Captain Stewart. Originally called Camp Illinois, the post was soon designated Fort Wayne. Work on the post was suspended in June, 1840, and a new site was chosen near Spavinaw (Flag) Creek, near the Arkansas line and close to the present town of Marysville. The new post was established on July 20, 1840, by Lieutenant Colonel Richard B. Mason, 1st U.S. Dragoons. The post, in both locations, was intended for the protection of the military road which was to run from Fort Snelling, Minnesota, to Fort Towson, near the Red River. Abandoned on May 26, 1842, because the War Department considered the post poorly located and of no real purpose. The garrison was moved north to establish what was to become Fort Scott, Kansas. The abandoned post was placed in the custody of the quartermaster at Fort Gibson and deteriorated rapidly. The old fort was used by the Confederate Cherokee general, Stand Watie, as a recruiting base in 1861. The military reservation, although never formally declared, was transferred to the Interior Department on March 26, 1871, to be sold.

OREGON

BAILEY. Located in the Grave Creek Hills about twenty-five miles south of the town of Roseburg and above Cow Creek. The post was a tavern which was occupied by volunteer Oregon troops during the Rogue River Indian War of 1855. It was called Fort Bailey for Captain Joseph Bailey, Company A, 1st Battalion, Mounted Volunteers.

DALLES. Established May 21, 1850. Located on the left bank of the Columbia River on Mill Creek at The Dalles. A trading post, not called a fort, had been located at the site by the Northwest Company in 1820 but was later abandoned. The Whitman massacre of November, 1847, and the Cayuse War which followed it, led to the establishment of a stockade by volunteer troops at The Dalles in January, 1848. This post was called Fort Lee for Major Henry A. G. Lee of the Oregon Rifles; also Fort Wascopam, from the Indian name for a nearby spring. The regular military post was first called Camp Drum, then, in April, 1853, Fort Drum, probably for Captain Simon H. Drum, 4th U.S. Artillery, killed in the assault on Mexico City, September 13, 1847. It was established by two companies of Mounted Riflemen, under the command of Captain Stephen S. Tucker, by order of Lieutenant Colonel William W. Loring, Mounted Riflemen, commanding the department.

In July, 1853, the post was designated Fort Dalles. It was substantially rebuilt, beginning in 1856. By 1852 a town had grown up around the post, and in 1857 it was granted a charter under the name Fort Dalles—which was soon changed to Dalles City—but listed by the Post Office Department as The Dalles. The name "Dalles" (flagstones) was applied to the stretch of the Columbia River, where both post and town were located, by French *voyageurs*. The post was not regularly garrisoned after 1861 but was used as a quartermaster's depot for the transshipment of supplies to interior posts and for public animals awaiting distribution. Apparently the last time the post was garrisoned was from March 27 to May 22, 1867. On March 28, 1877, the military reservation was transferred to the Interior Department.

HARNEY. Established August 16, 1867. Located on the right side of Rattlesnake Creek, about two miles above its sink in Harney Lake Valley, some twelve miles east of the present town of Burns. The base was established for operations against hostile Indians in southeastern Oregon. Earlier in the year a depot had been established on Harney Lake by Lieutenant Colonel George Crook, 23rd U.S. Infantry. The post was first called "Camp on Rattlesnake Creek;" then Camp Steele, for Colonel Frederick Steele, 20th U.S. Infantry, commanding the department; then Camp Crook, for Colonel Crook; and, on September 14, 1867, Camp Harney. The post was designated a fort on April 5, 1879. Named for Brigadier General William S. Harney. Abandoned on June 13, 1880. The military reservation was restored to the public domain on March 2, 1889.

HENRIETTA. Established November 18, 1855. Located near the west bank of the Umatilla River at the present town of Echo. The post was erected by a detachment of the 1st Oregon Mounted Rifles, commanded by Major Mark A. Chinn, in connection with the campaign to suppress the general Indian uprising in eastern Oregon and Washington in 1855. It consisted of a stockade with two bastions, erected on the Umatilla Indian Reservation. The agency buildings

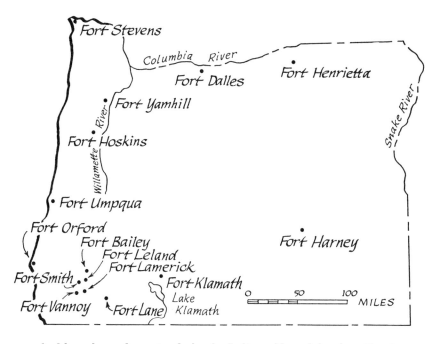

Fort Stevens

Columbia River

Fort Dalles

Fort Henrietta

Fort Yamhill

Willamette River

Fort Hoskins

Snake River

Fort Umpqua

Fort Orford

Fort Bailey

Fort Leland

Fort Lamerick

Fort Harney

Fort Smith

Fort Klamath

Lake Klamath

Fort Vannoy

Fort Lane

0   50   100   MILES

had been burned previously by the Indians. Named for the wife of Captain Granville O. Haller, 4th U.S. Infantry. Abandoned in 1856.

HOSKINS. Established July 26, 1856. Located in Kings Valley on the Luckiamute River, a confluent of the Willamette, near the mouth of Bonner Creek, about twelve miles northwest of the town of Corvallis. Established by Captain Christopher C. Augur, 4th U.S. Infantry. The post was erected after the Indians were concentrated at the Siletz Agency, following the Rogue River War, to control and protect the Indians and to protect the settlers of the area. A blockhouse on the Siletz River, connected with the fort by a trail built under the supervision of Second Lieutenant Phil Sheridan, 4th U.S. Infantry, was a sub-post of Fort Hoskins and was intended to provide immediate protection for the Indian agency. The post was named for First Lieutenant Charles Hoskins, 4th U.S. Infantry, killed on September 21, 1846, in the Battle of Monterrey, Mexico. Evacuation of the post was ordered by Brigadier General Benjamin Alvord on September 23, 1864. Abandoned on April 10, 1865, the last troops departing on April 13. The military reservation, never formally declared, was transferred to the Interior Department on February 16, 1881.

KLAMATH. Established September 5, 1863. Located about eight miles north of Upper Klamath Lake and some twenty miles south of the Rogue River trail on the east side of Wood River. The Klamath Indian Agency was located some five miles to the south. The site was selected and the post established by Major Charles C. Drew, 1st Oregon Cavalry, by order of Brigadier General George Wright, commanding the department. The post was constructed under the supervision of Captain William Kelly, 1st Oregon Cavalry. It was strategically located near roads leading to both Idaho and California and was intended to control the Indians of the area. It was an important center during the Modoc War of 1873. The military reservation was transferred to the Interior Department on May 4, 1886, but steps to open the land to public sale were suspended. The garrison was withdrawn in July, 1889, except for a small detachment which remained until 1890.

LAMERICK. Established May 1, 1856. Located at Big Meadows, about two miles north of the Rogue River. Established by Oregon volunteers during the Rogue River War of 1855–56. Named for Brigadier General John K. Lamerick of the Oregon Volunteers. Apparently the post was little more than a low breastwork of logs, enclosing a camping place. Since the war ended in the summer of 1856, the post was short lived.

LANE. Established September 28, 1853. Located on the south bank of the Rogue River near the mouth of Bear Creek. Established by

Captain Andrew J. Smith, 1st U.S. Dragoons. The Rogue River Indian Reservation was located on the north side of the Rogue River opposite the post. The post was intended to protect the agency and control the Indians of the area. It was designated Fort Lane for Brigadier General Joseph Lane, first territorial governor of Oregon. A temporary post, Camp Stuart, had been established near the site of Fort Lane by Captain Phil Kearny, 1st U.S. Dragoons, in June, 1851. It was named for Second Lieutenant James Stuart, Mounted Riflemen, who died of wounds received in an engagement with the Rogue River Indians on June 17, 1851. The immediate predecessor of Fort Lane was Camp Alden, named for Captain Bradford R. Alden, 4th U.S. Infantry, located near Upper Table Rock. It existed for a few months and was abandoned when Fort Lane was established. Fort Lane was abandoned on September 17, 1856. The military reservation was transferred to the Interior Department on March 25, 1871.

LEE. See Dalles.

LELAND. Established in the fall of 1855. Located on Grave Creek. Used as a center of operations by the mounted Oregon volunteers during the Rogue River War of 1855–56. The post was normally a tavern called Grave Creek House, belonging to McDonough Harkness and Jesse H. Twogood. The tavern had been provided with a stout stockade for protection against the Indians, and this, apparently, was the fort. The name Leland was derived from Martha Leland Crowley, member of an emigrant party, who died in 1846 and was buried at Grave Creek.

ORFORD. Established September 14, 1851. Located at the head of Trichenor Bay at Port Orford. Established because the Indians of the area were hostile. It was also intended that the post be developed into a sub-depot for the supply of a post or posts to be established in the interior of southern Oregon on the Oregon-California route. The latter plan was abandoned when it proved impossible to find a route suitable for a wagon road back through the coast mountains from Port Orford. Established by Second Lieutenant Powell T. Wyman, 1st U.S. Artillery. The post was constructed by the troops from lumber shipped from San Francisco and cedar logs cut locally. The settlement of Port Orford had been founded by Captain William Trichenor of the *Seagull* in June, 1851. The settlers, in July, 1851, erected two blockhouses on Fort Point. These were entirely separate from the military post. The military post was abandoned on July 10, 1856.

SMITH. A post of the Oregon volunteers during the Rogue River War of 1855–56. Located at the house of William Henry Smith on Cow Creek, about four miles above the present town of Glendale. The post probably consisted of a stockade.

STEVENS. The military reservation was declared on February 26, 1852; construction commenced in 1863; and the post was first garrisoned on April 25, 1865. Located on Point Adams, near the mouth of the Columbia River, about nine miles west of Astoria. The post was constructed under the supervision of Captain George H. Elliot, Corps of Engineers. Named in honor of Isaac I. Stevens, first territorial governor of Washington, who, as a major general, Volunteers, was killed on September 1, 1862, while leading the 79th New York Infantry at Chantilly, Virginia. The garrison was withdrawn in 1883 and the post placed in charge of an ordnance sergeant.

UMPQUA. Established July 28, 1856. Located on the west bank of the Umpqua River about two miles above its mouth. The post was one of three established to watch over the Indians of the Grand Ronde and Siletz agencies and to prevent their escape to the south. It was originally useful in suppressing Indian hostilities in southern Oregon. Established by Captain Joseph Stewart, 3rd U.S. Artillery, on a site selected by Captain John F. Reynolds, 3rd U.S. Artillery. The original buildings of the post consisted of structures moved from the abandoned Fort Orford. It is said that the paymaster arrived at the post in the summer of 1862 to find everyone stationed there absent on a hunting trip. On June 6, 1862, Colonel Justus Steinberger, 1st Washington Infantry, commanding the District of Oregon, recommended the abandonment of the post. Abandoned on July 16, 1862. The reservation was privately claimed.

VANNOY. Established in October or November, 1855. Located on the right bank of the Rogue River about four miles west of the town of Grants Pass, although the exact site is not known. This was one of the more important posts of the Oregon Volunteers during the Rogue River War of 1855–56, since it served as a headquarters camp for the volunteers. It consisted of a group of log houses with, possibly, a log breastwork or a low stockade. It was located on the Margaret Vannoy donation land claim, which adjoined the James N. Vannoy claim.

WASCOPAM. See Dalles.

YAMHILL. Established late in 1855. Located on a hill, now called Fort Hill, near the Yamhill River, in the Grand Ronde Valley, about twenty-five miles southwest of the town of Dayton. The original fort was a blockhouse, erected by settlers of the area, who were fearful that the Indian uprising so general in Oregon and Washington might spread to the Indians gathered at the Grand Ronde Reservation. The post became a U.S. Army fort on August 30, 1856, and was first garrisoned by a detachment under the command of Brevet Second Lieutenant William B. Hazen, 4th U.S. Infantry. Intended to control the Indians of the Grand Ronde and Siletz agencies. When the post was completed, it consisted of a blockhouse surrounded by a stockade. Named for the Yamhill River and the Yamhill Indians (Yamhel-as, Yellow River). Abandoned on June 30, 1866. The blockhouse was later moved about three miles to the Indian agency where it served as a jail. In 1911 it was moved to the town of Dayton where it now stands in a city park.

SOUTH DAKOTA

BENNETT. Established May 17, 1870. Located on the right bank of the Missouri River, about thirty miles above Fort Sully and below the mouth of the Cheyenne River, on the Cheyenne River Indian Reservation. Established by Captain Edward P. Pearson, 17th U.S. Infantry, to protect the agency. Originally called Cheyenne (or Cheyenne River) Agency. On December 30, 1878, the post was designated Fort Bennett, in honor of Captain Andrew S. Bennett, 5th U.S. Infantry, killed on September 4, 1878, in a skirmish with Bannock Indians in Montana. Abandoned on November 18, 1891.

DAKOTA. Established May 1, 1865. Located at Sioux Falls on the left bank of the Big Sioux River. Established by Captain Daniel F. Eicher, 6th Iowa Cavalry, by order of Brigadier General Alfred Sully, to serve as one of the chain of posts from Minnesota to the Missouri River to guard the frontier between the area of settlement and the Sioux country. The name is derived from the Dakota Sioux. Abandoned on June 18, 1869. The military reservation was transferred to the Interior Department on June 10, 1869.

HALE. Established June 8, 1870. Located originally on the right bank of the Missouri River, above the present town of Fort Lookout, on the Lower Brulé Indian Reservation. On July 21, 1870, the post was moved about fifteen miles upstream to a site opposite the mouth of Crow Creek. Established by Captain George W. Hill, 22nd U.S. Infantry. Originally called Lower Brulé Agency. On December 30, 1878, the post was designated Fort Hale, in honor of Captain Owen Hale, 7th U.S. Cavalry, killed on September 30, 1877, in a skirmish with Nez Percé Indians. Abandoned on May 20, 1884, except for a small detachment which remained to close the affairs of the post. The

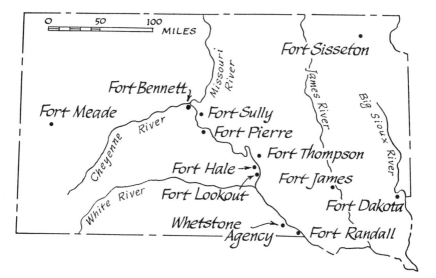

buildings were turned over to the Indian agent on July 7, 1884, and the detachment was withdrawn the following day.

JAMES. Established in September, 1865. Located at the junction of Fire Steel Creek with the James River on the right side of the James at the present town of Rockport. Established by Captain Benjamin King, 6th Iowa Cavalry, by order of Brigadier General Alfred Sully. It served as one of the chain of posts guarding the frontier between the area of settlement and the Sioux Indian country. Abandoned in October, 1866.

LOOKOUT. Established July 31, 1856. Located on the right bank of the Missouri River, about ten miles above the present town of Chamberlain, near the site of the former Columbia Fur Company trading post of the same name. Established by Captain Nathaniel Lyon, 2nd U.S. Infantry, by order of Colonel William S. Harney, 2nd U.S. Dragoons. Intended to control the Indians of the area.

135

Harney called the post Fort Lookout because of its proximity to the earlier trading post. Abandoned on June 17, 1857. Much of the post was dismantled and the materials shipped down river for use at Fort Randall.

LOWER BRULÉ. See Hale.

MEADE. Established August 28, 1878. Located on the east side of Bear Butte Creek, in the Black Hills, fourteen miles northeast of the town of Deadwood. Established by Major Henry M. Lazelle, 1st U.S. Infantry, on a site selected by Lieutenant General Phil Sheridan. Established to control the Sioux Indians and to protect the Black Hills mining district. Originally called Camp Ruhlen, the post was designated Fort Meade on December 30, 1878. Named in honor of Major General George Gordon Meade. Since 1944 the buildings have been used as a hospital by the Veterans Administration.

PIERRE. Established as a trading post in 1831 by Bernard Pratte and Company. Located on the right side of the Missouri River, a quarter of a mile from the river and about three miles above the mouth of the Bad (Teton) River, some three miles northwest of the present town of Pierre. Named for Pierre Chouteau, Jr. The post was purchased by the government for the use of the military on April 14, 1855. It was first occupied by troops on June 7, 1855, under the command of Major Albermarle Cady, 6th U.S. Infantry. Because of insufficient grass, timber, and hay, the post was considered unsatisfactory for army use and was abandoned on May 16, 1857. Some of the materials from the post were used in the construction of Fort Randall.

RANDALL. Established June 26, 1856. Located on the right bank of the Missouri River on a plateau one-quarter of a mile from the river, just north of the point where the river crosses the Nebraska line. The post was rebuilt in 1870–72, about one-quarter of a mile farther from the river and slightly downstream from the original site. Established to replace Fort Pierre. Intended to keep peace among the Sioux, Ponca, and other warlike tribes and to protect the advancing line of settlement. The Yankton Sioux Reservation was established north and east of the post in 1878 and the Ponca Reservation south and east at a later date. Established by First Lieutenant George H. Paige, 2nd U.S. Infantry, on a site selected by Colonel William S. Harney, 2nd U.S. Dragoons. Named for Lieutenant Colonel Daniel D. Randall, deputy paymaster general of the army, who died on December 17, 1851. Much of the military reservation was relinquished on July 22, 1884, and the garrison of the post was reduced in size after that date. Abandoned on December 7, 1892. The military reservation was transferred to the Interior Department on October 20, 1893.

SISSETON. Established August 1, 1864. Located on the elevated tableland known as Coteau des Prairies, near Kettle (Fort) Lakes. Established to control the hostile Indians along the northern frontier, to permit settlement east of the James River, and to protect the wagon route to the newly discovered gold fields in Idaho and Montana. Established by Major John Clowney, 30th Wisconsin Infantry, by order of Brigadier General John Pope, commanding the department. Originally designated Fort Wadsworth, in honor of Brigadier General James S. Wadsworth, who died on May 8, 1864, of wounds received in the Battle of the Wilderness. On August 29, 1876, the name was changed to Fort Sisseton because a post named Fort Wadsworth already existed in New York. The name was derived from the Sisseton band of Sioux. Abandoned on June 9, 1889. The military reservation was transferred to the Interior Department on April 22, 1889.

SULLY. Established September 14, 1863. Originally located on the left bank of the Missouri River, about six miles below the present town of Pierre. Established by Brigadier General Alfred Sully, for whom the post was named, during his campaign of 1863 against the Sioux. The post was temporary and served primarily as headquarters for the troops stationed in the vicinity. Abandoned on July 25, 1866, because the site was considered to be inconvenient and unhealthful, and relocated the following day on the left bank of the Missouri River, twenty-eight miles above Pierre and thirty miles below the mouth of the Cheyenne River. The new site was chosen and the post established by Lieutenant Colonel George L. Andrews, 13th U.S. Infantry. Construction of the new post began in August, 1866. Abandoned on October 30, 1894, except for a small detachment which remained until November 30, 1894, to close the affairs of the post. The military reservation was transferred to the Interior Department on November 14, 1894.

THOMPSON. Established in September, 1864. Located on the left side of the Missouri River at the mouth of Soldier Creek, on the Crow Creek Indian Reservation, some twenty miles above the present town of Chamberlain. The post served as agency headquarters for the reservation and was also called Crow Creek Agency. Named for Colonel Clark W. Thompson, superintendent of Indian affairs at St. Paul, Minnesota. The military post was established by Captain Nelson Minor, Dakota Cavalry. Abandoned as a separate post on June 9, 1867, and the garrison transferred to Fort Sully. A detachment from Fort Sully was stationed at the post for a time after the garrison was withdrawn.

WADSWORTH. See Sisseton.

WHETSTONE. Established May 10, 1870. Located on the right bank of the Missouri River about thirty miles above Fort Randall on the Whetstone Indian Reservation, now a part of the Rosebud Indian Reservation. Troops were stationed at the post to protect the agency and control the Sioux Indians. Properly called the Whetstone

Agency, the post was never officially designated a fort. Troops from Fort Randall, under the command of Captain DeWitt C. Poole, 25th U.S. Infantry, who also served as Indian agent, garrisoned the post. Abandoned on April 30, 1872.

TEXAS

ALTAR, DEL. It is alleged that a Spanish post by this name existed near the headwaters of the Devils (San Pedro) River. It appears on Disturnell's map of 1847. In 1849, Second Lieutenant William H. C. Whiting, Corps of Engineers, led a military expedition which examined the river from its source to near its mouth but could find no trace of the fort. There seems to be nothing to authenticate its existence. A presidio of this name was located in Sonora.

ANÁHUAC. Established in 1831. Located on the east shore of Galveston Bay near the mouth of the Trinity River. Established by order of General Manuel de Mier y Terán. This was one of the series of Mexican posts erected to block the illegal entry of persons and goods from the United States into Texas. It was erected under the direction of Colonel John Davis Bradburn. The post, thirty by forty feet in size, was built of adobe brick and overlooked the bay. It mounted two cannon, probably six-pounders. It was evacuated on July 13, 1832, following a revolt of the garrison, but reoccupied in January, 1835, by a collector of customs and a small garrison commanded by Captain Antonio Tenorio. Captured by irregular Texan forces under the command of William B. Travis on July 30, 1835. The post was named for the Valley of Anáhuac (Valley of Mexico).

BAHÍA DE ESPÍRITU SANTO, PRESIDIO DE NUESTRA SEÑORA DE LORETO DE LA. Established April 4, 1721. Located on the right bank of Garcitas Creek, about five miles above its mouth, on the site of La Salle's Fort St. Louis. Established by Captain Domingo Ramón by order of the Marqués de San Miguel de Aguayo, governor of

Fort Preston   Fort Johnson

Bird's Fort

Fort Houston

Presidio de Nuestra Señora del Pilar
y Gloriosa San José

Fort Milam
Little River Fort   Fort Tenoxtitlán

Presidio de San Luis
de las Amarillas   Presidio de
San Xavier

Fort Coleman

Presidio de Nuestra
Señora de los Dolores
de los Tejas

Presidio de
San Augustín
de Ahumada

Fort Anáhuac

Presidio de San Antonio
de Bejar

Fort Santa Cruz   Fort St. Louis   Fort Velasco

Presidio de Nuestra
Señora de Loreto
de la Bahía de
Espíritu Santo

Fort Lipantitlán

0   50   100
MILES

TEXAS POSTS
ESTABLISHED
PRIOR TO 1846

Coahuila y Texas. Actual construction of the fortification did not
commence until April 6, 1722. The post was intended to be a permanent establishment in connection with the nearby mission of
Nuestra Señora del Espíritu Santo de Zuñiga. The original establishment was made as part of Spain's effort to stop French encroachment on her territory and to serve the Karankawa Indians. In 1726
both the presidio and the mission were moved, as a result of orders

140

TEXAS POSTS
ESTABLISHED
1846–1898

issued on August 29 of that year, to a new location in the Mission Valley near the Guadalupe River, about thirteen miles above the present town of Victoria. By the autumn of 1749, they had been moved again—for the last time—to the right bank of the San Antonio River, opposite the town of Goliad. By a royal decree issued September 10, 1772, the presidio was made a *plaza fuerte* and so remained as long as Spain held her colonies. During the Mexican

141

independence movement, the presidio was held for a time by Bernardo Gutiérrez de Lara, one of the insurgent leaders. It remained a presidio under the Republic of Mexico and was the scene of fighting during the Texas independence movement. The mission has been restored, and the presidio is well preserved.

BELKNAP. Established June 24, 1851. Located on the left bank of the Salt (Red) Fork of the Brazos River, ten miles above its junction with the Clear Fork in Young County. The first troops for the establishment of the post, commanded by Captain Carter L. Stevenson, 5th U.S. Artillery, encamped near the site on June 13, 1851. On June 24, 1851, Lieutenant Colonel William G. Belknap, 5th U.S. Infantry, for whom the post was named, selected the site for the permanent post. Colonel Belknap died on November 10, 1851. The post was erected to protect the emigrant route from Fort Smith, Arkansas, to Santa Fe, and to protect the settlers of the area from marauding Indians. Originally called Camp Belknap, the post was designated a fort on November 1, 1851. Abandoned by order of Brigadier General David E. Twiggs on February 23, 1859, because of the shortage of water at the post, and the garrison transferred to Camp Cooper. The post was occupied by Texan forces at times during the Civil War. It was reoccupied by regular U.S. Army troops in May, 1867, but was not regularly garrisoned after the establishment of Fort Griffin later in the year. It was maintained as a picket post to protect the mail line, as a temporary base of operations against the Indians, and for escort duty. Abandoned as a regular post in September, 1867, because of the insufficiency of good water.

BIRD'S FORT. Established in the winter of 1840–41. Located some two or three miles east of the later town of Birdsville, northwest of the present Dallas, on the main fork of the Trinity River. Established by Captain John Bird and a company of Texas Rangers. The post, which consisted of a stockade, was intended to encourage settlement in the area. The period of enlistment of the Rangers expired shortly after the post was established and they returned to their homes, leaving the post unoccupied. In 1841 several families settled at Bird's Fort, the first permanent settlement on the upper Trinity.

BLISS. Established September 8, 1849. The post has occupied six separate locations. The original post was located at Ponce's Ranch[1] (Franklin) by Captain Jefferson Van Horn, 3rd U.S. Infantry, by order of Colonel William Jenkins Worth, 8th U.S. Infantry, commanding the department. It was called the Post of El Paso because of its proximity of the Mexican town of El Paso del Norte (Ciudad Juárez). A part of the frontier defense system, the post was less to guard against possible Mexican raids than to deal with the Indians and to protect the important southern route to California. The post was evacuated in September, 1851, and the garrison transferred to Fort Fillmore, New Mexico. A small guard remained until the fall of 1852 to protect public property.

The second post was established January 11, 1854, at Magoffinsville. On March 8, 1854, it was designated Fort Bliss, in honor of Captain William Wallace Smith Bliss, 4th U.S. Infantry, who had served as adjutant general under Major General Zachary Taylor during the Mexican War, and was Taylor's son-in-law. Fort Bliss was surrendered to the Confederacy on March 31, 1861, by order of Brigadier General David E. Twiggs. It was evacuated by the Confederates and largely destroyed by them in the summer of 1862. The United States flag was raised over the post by Union troops under the command of Brigadier General James H. Carleton, in June, 1862.

---

[1] Juan María Ponce de León, a resident of El Paso del Norte, received a land grant and erected the first buildings north of the Río Grande in this area in 1827. Ponce's ranch was purchased by Ben Franklin Coons in 1848 or 1849. It was in his possession when Van Horn established the Post of El Paso in 1849. In 1853 the ranch was occupied by William "Billy" Smith, from whom the name "Smith's Ranch" was derived. It was one of four settlements of United States citizens in the immediate vicinity, the others being Magoffinsville (James W. Magoffin), Hart's Mill (Simeon Hart), and Stephenson's Ranch (Hugh Stephenson).

Work of rebuilding the post commenced in June, 1864, and was completed in February, 1866. Until October 15, 1865, when Fort Bliss was reoccupied, the garrison had been stationed at Franklin or Hart's Mill. The second location was abandoned on March 1, 1868, because the Río Grande was eating into the site and several of the buildings had been destroyed.

The post was moved to its third location, Concordia Ranch, part of the old Stephenson's Ranch, three miles east of El Paso (Franklin) and named Camp Concordia. The name Fort Bliss was resumed in 1869. Orders to abandon the post were issued in December, 1876, and it was evacuated in January, 1877.

Indian activities and the Salt War of 1877 led to the re-establishment of the post on January 1, 1878. The facilities at Concordia Ranch were considered to be uninhabitable, and buildings were leased in El Paso to quarter the troops. In 1879 arrangements were made to purchase a tract of land at Hart's Mill for the construction of a new post. This was the first site owned by the government, all previous sites having been leased. Expansion of the post led to the authorization, on March 1, 1890, to purchase a new site. The new post was first occupied by a small number of troops in October, 1893, and the post at Hart's Mill was completely evacuated on May 31, 1894. The post is still operative. All of the sites it has occupied, except the present, lie within the limits of the city of El Paso.

BROWN. Established March 28, 1846. Located at the present Brownsville, across the Río Grande from Matamoros. Established by Colonel Zachary Taylor, 6th U.S. Infantry, just prior to the beginning of the Mexican War. Construction of the post was under the direction of Captain Joseph K. F. Mansfield, Corps of Engineers. Originally called Fort Taylor, the name was changed to Fort Brown, in honor of Major Jacob Brown, 7th U.S. Infantry, who died on May 9, 1846, of wounds received during the Mexican bombardment of the fort.

Brownsville Barracks was established adjacent to the fort in 1848.

The post was abandoned by order of Brigadier General David E. Twiggs, dated February 5, 1859, and the garrison transferred to Fort Duncan. Reoccupied on December 5, 1859, as a result of the activities of Juan Nepomuceno Cortinas along the Mexican border. Evacuated by Union troops, beginning March 9 and completed on March 20, 1861. Occupied by the Confederates until November 3, 1863, when it was evacuated and burned by order of Brigadier General Hamilton P. Bee, Confederate States of America (C.S.A.). The town of Brownsville was occupied by Union troops on November 7, 1863, but it was retaken by the Confederates on July 30, 1864, and retained by them until the end of the war. It was reoccupied and rebuilt by the United States following the Civil War. On April 26, 1895, the site occupied by the post was purchased by the United States government. Because of bad feelings between the garrison and the citizens of Brownsville, which resulted in some bloodshed, the post was evacuated in 1906, and the military reservation was transferred to the Department of Agriculture. By executive order, dated October 14, 1911, the post was transferred to the Interior Department. It was again occupied by troops during the border troubles with Mexico, beginning on February 26, 1913. Abandoned in 1944.

BUFFALO SPRING. See Richardson.

CHADBOURNE. Established October 28, 1852. Located on the east side of Oak Creek about three miles above its junction with the Colorado River and about four miles northeast of the present town of Fort Chadbourne. Established to protect the emigrant route from Fort Smith, Arkansas, to Santa Fe. Established by Captain John Beardsley, 8th U.S. Infantry. Named for Second Lieutenant Theodore L. Chadbourne, 8th U.S. Infantry, killed on May 9, 1846, in the Battle of Resaca de la Palma. Surrendered to the Confederacy on March 23, 1861, by order of Brigadier General David E. Twiggs.

Reoccupied by the United States on May 25, 1867, and partly rebuilt. Abandoned as a regular post on December 18, 1867, because of the failure of the water supply, but irregularly used as a picket-post and garrisoned from Fort Concho for about a year thereafter.

CIBOLO. Located a few miles west of the town of Shafter in Presidio County. The fort consisted of a building erected by ranchers of the area. It was often temporarily occupied by detachments of United States troops moving between Fort Davis and Fort Leaton, the latter a trading post near Presidio on the Río Grande. The name was derived from Cibolo Creek.

CLARK. Established June 20, 1852. Located on the right side of Las Moras Creek, near its head, at the present town of Brackettville. The post was a link in the frontier defense system and helped to guard the San Antonio–El Paso road. First called Fort Riley, it was designated Fort Clark on July 16, 1852, in honor of Major John B. Clark, 1st U.S. Infantry, who died on August 23, 1847. Established by Captain William Edgar Prince, 1st U.S. Infantry. The first permanent buildings were not erected until 1857. Surrendered to the Confederacy on March 19, 1861, by order of Brigadier General David E. Twiggs. Except for a brief period of Confederate occupancy the post was not garrisoned again until December 10, 1866, when it was occupied by Union troops commanded by Captain John A. Wilcox, 4th U.S. Cavalry. Abandoned in 1946.

COLEMAN. Established in June, 1836. Located on Walnut Creek, a confluent of the Colorado River, about six miles below and to the east of Austin. Erected by a body of Texas Rangers, commanded by Captain Robert M. Coleman, for whom the post was named. Established to provide defense against hostile Indians, the post consisted of a group of log cabins enclosed in a heavy stockade with blockhouses at opposite corners. The post was also called Fort Colorado. Abandoned in November, 1838.

COLORADO. See Coleman.

CONCHO. Established December 4, 1867.[1] The forerunner of Fort Concho, which came to be known as Permanent Camp, was established by First Lieutenant Peter M. Boehm, 4th U.S. Cavalry, on June 8, 1867. It was located on the middle branch of the Concho River, some eighteen miles above the junction of the North and South Concho, probably near the mouth of East Rocky Creek. Permanent Camp was an outpost of Fort Chadbourne. The permanent post was located between and at the junction of the North and South Concho Rivers at the present town of San Angelo. Established by Captain George G. Huntt, 4th U.S. Cavalry, when Fort Chadbourne was abandoned. The post was part of the frontier defense system and the center of the line of posts extending from El Paso to the Red River. First called Camp Hatch, for Major John Porter Hatch, 4th U.S. Cavalry; then, in January, 1868, Camp Kelly, for Captain Michael J. Kelly, 4th U.S. Cavalry; and, finally, on February 5, 1868, Fort Concho, after the stream on which it was located. Abandoned on June 20, 1889.

COOPER. Established January 2, 1856. Located on the Clear Fork of the Brazos, five miles east of the mouth of Otey's Creek on the Comanche Indian Reservation. Established to protect the El Paso–Red River Trail, laid out by Captain Randolph B. Marcy, 5th U.S. Infantry, from the Comanche Indians and to control the Indians on the reservation. Established by Major William J. Hardee, 2nd U.S. Cavalry. Named for Colonel Samuel Cooper, adjutant general, U.S. Army. The post was a camp and was never officially designated a fort. Surrendered to the Confederacy on February 21, 1861, by order of Brigadier General David E. Twiggs. The post was not reoccupied after the Civil War.

[1] The biographer of Fort Concho is of the opinion that "the camp which was to become Fort Concho was established late in November, instead of in December, as the authorities usually show." J. Evetts Haley, *Fort Concho and the Texas Frontier*, 128.

147

CROGHAN. Established March 18, 1849. Located on the right bank of Hamilton Creek, a tributary of the Colorado, fourteen miles above its mouth, at the present town of Burnet. The post formed part of the frontier defense system. Established by Brevet Second Lieutenant Charles H. Tyler, 2nd U.S. Dragoons. Named for Colonel George Croghan, inspector general, U.S. Army, who died on January 8, 1849. The post was originally called "Post on Hamilton Creek," but was designated Fort Croghan in 1850. Abandoned in December, 1853.

DAVIS. Established October 7, 1854. Located at the mouth of a canyon about one-half mile south of Limpia Creek in the Limpia (Davis) Mountains, north of the present town of Fort Davis. Lieutenant Colonel Washington Seawell, 8th U.S. Infantry, occupied the site on October 7, 1854. By an order dated October 23, 1854, he was directed to establish a fort at the site. The post was intended to protect the El Paso–San Antonio road and to control the Indians, especially the Comanches and Apaches. Named in honor of Jefferson Davis, who was secretary of war at the time the post was established. Evacuated on April 13, 1861, by order of Brigadier General David E. Twiggs. Temporarily occupied by Confederate troops, then by roving bands of Mexicans and Indians who largely destroyed the post. The United States flag was raised over the post by Captain Edmund D. Shirland, 1st California Cavalry, in September, 1862, but the post was not reoccupied at that time. Reoccupied by Federal troops under the command of Lieutenant Colonel Wesley Merritt, 9th U.S. Cavalry, on July 1, 1867, and completely rebuilt. Abandoned on June 30, 1891, by which time it was no longer considered necessary.

DEL ALTAR. See Altar, del.

DUNCAN. Established March 27, 1849. Located on the left bank of the Río Grande at Eagle Pass. The first permanent buildings were not erected until 1850. Established by Captain Sidney Burbank, 1st U.S. Infantry. The post was named for Colonel James Duncan, Inspector General's Department. Evacuated by Federal troops on March 20, 1861, by order of Brigadier General David E. Twiggs. Garrisoned during part of the Civil War by Confederate troops. Reoccupied by Federal troops on March 23, 1868. The site occupied by the post was rented, and for years the government sought to purchase it, but could not come to an agreement with the owners as to a price. Largely for that reason, the post was abandoned on August 31, 1883. In subsequent years the department commanders urged reoccupation of the post because of its location on one of the main routes of travel into Mexico and its usefulness in observing and patrolling the Río Grande. In 1891 a cavalry post was established at Eagle Pass and designated "Post at Eagle Pass," or "Camp Eagle Pass." Efforts to purchase the site of old Fort Duncan were renewed in 1891, and the site was finally acquired by the government in 1894. By this time the buildings were in ruinous condition. The post, again called Fort Duncan, was occupied irregularly during the border troubles with Mexico following the outbreak of the Mexican Revolution. It was permanently abandoned in 1916.

ELLIOTT. Established February 3, 1875. The post, in its original location, was established on February 3, 1875, and was known as "Cantonment North Fork of the Red River." On June 5, 1875, it was relocated north of and near to the headwaters of Sweetwater Creek, a confluent of the North Fork of the Red River, near the present town of Mobeetie. The site was selected by Major James Biddle, 6th U.S. Cavalry. Established by Major Henry Cary Bankhead, 4th U.S. Cavalry, by order of General William Tecumseh Sherman, who had in mind the opening of a route for Texas cattle west of the settlements in Kansas. The post was intended to prevent the re-entry of Indians into west Texas and to force them to remain on their reservation.

Originally a sub-post of Fort Sill, Oklahoma, the post was first called "New Cantonment" and "Cantonment on Sweetwater." It was designated Fort Elliott on February 21, 1876, for Major Joel H. Elliott, 7th U.S. Cavalry, who was killed on November 27, 1868, in action on the Washita River, Indian Territory. Abandoned on October 1, 1890, the last troops leaving the post on October 21. The military reservation was transferred to the Interior Department on October 14, 1890, and the buildings sold at public auction on March 20, 1900.

EWELL. Established May 18, 1852. Located on the right side of the Nueces River at the point where the San Antonio–Laredo road crossed the river, in the present La Salle County. Established by Lieutenant Colonel William W. Loring, Mounted Riflemen. Named for Captain Richard S. Ewell, 1st U.S. Dragoons, who had served in the Mexican War and was later a lieutenant general in the Confederate Army. The post was built of adobe. Captain William Grigsby Freeman, 4th U.S. Artillery, who inspected the post in 1853, wrote of it, "Indeed a less inviting spot for occupation by troops cannot well be conceived." Abandoned on October 3, 1854.

GATES. Established October 26, 1849. Located on the left bank of the Leon River in the present Coryell County, about six miles southeast of the present town of Gatesville. Established as a part of the frontier defense system. Established by Captain William R. Montgomery, 8th U.S. Infantry. The post was probably named for Captain Collinson R. Gates, 8th U.S. Infantry, a veteran of the Mexican War, who died on June 28, 1849. Abandoned in March, 1852.

GRAHAM. Established March 27, 1849. Located about a mile from the east bank of the Brazos River, northwest of the present town of Hillsboro, at José María village, an Anadarko Indian encampment. Established as part of the frontier defense system. Established by Captain Ripley A. Arnold, 2nd U.S. Dragoons, by order of Colonel

William S. Harney, 2nd U.S. Dragoons. Probably named for Lieutenant Colonel William M. Graham, 11th U.S. Infantry, killed on September 8, 1847, in the Battle of Molino del Rey. Abandoned on October 6, 1853.

GRIFFIN I. This was a Texas Ranger post, located on the Little River. It was in existence in 1839.

GRIFFIN II. Established July 31, 1867. Located on a hill about half a mile west of the Clear Fork of the Brazos River in the present Shackelford County. Established by Lieutenant Colonel Samuel D. Sturgis, 6th U.S. Cavalry, by order of Lieutenant Colonel George L. Hartsuff, assistant adjutant general, U.S. Army. The post was established to replace Fort Belknap. It served as an important supply point for buffalo hunters and provided protection for the cattle trails and for settlers. First called Camp Wilson, for Second Lieutenant Henry Hamilton Wilson, 6th U.S. Cavalry, who died on December 24, 1866. In 1868 the post was designated Fort Griffin, in honor of Colonel Charles Griffin, 35th U.S. Infantry, commanding the department, who died on September 15, 1867. Abandoned on May 31, 1881. The site is now a state park.

HANCOCK. Established June 9, 1882. Located on the left bank of the Río Grande, at the present town of Fort Hancock, about forty miles below El Paso. Originally a sub-post of Fort Davis, it was established to protect the area against incursions by Indians or bandits from across the Río Grande. First called Camp Rice, it was designated Fort Hancock on May 14, 1886. Named in honor of Major General Winfield Scott Hancock, who died on February 9, 1886. Abandoned on December 6, 1895. The military reservation was transferred to the Interior Department on November 1, 1895.

HOUSTON. Established in 1836. Located at the present town of Palestine. This was a military post of the Republic of Texas, established immediately after the Battle of San Jacinto by order of General Sam Houston, for whom it was named. It was described as being a rude blockhouse.

HUDSON. Established June 7, 1857. Located on the right bank of the Devils River, some forty miles northwest of the town of Del Rio on the lower San Antonio–El Paso road. Established as part of the frontier defense system. Established by First Lieutenant Theodore Fink, 8th U.S. Infantry. Named in honor of Second Lieutenant Walter W. Hudson, 1st U.S. Infantry, who died on April 19, 1850, of wounds received in action with Indians near Laredo. The post was a camp and was never officially designated a fort, although it was sometimes so called in official documents. Evacuated by Federal troops on March 17, 1861, by order of Brigadier General David E. Twiggs. It was briefly occupied by Federal troops after the Civil War and was permanently abandoned on April 12, 1868.

INGE. Established March 13, 1849. Located on the left bank of the Leon River, above the crossing, near the present town of Uvalde. The post was important because of its location on the great inland commercial route at the point where the road to Eagle Pass branched off from the lower San Antonio-El Paso road. Established by Captain Sidney Burbank, 1st U.S. Infantry. The post was named for First Lieutenant Zebulon M. P. Inge, 2nd U.S. Dragoons, killed on May 9, 1846, in the Battle of Resaca de la Palma. Abandoned on May 24, 1855, but regarrisoned intermittently until March 19. 1861, when it was evacuated by Federal troops. Occupied by Confederate troops during the Civil War and reoccupied by Federal troops in 1866. Abandoned February 28, 1869.

JOHNSON. Established in the winter of 1840–41. Located on the right bank of the Red River opposite the mouth of the Washita, near the present town of Denison. Albert Sidney Johnston, secretary of war of the Republic of Texas, planned a series of forts along the Texas frontier, much harrassed by raids by the Comanche Indians. Fort Johnson was the northernmost of these. Established by Colonel William G. Cooke. Probably named for Colonel Benjamin H. Johnson, purportedly killed by Mexicans in 1839. Abandoned in May, 1841.

LA BAHÍA DE ESPÍRITU SANTO. See Bahía.

LAMAR. A fort of the Texas Republic period. It was in existence in 1839. Probably named for Mirabeau Buonaparte Lamar, president of the Republic of Texas.

LANCASTER. Established August 20, 1855. Located on Live Oak Creek, one-half mile above its junction with the Pecos River. Intended to guard the San Antonio–El Paso road and to protect the movement of supplies and emigrants from Indian hostilities. Established by Captain Stephen D. Carpenter, 1st U.S. Infantry. Originally called Camp Lancaster, the post was designated a fort in 1856. Evacuated by Federal troops on March 19, 1861. Apparently the post was not occupied after the Civil War.

LINCOLN. Established July 7, 1849. Located on the west bank of the Río Seco, about fifty miles west of San Antonio and two miles west of the settlement of D'Hanis, the present village of Old D'Hanis, which it was erected to protect. Established by First Lieutenant James Longstreet, 8th U.S. Infantry. Named for Captain George Lincoln, 8th U.S. Infantry, killed on February 23, 1847, in the Battle of Buena Vista. Abandoned on July 20, 1852.

LIPANTITLÁN. Established in 1831. Located near the mouth of the Nueces River. Established by order of General Manuel de Mier y Terán. Intended to block the illegal entry of persons and goods from the United States and to promote colonization. The fort is described as a simple embankment, miserably constructed. It was surrendered to the Texans on November 13, 1835, without attempting a defense. The fortifications were probably destroyed at this time. The name appears to be derived from the Lipan Apaches in combination with the Nahuatl suffix meaning "place of."

LITTLE RIVER FORT. Established late in 1836. Located near the Three Forks of the Little River. Established to protect the settlers in the vicinity. The site was selected by Captain Robert M. Coleman. The post, a blockhouse or log fort, was erected by Lieutenant George B. Erath and a small detachment of Texas Rangers. Apparently abandoned in 1837.

McINTOSH. Established March 3, 1849. Located on the left bank of the Río Grande at Laredo. Originally called Camp Crawford, it was designated Fort McIntosh on January 7, 1850, in honor of Lieutenant Colonel James S. McIntosh, 5th U.S. Infantry, who died on September 26, 1847, of wounds received in the Battle of Molino del Rey. It was one of the line of posts established along the Río Grande and western frontier at the close of the Mexican War. Intended to guard the frontier and to block the movement of Indians from the United States into Mexico. Established by Second Lieutenant Egbert Ludovicus Viele, 1st U.S. Infantry. The post was abandoned in 1858, reoccupied, again abandoned, then reoccupied in December, 1860. Evacuated by Federal troops on March 12, 1861, by order of Brigadier General David E. Twiggs. The post was occupied by Confederate troops until the close of the Civil War. Reoccupied by Federal troops on October 23, 1865. The post was completely rebuilt in the period 1868–77. Discontinued as an army post on May 31, 1946.

McKAVETT. Established March 14, 1852. Located on a high bluff on the right bank of the San Saba River, near its source, at the present town of Fort McKavett. Erected as part of the defense system to protect the frontier from the Indians. Established by Major Pitcairn Morrison, 8th U.S. Infantry. First called Camp San Saba, it was later designated Fort McKavett, in honor of Captain Henry McKavett, 8th U.S. Infantry, killed on September 21, 1846, in the

Battle of Monterrey. Abandoned on March 22, 1859, by order of Brigadier General David E. Twiggs, and the garrison transferred to Camp Cooper. Occupied by Confederate troops during the Civil War. Reoccupied by Federal troops on April 1, 1868, at which time the post was in a state of disrepair, only one building being fit for occupancy. Rebuilt under the direction of Colonel Ranald S. Mackenzie, 41st U.S. Infantry. Abandoned on June 30, 1883.

MARTIN SCOTT. Established December 5, 1848. Located on Baron's Creek, a confluent of the Pedernales River, about two miles south of Fredericksburg. Established to protect the Fredericksburg–San Antonio road. Established by Captain Seth Eastman, 1st U.S. Infantry, who, prior to the establishment of the post, had been stationed with his command at Fredericksburg. Named in honor of Major Martin Scott, 5th U.S. Infantry, killed on September 8, 1847, in the Battle of Molino del Rey. After April, 1853, the post was frequently occupied by a very small garrison and served more as a forage depot than a defense post. Evacuated by Federal troops at the beginning of the Civil War and held by the Confederates, 1861–65. Permanently abandoned in December, 1866.

MASON. Established July 6, 1851. Located two miles west of Comanche Creek, eight miles above its confluence with the Llano River, in the present Mason County. Established by Captain Hamilton W. Merrill, 2nd U.S. Dragoons. The post, which was situated on the upper San Antonio–El Paso road, was established to protect the German settlements in the area. Named for Second Lieutenant George T. Mason, 2nd U.S. Dragoons, killed on April 25, 1846, in the skirmish at La Rosia, near Fort Brown. Brigadier General David E. Twiggs ordered the post abandoned on February 5, 1859, but it was occupied irregularly until March 28, 1861, when it was evacuated by Federal troops. Reoccupied following the Civil War, it was permanently abandoned on March 23, 1869.

MERRILL. Established March 1, 1850. Located near the right bank of the Nueces River about fifty miles above its mouth at the point where the San Antonio–Corpus Christi road crossed the river. It was one of the line of posts established for the defense of the frontier. Established by Captain Samuel M. Plummer, 1st U.S. Infantry. Named in honor of Captain Moses E. Merrill, 5th U.S. Infantry, killed on September 8, 1847, in the Battle of Molino del Rey. Abandoned on December 1, 1855.

MILAM. A Ranger post of the Texas Republic period. Located near the falls of the Brazos River, about two miles from the present town of Marlin. Named for Colonel Benjamin Rush Milam, killed on December 7, 1835, in the attack on San Antonio.

NUESTRA SEÑORA DEL PILAR Y GLORIOSA SAN JOSÉ, PRESIDIO OF. Established in 1773. Located at San Elizario, on what was then the southern end of an island in the Río Grande. The river has since changed its course and San Elizario is now on its left bank a few miles below El Paso. The presidio was occupied during the Mexican period and remained in the hands of Mexico after Texas gained its independence. It was garrisoned by United States troops, under the command of Captain William S. Henry, 3rd U.S. Infantry, on September 15, 1849. The garrison was withdrawn in September, 1851. The presidio was occupied irregularly during the Civil War, first by Confederate and later by Union troops. The presidio, which was commonly known as the Presidio of San Elizario, was initially established to protect the settlers of the area, notably the Pueblo Indians who had moved there at the time of the Pueblo Revolt in New Mexico, and to protect the missions from hostile Indians, particularly the Apaches.

ORCOQUISAC. See San Agustín de Ahumada.

PHANTOM HILL. Established November 14, 1851. Located between the Elm and Clear Forks of the Brazos River, about a mile above their junction. Established by Major John Joseph Abercrombie, 5th U.S. Infantry. This was one of the posts established to protect the emigrant route from Fort Smith, Arkansas, to Santa Fe. The post was referred to officially as both Fort Phantom Hill and "Post on the Clear Fork of the Brazos." The origin of the name "Phantom Hill" is obscure, but, presumably, it refers to the configuration of the local terrain. Abandoned as a permanent post on April 6, 1854. The site was a station on the Butterfield Overland stage route from 1858 until the outbreak of the Civil War. After the establishment of Fort Griffin in 1867, it was used from time to time as a picket post until 1880. After its abandonment in 1854, the buildings were burned so that as a sub-post of Fort Griffin it consisted of tents.

POLK. Established March 26, 1846. Located at Point Isabel at the mouth of the Río Grande. The post included troop quarters, warehouses, and dock facilities and was intended as a depot from which to supply the forces along the lower Río Grande. Established by Colonel Zachary Taylor, 6th U.S. Infantry. The post was named in honor of President James K. Polk. Abandoned on February 19, 1850.

PRESTON. Established in 1840. Located in a great bend of the Red River west of the present town of Denison near the spot where Colonel Holland Coffee had established a trading post in the 1830's. The post was a Ranger post of the Texas Republic period.

QUITMAN. Established September 28, 1858. Located on the left bank of the Río Grande, about seventy miles below El Paso. Established to protect the stage line and the east-west emigrant route. The post was built of adobe and was usually in a poor state of repair. Probably established by Captain James V. Bomford, 8th U.S. Infantry. Named in honor of Major General John Anthony Quitman, who died on July 17, 1858. Evacuated by Federal troops on April 5, 1861, by order of Brigadier General David E. Twiggs, and occupied by Confederate troops. Reoccupied by Federal troops under the command of Captain John C. Cremony, 2nd California Cavalry, on August 22, 1862. The troops were withdrawn in 1863, and the post was not again garrisoned until January 1, 1868. Permanently abandoned on January 5, 1877.

RICHARDSON. Established November 26, 1867. Located on the right bank of Lost Creek, a tributary of the Trinity River, about seven miles above its mouth, adjacent to the town of Jacksboro. The first troops stationed at Jacksboro were units of the 6th U.S. Cavalry, commanded by Major Samuel H. Starr, who arrived on July 4, 1866. The garrison was withdrawn from the town in the spring of 1867. Part of the troops were sent to regarrison Fort Belknap and some to Buffalo Springs (Camp Wichita). The post at Buffalo Springs, sometimes erroneously referred to as Fort Buffalo Springs, was established by Captain Benjamin T. Hutchins, 6th U.S. Cavalry, on April 18, 1867. It was abandoned on March 10, 1868, because of the shortage of water and difficulties of transportation. Fort Richardson was part of the defensive system intended to control hostile Indians, especially the Kiowas and Comanches, and it served also to protect the cattle trade. It was named for Major General Israel B. Richardson, who died on November 3, 1862, of wounds received in the Battle of Antietam. The post was sometimes referred to as Fort Jacksboro. Abandoned on May 22, 1878. Some of the post buildings have been restored.

RILEY. See Clark.

RINGGOLD. Established October 26, 1848. Located on the left bank of the Río Grande at David's Landing, about one-half mile below Río Grande City at the head of navigation on the river. It was one of the line of posts established along the Río Grande and the western frontier at the close of the Mexican War. Established by Captain

Joseph H. La Motte, 1st U.S. Infantry. First called "Post at David's Landing," then "Camp Ringgold," and, finally, on July 16, 1849, "Ringgold Barracks." It was designated Fort Ringgold on December 30, 1878. The post was named for Captain Samuel Ringgold, 3rd U.S. Artillery, who died on May 11, 1846, of wounds received in the Battle of Palo Alto. Abandoned on March 3, 1859, by order of Brigadier General David E. Twiggs, and the garrison transferred to Camp Hudson. Reoccupied on December 9, 1859, because of the activities of Juan Nepomuceno Cortinas along the Mexican border. Evacuated by Federal troops on March 7, 1861, and reoccupied in June, 1865. Rebuilt in 1869 on a location a little above the original site. The land occupied by the post was purchased by the federal government in 1881. Abandoned in October, 1906, and placed in charge of a caretaker. The post was occupied irregularly during the border difficulties with Mexico, 1913–17. In 1944 the post was declared surplus and deactivated.

SAM HOUSTON. Established in 1879. Located at San Antonio. As early as 1845 the government recognized the desirability of establishing a military post at San Antonio. Following the Mexican War, a depot was maintained there, and much of the time San Antonio served as departmental headquarters. In 1870 the city donated land for the establishment of a permanent post, and additional land was donated in 1871 and 1875. Erection of the post commenced in 1876. The original post was the San Antonio Quartermaster Depot. Permanent quarters to house the headquarters staff for the department were added, beginning in 1881, and occupied the same year. In 1885 construction of barracks, officers' quarters, and other facilities for the housing of twelve cavalry companies was undertaken. The post, including all of the establishments thereon, was at this time known as Post of San Antonio. It was designated Fort Sam Houston on September 10, 1890, in honor of the man who had played so prominent a role in the military and political history of Texas. The post is still operative.

SAN AGUSTÍN DE AHUMADA, PRESIDIO OF. Established late in May or June, 1756. Located at El Orcoquisac, a short distance east of the Trinity River and a few miles above its mouth. Established by Jacinto de Barrios y Jáuregui, governor of the province of Texas. Established to counter French activities among the Orcoquisa Indians and to afford protection for the Mission of Nuestra Señora de la Luz del Orcoquisac. Named for Agustín de Ahumada y Villalón, Marqués de las Amarillas, viceroy of New Spain. Also referred to as Presidio del Orcoquisac. The presidio was abandoned in 1772 on the recommendation of the Marqués de Rubí, who examined all of the Texas posts in 1767.

SAN ANTONIO DE BÉJAR, PRESIDIO OF. Established May 5, 1718. Located on the right side of the San Antonio River, two miles above the Mission of San Antonio de Valero, near San Pedro Spring. Established by Martín de Alarcón, governor of Coahuila y Texas. Established to protect the missions and settlers in the area. In 1722 the Marqués de San Miguel de Aguayo, governor of Coahuila y Texas, had the presidio moved to a new site almost directly across the San Antonio River from the Mission of San Antonio de Valero. Following the abandonment of the mission, the mission buildings were occupied by a presidial company from Alamo de Parras, Coahuila. Because of this, the former mission came to be known as the Alamo. Although the Alamo became an important post, it was not designated a presidio. The garrison at San Antonio de Béjar was continued.

SAN ELIZARIO, PRESIDIO OF. See Nuestra Señora del Pilar y Gloriosa San José.

SAN LUIS DE LAS AMARILLAS, PRESIDIO OF. Established by May 4,

1757. Located on the left bank of the San Saba River, a little west of the present town of Menard. Established by Colonel Diego Ortiz de Parilla. The presidio was intended to protect the Mission of San Sabá, founded south of the river at the same time. It was located also on the route between San Antonio and Santa Fe, and was intended to safeguard the opening of supposedly rich silver mines in the area. The purpose of the presidio failed, ten soldiers and settlers and two priests being killed in an Indian attack a year later. Further hostilities led to the campaign in which Ortiz de Parilla marched to the Red River in 1759. The original wooden buildings of the presidio were replaced by a fort of stone and mortar in 1761. Named for Agustín de Ahumada y Villalón, Marqués de las Amarillas, viceroy of New Spain. Also called Presidio of San Sabá. Abandoned in 1772.

SAN SABÁ, PRESIDIO OF. See San Luis de las Amarillas.

SAN XAVIER, PRESIDIO DE. Established in 1751. Located south of the San Xavier (San Gabriel) River, near the present town of Rockdale. Established to protect the three missions founded in the immediate vicinity. Established by Captain Felipe de Rábago y Terán. Although the missions, founded in 1747, had been protected by a mission guard, the presidio itself was not erected until 1751. In the latter part of 1755 the garrison was removed, though without official sanction. On May 18, 1756, the formal decree of the viceroy gave permission for the abandonment of San Xavier and the establishment of a new presidio on the San Saba River.

SANTA CRUZ. Established in 1772. Located on the Arroyo del Cíbolo (Cibolo Creek) between San Antonio and the Presidio de la Bahía. Established as part of the program to reorganize and strengthen the defenses of the entire northern frontier of New Spain from the Gulf of California to the Gulf of Mexico. The post consisted of a stockade and was garrisoned by twenty men. It occupied an intermediate point between the Presidios of San Antonio de Béjar and Bahía del Espíritu Santo.

St. Louis. Established in 1685. A temporary fort, also called St. Louis, was built on Matagorda Bay, close to the shore and slightly south of the mouth of Garcitas Creek. The permanent post was erected on a high bluff on the right side of Garcitas Creek, about five miles above its mouth. Established by René Robert Cavalier, Sieur de la Salle, in his ill-fated attempt to plant a French settlement at the mouth of the Mississippi River. Most of the soldiers and settlers were either killed or taken captive by the Indians. The fort, as described by Captain Alonzo de León, commander of the Spanish expedition which reached it in 1689, was made from the hulk of a wooden vessel. It was burned by the Spaniards in 1690.

Stockton. Established March 23, 1859. Located at Comanche Springs on Comanche Creek at the present town of Fort Stockton. Designed to protect the San Antonio–El Paso stage route. Established, probably, by First Lieutenant Walter Jones, 1st U.S. Infantry. Originally called Camp Stockton, it was later designated a fort, probably in 1859. Named for Commodore Robert H. Stockton, U.S. Navy. Most of the buildings of the post, which was not fortified, were constructed of adobe. Evacuated by Federal troops in April, 1861, by order of Brigadier General David E. Twiggs. Occupied briefly by Confederate troops, then burned by them. Reoccupied by Federal troops commanded by Colonel Edward Hatch, 9th U.S. Cavalry, on July 7, 1867, and completely rebuilt. Abandoned on June 30, 1886, by which time it was no longer considered useful.

Taylor. See Brown.

Tejas, Presidio of Nuestra Señora de los Dolores de los. The original post was a temporary encampment, established by Captain Domingo Ramón in 1716. It was located on a small plain near

Thomas Creek, a few miles east of the Neches River. The temporary site was chosen on June 30, 1716, and three months later the permanent site was selected a little east of the Angelina (Nuestra Señora de Asunción) River. Four missions were founded in the same general area. Abandoned in 1719. Re-established on the same site on August 15, 1721, by Joseph de Azlor y Virto de Vera, Marqués de San Miguel de Aguayo. At this time, seven missions existed in the general area. The decree for the abandonment of the presidio was issued by the viceroy of New Spain on April 26, 1729, on the recommendation of Brigadier General Pedro de Rivera, who had inspected the Texas presidios in 1727. The actual abandonment apparently took place in June, 1729.

TENOXTITLÁN. Established in the fall of 1830. Located on the Brazos River near the point at which the San Antonio–Nacogdoches road crossed the river. Established by Colonel Francisco Ruíz by order of General Manuel de Mier y Terán. The post was established to block the illegal entry of persons and goods from the United States and to encourage settlement. Probably abandoned in August, 1832. The name is that of the ancient capital of the Aztecs, now Mexico City.

TERÁN. Established in 1831. Located on the right bank of the Neches River, about two miles upstream from the present town of Rockland. Established by order of General Manuel de Mier y Terán, for whom the post was named. The post was established to block the illegal entry of persons and goods from the United States and to encourage settlement.

TERRETT. Established February 5, 1852. Located on the east bank of the North Fork of the Llano River, about two hundred yards from its source, in the present Sutton County. Established for the defense of the frontier. Established by Lieutenant Colonel Henry Bainbridge, 1st U.S. Infantry. Named for First Lieutenant John C.

Terrett, 1st U.S. Infantry, killed on September 21, 1846, in the Battle of Monterrey. Abandoned on February 26, 1854.

VELASCO. Established in 1832. Located on the left bank of the Brazos River at its mouth, at the town of Velasco. The site is now some distance from the Gulf because of the extension of the shoreline. Established by Colonel Dominic Ugartachea, by order of General Manuel de Mier y Terán. Established to block the illegal entry of persons and goods from the United States and to promote settlement. This was the last of the series of posts established for the purpose. Evacuated on June 27, 1832, following an attack by Texan supporters of Santa Anna, led by John Austin. Ugartachea and his men held out until their ammunition was nearly exhausted before surrendering the post. There is some question as to whether it was occupied by Texas troops after Texas secured its independence, but there is evidence that it was. During the Civil War the remains of the fort were torn down by the Confederates for metal and firewood.

WORTH. Established June 6, 1849. Located on the Trinity River immediately below the mouth of the Clear Fork of the Trinity at the present city of Fort Worth. In August, 1849, the post was moved from the river bottom, because of flooding, to a site on the bluff. Established by Captain Ripley A. Arnold, 2nd U.S. Dragoons. First called Camp Worth, the post was designated a fort on November 14, 1849. Named in honor of Colonel William Jenkins Worth, 8th U.S. Infantry, commanding the department, who died on May 7, 1849. The post, constructed of logs, was designed to protect the sparsely settled area from Indian hostilities. Abandoned on September 17, 1853, and the garrison transferred to Fort Belknap.

UTAH

CAMERON. Established May 25, 1872. Located on the right side of the Beaver River, two miles east of the town of Beaver. Established to

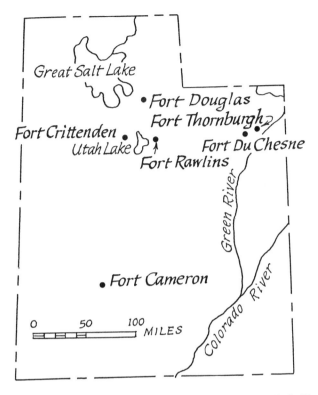

protect the recently opened mining district in southern Utah. Established by Major John D. Wilkins, 8th U.S. Infantry. The post was originally called Camp Beaver or "Post near Beaver City." It was designated Fort Cameron on June 30, 1874, for Colonel James Cameron, 79th New York Infantry, who was killed on July 21, 1861, at Bull Run. Abandoned on May 1, 1883, because the influx of settlers into the area rendered further protection unnecessary. The military reservation was transferred to the Interior Department on July 2, 1885.

CRITTENDEN. Established August 24, 1858. Located in Cedar Valley, west of Utah Lake, near the present town of Fairfield. Established by Colonel Albert Sidney Johnston, 2nd U.S. Cavalry, during the Mormon campaign (Utah War). Originally called Camp Floyd, for Secretary of War John B. Floyd, the post was designated Fort Crittenden on February 6, 1861, after Floyd had cast his lot with the Confederacy. Named for Senator John J. Crittenden of Tennessee. Abandoned on July 27, 1861. Briefly reoccupied in October, 1862, by Colonel Patrick E. Connor, 3rd California Infantry, and his command. By the time the post was reoccupied, some of the buildings had been sold to the Overland Mail Company and many of the others had been destroyed. The post was abandoned and replaced by Camp Douglas (*q.v.*). The military reservation was transferred to the Interior Department on July 22, 1884.

DOUGLAS. Established October 26, 1862. Located on a bench just north of Red Butte Creek, to the east of and overlooking Salt Lake City. Established to protect the Overland Mail and telegraph, to prevent Indian hostilities, and to keep an eye on the Mormons, whose loyalty was suspected by Secretary of War Edwin M. Stanton. Established by Colonel Patrick E. Connor, 3rd California Infantry. Originally called Camp Douglas, the post was designated a fort on December 30, 1878. Named for Senator Stephen A. Douglas of Illinois. The post is still operative.

DU CHESNE. Established August 20, 1886. Located on a site chosen by Brigadier General George Crook, about three miles above the junction of the Du Chesne and Uintah rivers. Established to control the Uncompahgre and White River Utes who had become restless and resistant to the authority of their agent. Established by Major Frederdick W. Benteen, 9th U.S. Cavalry. The post was ordered abandoned in 1892, but the order was rescinded before it was carried out. Abandoned in 1910, at which time the former post buildings became the agency headquarters for the Uintah and Ouray Indian Reservation.

FLOYD. See Crittenden.

RAWLINS. Established July 30, 1870. Located on the north bank of the Timpanogos River, two miles from the town of Provo, near the base of the Wasatch Mountains. Named for Secretary of War John A. Rawlins, who died on September 6, 1869. Two companies of the 13th U.S. Infantry, under the command of Captain Nathan W. Osborne, were sent to establish the post. Although the site was selected, no buildings were erected, the garrison being quartered in tents in Provo. Abandoned on July 9, 1871, the post no longer being deemed necessary.

THORNBURGH. Established in September, 1881. Originally located at the junction of the Green and White rivers. At the request of the Interior Department, the post was moved north to a site on Ashley Creek. Established to control the Ute Indians and to provide protection for their agents, after the removal of the Uncompahgre and White River Utes from Colorado to a new agency located at the junction of the Green and White rivers. Established by Captain Hamilton S. Hawkins, 6th U.S. Infantry. Named for Major Thomas T. Thornburgh, 4th U.S. Infantry, killed by Ute Indians on September 29, 1879, during the course of the campaign which included the White River massacre. Although a military reservation was declared, it proved impossible for the government to secure valid title to all of the land, and the post was abandoned in 1883. The military reservation was transferred to the Interior Department on July 22, 1884.

WASHINGTON

BELLINGHAM. Established August 26, 1856. Located at the present town of Bellingham, on Bellingham Bay, about twenty-five miles south of the Canadian border. In 1855 a small blockhouse was erected by the settlers of the area because of the widespread Indian disorders in the Pacific Northwest. In response to the appeal of the settlers, United States troops were sent under the command of Captain George E. Pickett, 9th U.S. Infantry, and the military post was established. It was considered a temporary post, its chief purpose being to protect the Whatcom coal mining district from Indian depredations. Abandoned on April 28, 1860.

BENNETT. After the "Battle of Frenchtown," which occurred near the site of Waiilatpu Mission in December, 1855, Fort Bennett was established by Lieutenant Colonel James K. Kelley and a force of Oregon volunteers. The fort, so-called, was a hastily erected stockade, designed as winter quarters for the volunteers. It was located about two miles east of the mission, which was some six miles west of the present town of Walla Walla. Named for Captain Charles Bennett, Oregon Volunteers, who had been killed in the fighting on December 7. Abandoned in 1856.

BLOCKHOUSES. The Indian uprising of the winter of 1855–56 led Territorial Governor Isaac I. Stevens to urge the settlers not to abandon their homes but, wherever three or more families were located sufficiently close together, to build blockhouses for their protection. Before the hostilities were brought under control, the settlers had erected twenty-three blockhouses or stockades, the volunteer troops thirty-five, and the regular troops seven. Many of these fortifications were referred to as forts. About July 20, 1856, the volunteers were disbanded, the hostile Indians having been driven east of the mountains.

FORTIFICATIONS ERECTED BY THE REGULAR TROOPS

Maloney. Located on the Puyallup River. Erected under the di-

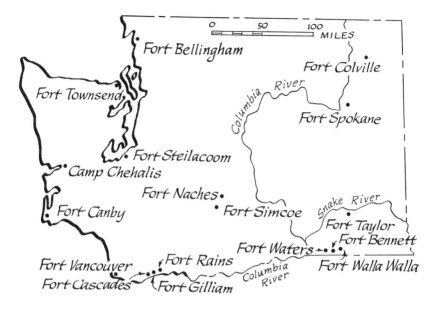

rection of Captain Maurice Maloney, 4th U.S. Infantry, for whom it was named.

Slaughter. Located on Muckleshoot Prairie, near the junction of the White and Green rivers. Erected under the direction of Captain Erasmus Darwin Keyes, 3rd U.S. Artillery. Named for First Lieutenant William A. Slaughter, 4th U.S. Infantry, who was killed by the Indians on December 4, 1855. This blockhouse was maintained until August, 1857. In official reports it is usually referred to as Muckleshoot Prairie.

Thomas. Located on the Green River.

Blockhouses, apparently not called forts, were erected on the Black River, and in the Yakima and Walla Walla valleys. (See also Fort Cascades.)

FORTIFICATIONS ERECTED BY THE VOLUNTEER TROOPS

Alden. Located above the falls of the Snoqualmie River. Erected by the northern battalion of the second volunteer regiment. Named for Captain James Alden.

Ebey. Located eight miles above the mouth of the Snohomish River. Named for Isaac N. Ebey, United States customs collector, who was later murdered and dismembered by Indians in 1857.

Hays. Located on Connell's Prairie, south of the White River. Erected by the central battalion of the volunteers. Named for Major Gilmore Hays, 2nd Regiment.

Hicks. Located about twelve miles east of Fort Steilacoom.

Kitsap. Located at Port Madison on a western arm of Puget Sound. Named for Kitsap, a friendly Yakima chief.

Lander. Located on the Dwamish River. Erected under the direction of Captain Edward W. Lander, 2nd Regiment, for whom it was named.

McAllister. Located on South Prairie.

Mason. Located in the Walla Walla Valley. Probably named for Charles H. Mason, secretary of the territory and acting governor at the time the Indian uprising commenced.

Miller. Located on Tanalquot Prairie. Named for W. W. Miller, quartermaster and commissary general, 2nd Regiment.

Pike. Located at the crossing on White River. Erected by the central battalion.

Posey. Located at the crossing on White River. Erected by the central battalion.

Preston. Located on Michel Fork of the Nisqually River.

Stevens. Located on Yelm Prairie. Erected by the central battalion. Named for Governor Isaac I. Stevens.

Tilton. Located below the falls of the Snoqualmie River. Erected by the northern battalion. Named for Major James Tilton, surveyor general, Volunteers.

White. Located at the emigrant crossing of the Puyallup River. Erected under the direction of Major Gilmore Hays. Named for Captain Joseph A. White, Pioneer Company, 2nd Regiment.

The remaining fortifications erected by the volunteers apparently were not called forts.

FORTIFICATIONS ERECTED BY THE SETTLERS

Only two of these seem to have been called forts: HENNESS, located on Grand Mound Prairie and named for Captain Benjamin L. Henness of the central battalion; and ARKANSAS, located on the Cowlitz River.

CANBY. Construction of the post commenced in July, 1863. It was first garrisoned on April 5, 1864. Located on Cape Disappointment, within the mouth of the Columbia River. The quarters for the officers and men were located around the shores of Baker Bay. The site was chosen by Colonel René E. de Russy, Corps of Engineers, in charge of Pacific coastal defenses. The post was originally designated Fort Cape Disappointment by Brigadier General Benjamin Alvord. On January 28, 1875, the name was changed to Fort Canby, in honor of Brigadier General Edward R. S. Canby, who was killed by Modoc Indians on April 11, 1873, while engaged in peace negotiations. The post was designed to guard the entrance to the Columbia River, in conjunction with Fort Stevens, Oregon. It was not garrisoned in 1888, but was reoccupied the following year.

CAPE DISAPPOINTMENT. See Canby.

CASCADES. Established September 30, 1855. Located on the right bank of the Columbia River at the foot of the Cascades, near the present Bonneville Dam. The Cascades are the lower of the two rapids in the Columbia which interrupt the navigation of the river. Established to protect the movement of persons and supplies along the river. In addition to the fort itself, two blockhouses were erected on the north bank of the river, one about midway along the rapids and the other at the head of the rapids, some five miles above the fort. These blockhouses accommodated small garrisons. Established by Captain Granville O. Haller, 4th U.S. Infantry. Evacuated on June 14, 1861. Reoccupied on August 20, 1861, because of the threatened renewal of Indian hostilities. Finally abandoned on November 6, 1861. The military reservation, which was privately claimed, was relinquished on February 2, 1867.

CHEHALIS. Established February 11, 1860. Located at Gray's Harbor near the mouth of the Chehalis River. Established when the Chehalis Indians threatened the settlement recently established at the mouth of the river. Established by Captain Maurice Maloney, 4th U.S. Infantry. The post was a camp and was never officially designated a fort. Abandoned on June 19, 1861, by order of Colonel George Wright, 9th U.S. Infantry. Reoccupied in August, 1861, to restore the confidence of the settlers in the vicinity and to protect the Indian agent while an agency was being established nearby. Permanently abandoned before the end of the year. In 1868 the government ordered the buildings at the post sold.

COLVILLE. Established June 15, 1859. Located on a flat on the left side of Mill Creek, seven miles above its confluence with the Colville River and about three miles east of the present town of Colville. Established to control the Indians of the area, who had been very hostile, and to provide a base for the northwest boundary commission. Established by Captain Pinkney Lugenbeel, 9th U.S. Infantry, by order of Brigadier General William S. Harney. First called Harney Depot, the post was later designated Camp Colville, then Fort Colville. The name was derived from the earlier Hudson's Bay Company post, which was named for Andrew Colville, an official of the company. Abandoned in 1883. The military reservation was transferred to the Interior Department on February 26, 1887.

GILLIAM. Established in January, 1848. Located on the right bank of the Columbia River near the present Bonneville Dam, not far from the site of the later Fort Cascades. Established during the Cayuse War by the Oregon volunteers to serve as a supply station and a base of operations for troops sent up the river from Oregon City. Named for Colonel Cornelius Gilliam, Oregon Volunteers, who established the post. The post consisted of a few log cabins and was usually referred to simply as "the Cabins."

NACHES. Established in May, 1856. Located about nine miles above the mouth of the Naches River, a confluent of the Yakima. Established as a base of operations during the Indian campaign of 1856. Established by Colonel George Wright, 9th U.S. Infantry. The fort consisted of a fieldwork constructed of large wickerworks of willow filled with earth (gabions). Because of the way it was constructed, the post was called the "basket fort" by the settlers of the area. Wright called it "Fort Na-chess." In official listings it is called "Camp on Nechess River." It was a temporary post, abandoned at the close of the campaign.

RAINS. Established in 1856. Located on Sheridan's Point on the north side of the Columbia River, a little to the east of the present town of North Bonneville. The post consisted of a blockhouse erected for the protection of the settlers of the area. Erected by Major Gabriel Rains, 4th U.S. Infantry, who had been appointed Brigadier General of the Oregon Volunteers during the Indian wars of 1855–56. The post was not a U.S. Army post and was, apparently,

173

never garrisoned. It was washed away during a period of high water in 1876.

SIMCOE. Established August 8, 1856. Located in the Simcoe Valley, roughly midway between Simcoe and Toppenish creeks, in the present Yakima County. Established during the Yakima War as a base of operations against the Indians and for the protection of the settlers. Established by Colonel George Wright, 9th U.S. Infantry. Constructed under the supervision of Major Robert S. Garnett, 9th U.S. Infantry. The valley and creek, from which the name of the post was derived, were named for John Simcoe, the first lieutenant governor of Upper Canada. Abandoned on May 22, 1859, as it was no longer considered useful. The buildings were transferred to the Interior Department to serve as headquarters for the Yakima Indian Agency, which occupied the site until 1922.

SPOKANE. Established on October 21, 1880. Located near the junction of the Spokane and Columbia rivers. The post replaced Fort Colville and was intended to protect both the Indians and the settlers; however, by the time the post was established, friction between whites and Indians in the area was largely a thing of the past. Established by Major Leslie Smith, 2nd U.S. Infantry. Originally called Camp Spokane, the post was designated a fort in 1881. The garrison was withdrawn in 1898 at the time of the Spanish-American War, and the post was abandoned on August 26, 1899. The military reservation was transferred to the Interior Department on August 28, 1899, to be used as an Indian school.

STEILACOOM. Established August 28, 1849. Located at the present town of Steilacoom, a few miles south of Tacoma, near the head, but more than a mile east, of Puget Sound. Established to protect the settlers in the area, principally those in the vicinity of the Hudson's Bay Company's Fort Nisqually, from Indian depredations. Established by Captain Bennett H. Hill, 1st U.S. Artillery. The post was located on land belonging to the Hudson's Bay Company. Erected under the direction of Second Lieutenant Grier Tallmadge, 4th U.S. Artillery, acting assistant quartermaster. Originally referred to as the "Post on Puget Sound" or simply "Steilacoom." Named for the Steilacoom River, a small stream near the post. Abandoned on April 22, 1868. On April 15, 1874, a portion of the reservation was donated to the territory of Washington, which there established the Western State Hospital for the Insane. The remaining portion of the military reservation was transferred to the Interior Department on July 22, 1884. The post buildings were sold on January 15, 1870.

TAYLOR. Established August 11, 1858. Located on the left bank of the Snake River at the mouth of the Tucannon. Established by Colonel George Wright, 9th U.S. Infantry. Used as a base of operations in the campaign against the hostile Spokane, Coeur d'Alene, and Palouse Indians in the Spokane country. The post was built of basalt rock with hexagonal bastions of alder. Named for First Lieutenant Oliver Hazard Perry Taylor, 1st U.S. Dragoons, who was killed in action against the Spokane Indians on May 17, 1858. Abandoned on October 2, 1858, when Colonel Wright and his command re-crossed the Snake River at the close of the campaign.

TOWNSEND. Established October 26, 1856. Located on the west side of Port Townsend Bay at the entrance to Puget Sound. Established to protect the settlers in the area from hostile Indians. Established by Captain Granville O. Haller, 4th U.S. Infantry. Ordered abandoned on June 11, 1861. In May, 1862, the collector of customs at Port Townsend was authorized by Brigadier General George Wright to take possession of the buildings at the post and make use of them for a marine hospital until such time as they were required for military use. Re-established on July 1, 1874, when Camp Steele on San Juan Island was abandoned. Although the post was small, it was the only military post in the area and was considered necessary to protect the settlers from Indian depredations and to guard the Indian reservations on the west side of the sound from the encroachment of the settlers. The post was partly destroyed by fire in the winter of 1894–95, and the garrison was withdrawn for that reason. The military reservation was transferred to the Interior Department on June 28, 1895; however, the order was rescinded on May 1, 1896, and the reservation was returned to the War Department. The post was not regarrisoned.

VANCOUVER. Originally erected by the Hudson's Bay Company in 1824–25. Located at the present town of Vancouver, on the right bank of the Columbia River opposite Portland, Oregon, and 124 miles above the mouth of the river. Named Fort Vancouver on March 19, 1825, for Captain George Vancouver, English navigator and explorer. The company did not entirely withdraw from the post until 1860. Established as a United States military post on May 15, 1849. The first troops to arrive in the Oregon country were two companies of the 1st U.S. Artillery, commanded by Captain John S. Hatheway, who arrived at the mouth of the Columbia River by sea from New York on May 13, 1849. One company was stationed near Fort Vancouver and the other at Nisqually on Puget Sound. The post was first called Columbia Barracks. It was not garrisoned until 1850 because quarters were not available for troops. Colonel Persifor F. Smith, Mounted Riflemen, commanding the Pacific Division, ordered the erection of quarters, which were constructed under the supervision of Captain Rufus Ingalls, assistant quartermaster. The other buildings originally occupied by the military were leased from the Hudson's Bay Company. The military post was designated Fort Vancouver on July 13, 1853. Vancouver Arsenal was established in connection with the post in 1859. The name of the post was changed to Vancouver Barracks on April 5, 1879. Abandoned in 1947.

WALLA WALLA. Established September 23, 1856. Located in the Walla Walla Valley at the present town of Walla Walla. In 1858 the post was moved to a new site about one and a half miles from the original location. Established by Major Edward J. Steptoe, 9th U.S. Infantry. Intended to control the hostile Indians of the area and to protect the lines of transportation and travel. The post was garrisoned irregularly from 1864 to 1867. During the years from 1867 to 1873, it was used as a depot for wintering public animals. Reoccupied in August, 1873. Finally abandoned on March 31, 1911, and placed in the hands of a caretaker. The site is now occupied by a Veterans Administration hospital.

WATERS. Established March 2, 1848. Located on the site of Waiilatpu Mission, which had been destroyed following the Whitman massacre. Established by Lieutenant Colonel Cornelius Gilliam, Oregon Volunteers, to serve as a base of operations during the Cayuse War. The post was constructed from the remains of the mission buildings. It was named for Lieutenant Colonel James Waters of the Oregon Volunteers.

WYOMING

AUGUR. Established June 28, 1869. Located in the valley of the Popo Agie River at the present town of Lander. Established by First Lieutenant Patrick Henry Breslin, 4th U.S. Infantry. Intended to protect the Bannock and Shoshoni Indians as well as the settlers in the Sweetwater mining district. The post was named Camp Augur, for Brigadier General Christopher C. Augur, commanding the department, and was never officially designated a fort. It was originally a sub-post of Fort Bridger. Reorganized as a separate post on March 28, 1870, at which time the name was changed to Camp Brown, in honor of Captain Frederick H. Brown, 18th U.S. Infantry, who was killed on December 21, 1866, in the Fetterman massacre. The original site was abandoned in the spring of 1871 when the agency for the Shoshoni Indians was moved to the Little Wind River and a new post established. (See Fort Washakie.)

BRIDGER. Originally built as a trading post by Jim Bridger and Luis Vásquez in 1842. Located on the left bank of Black's Fork of the Green River at the present town of Fort Bridger. The Mormons charged that Bridger was selling powder and lead to the Indians and, in 1853, sent a posse after him. He departed before it arrived. The Mormons later claimed that they had purchased the fort from Vásquez. It was substantially rebuilt by the Mormons in 1855. They abandoned and burned the post in October, 1857, at the outset of the Utah War. Bridger leased the remains of the post to the United States government for the use of the military on November 18, 1857. Fort Bridger was formally designated an army post by Colonel Albert Sidney Johnston, 2nd U.S. Cavalry, on June 7, 1858, when he departed for Salt Lake City.

The post was rebuilt under the direction of Major William Hoffman, 6th U.S. Infantry, and his successor in command, Major Edward R. S. Canby, 10th U.S. Infantry. It served as a supply depot for the U.S. Army in Utah and was an important point on the Overland Trail, guarding, as it did, the stage route and later the construction of the Union Pacific Railway. The post was located on a Mexican land grant of nine square miles, but no money was paid to Bridger for it because of his inability to prove title to the land, although he was eventually paid $6,000 for the improvements. Abandoned on May 23, 1878. Reoccupied in June, 1880, because of the Ute Indian uprising and the Meeker massacre. Finally abandoned on November 6, 1890. The military reservation was transferred to the Interior Department on October 14, 1890.

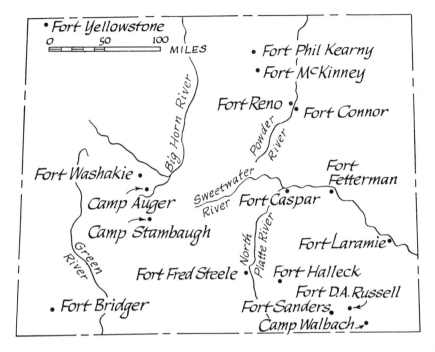

BROWN. See Augur and Washakie.

CARRINGTON. See Phil Kearny.

CASPAR. Established in May, 1862. Located on the south side of the North Platte River at the present town of Casper. From 1840 until 1847 the crossing point was known as Camp Platte and served as a convenient and natural camping place for emigrants following the Oregon Trail. In June, 1847, the Mormons established a ferry at this point and for the succeeding twelve years it was known as Mormon Ferry. Platte Bridge Station, consisting of adobe buildings, was erected at the same spot—the common crossing place—in 1858. From July 29, 1858, to April 20, 1859, troops were stationed there

179

to protect the emigrant trains, to keep open communciations with Salt Lake City, and to facilitate the movement of supplies for the Utah expeditionary force. The post was garrisoned by regular troops, Companies D and E of the 4th U.S. Artillery, Captain Joseph Roberts and Captain George W. Getty, commanding. In 1859, Louis Guinard completed the 1,000-foot bridge across the North Platte River from which the camp derived its name. In May, 1862, a garrison, consisting of troops of the 6th U.S. Volunteers, was provided to protect the crossing and the telegraph line from the Indians.

In the spring of 1865 the post, still called Platte Bridge Station, became permanent. The post became unusually active that same year when the Indians sought to halt all traffic along the Oregon Trail. On November 21, 1865, Major General John Pope, commanding the department, ordered that henceforth the post be known as Fort Caspar, in honor of First Lieutenant Caspar W. Collins, 11th Ohio Cavalry, killed in the Platte Bridge Station Battle, on July 26, 1865. The post was first garrisoned by regular troops on June 28, 1866, under the command of Captain Richard L. Morris, 18th U.S. Infantry. The name "Caspar" was often spelled "Casper" in government reports, and in that form was applied to the town which later grew up at the site. The post was rebuilt and enlarged in 1866. Abandoned on October 19, 1867, when it was replaced by Fort Fetterman. Immediately after Fort Caspar was abandoned, the buildings and the bridge across the North Platte were burned by the Indians. The fort has been reconstructed and the site is now a park.

CONNOR. See Reno.

FETTERMAN. Established July 19, 1867. Located on a sagebrush-covered plateau on the south bank of the North Platte River, near the mouth of La Prele Creek, at the point where the Bozeman Trail left the river and turned north. Intended to protect the various emigrant routes in the area and to aid in the control of the hostile Sioux Indians. Established by Major William McEntyre Dye, 4th U.S. Infantry. Named for Captain William J. Fetterman, 27th U.S. Infantry, killed by the Sioux Indians in the Fetterman massacre on December 21, 1866, near Fort Phil Kearny. The post buildings were sold on September 29, 1882, and military custody ceased on November 6, 1882. The military reservation was transferred to the Interior Department on July 22, 1884. The old post then became the nucleus for a hell-roaring cattle town which eventually declined and was deserted. Some of the buildings still stand.

HALLECK. Established July 20, 1862. Located west of the Medicine Bow River at the north base of Elk Mountain. The site was selected by and the post built under the command of Major John O'Ferrall, 11th Ohio Cavalry. It was established to protect the Overland Trail, the Denver–Salt Lake stage route, and the telegraph line from the Indians. Named for Major General Henry W. Halleck. Abandoned on July 4, 1866. The military reservation was transferred to the Interior Department on October 11, 1886.

JOHN BUFORD. See Sanders.

LARAMIE. Originally erected in 1834 as a trading post. First called Fort William, for William Sublette, William Anderson, and William Patton; then Fort John, presumably for John B. Sarpy. Located on the left bank of the Laramie River, about a mile above its junction with the North Platte. In March, 1849, United States Adjutant General Roger Jones directed Colonel David E. Twiggs, 2nd U.S. Dragoons, commanding the Western Division of the Army, to establish a post at or near Fort Laramie. Major Winslow F. Sanderson, Mounted Riflemen, who arrived at Fort Laramie on June 16, 1849, recommended the purchase of the trading post itself. The arrangement for the purchase was concluded on June 26, 1849.

The post was first garrisoned by two companies of Mounted Riflemen and one company of the 6th U.S. Infantry, arriving in detachments in June, July, and August, 1849. The name, Fort Laramie, which had long been the popular name for the post, was retained. The name was derived from the Laramie River, which was named for a French trapper, Jacques Laramie, who was killed by Arapaho Indians near its headwaters in 1821. The post was used to protect the Oregon Trail, which had become a major highway for the gold rush to California, and, later, to control the Indians of the northern plains. The buildings of the trading post were occupied by the army only until they could be replaced by other structures, the last being destroyed in 1862. The construction of the Union Pacific seventy miles to the south and the Chicago and Northwestern fifty miles to the north placed Fort Laramie off the main lines of travel and marked the beginning of its decline. Abandonment was ordered on August 31, 1889 although the last troops did not leave until March 2, 1890. Part of the military reservation was transferred to the Interior Department on June 9, 1890, and the remainder on November 4, 1897. Some of the buildings were dismantled; the rest were sold at public auction on April 9, 1890. The partly restored post is now a national monument.

MCKINNEY. Established October 12, 1876. After Brigadier General George Crook's Big Horn expedition had been stopped by Crazy Horse at the Rosebud, another column, the Powder River expedition, was organized under the command of Colonel Ranald Mackenzie, 4th U.S. Cavalry, to operate from Fort Fetterman as a base. A series of depots was established, one of which was Cantonment Reno, located three miles south of the abandoned Fort Reno. Established by Captain Edwin Pollock, 9th U.S. Infantry. On August 30, 1877, the post was designated Fort McKinney, for First Lieutenant John A. McKinney, 4th U.S. Cavalry, killed by Indians

182

on November 25, 1876. The site was considered unhealthful; hence, on June 17, 1878, authorization was given to relocate the post on the right bank of Clear Creek, a confluent of the Powder River, a little west of the present town of Buffalo. The last troops did not leave the old site, now called McKinney Depot, until late in 1879. The new post, also established by Captain Pollock, was a center for control of the Indians in the cattle country east of the Big Horn Mountains. Abandoned on November 9, 1894. In 1895 the post buildings and two sections of land were given to the state. In 1903 the old post became the State Soldiers' and Sailors' Home.

PHIL KEARNY. Established July 13, 1866. Located at the foot of the Big Horn Mountains, between Big and Little Piney creeks, just before they unite, about fifteen miles north of the present town of Buffalo. Established by Colonel Henry B. Carrington, 18th U.S. Infantry, as part of the protective system for the Bozeman Trail. First called Fort Carrington, the post was soon designated Fort Phil Kearny, in honor of Major General Philip Kearny, who was killed on September 1, 1862, in the Battle of Chantilly, Virginia. Abandoned on July 31, 1868,[1] as a result of the Fort Laramie Treaty of April 29, 1868, with the Sioux Indians. Immediately after it was evacuated, the buildings were burned by the Sioux Indians.

RENO. Established August 14, 1865. Located on a shelf rising some fifty feet above the left bank of Powder River, about four miles below the mouth of Dry Fork and about twenty-two miles northeast of the present town of Kaycee. Established by Brigadier General Patrick E. Connor, for whom the post was first called Fort Connor.

[1] President Andrew Johnson ordered the abandonment of the three Bozeman Trail forts—Reno, Phil Kearny, and C. F. Smith—on March 2, 1868, but lack of transportation facilities delayed the evacuation of the garrisons until midsummer. August 18, 1868, is sometimes given as the date of abandonment. War Department records do not seem to contain the specific dates. Peter C. Harris, adjutant general, stated that they were abandoned in August, 1868, prior to August 7, according to available records. Grace R. Hebard and E. A. Brininstool, *The Bozeman Trail*, II, 254, especially note 136.

The post was intended to protect the Bozeman Trail and served as a supply base for Connor's Powder River campaign. It was constructed under the direction of Colonel James H. Kidd, 6th Michigan Cavalry. On November 11, 1865, the post was officially designated Fort Reno, in honor of Major Jesse L. Reno, killed on September 14, 1862, in the Battle of South Mountain. On June 28, 1866, command of the post was assumed by Colonel Henry B. Carrington, 18th U.S. Infantry, commander of the Mountain District. He had intended to relocate the post but, instead, left a garrison of two companies under the command of Captain Joseph L. Proctor, under whose direction it was considerably enlarged. Abandoned on August 18, 1868, as a result of the Fort Laramie Treaty of April 29, 1868, with the Sioux Indians. The post was immediately burned by the Indians. Cantonment Reno (see Fort McKinney) was established near the site in 1876.

RUSSELL. D. A. Established July 21, 1867. Located three miles west of Cheyenne on the north bank of Crow Creek, a branch of the South Platte. In the summer of 1867, Major General Grenville M. Dodge selected the site of what was to become the city of Cheyenne for a construction camp for the Union Pacific Railway. Colonel Christopher C. Augur, 12th U.S. Infantry, commanding the department, chose the site for the post, which was established by Colonel John D. Stevenson, 30th U.S. Infantry. It was located northwest of the railway terminal, at the point where the Union Pacific was to cross Crow Creek, and was designed to protect the railway workers and the citizens of the new town. The post was designated Fort D. A. Russell, in honor of Brigadier General David A. Russell, on September 8, 1867. General Russell was killed on September 19, 1864, in the Battle of Opequon, Virginia. The post immediately became an important supply depot for the area. For that reason Camp Carlin, so called for Captain Elias B. Carling, assistant quartermaster, who selected the site and established the depot, also was established in

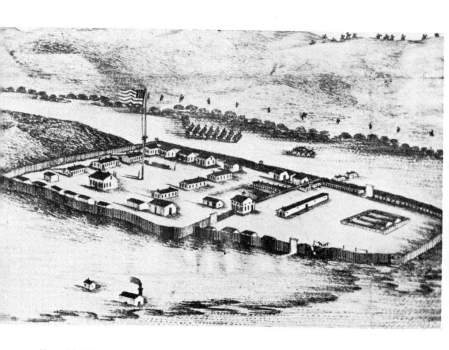

Fort Phil Kearny, as sketched in 1867 by Bugler Antonio Nicoli. It is an example of the type of post provided with stockades but not blockhouses.

Courtesy Archives and Western History Department, University of Wyoming Library

September, 1867. The depot, officially designated Cheyenne Depot, was located on the military reservation about midway between Fort Russell and the city of Cheyenne. The depot was dismantled in 1890. On January 1, 1930, the fort was renamed Fort Francis E. Warren, for a Civil War veteran who was the first governor of the state of Wyoming. The post is still operative and is now the Francis E. Warren Air Force Base.

SANDERS. Established July 10, 1866. Located one and three-quarters miles east of the Laramie River and about three miles south of the town of Laramie. The post was intended to protect the Overland and Lodgepole Creek emigrant routes, the Denver–Salt Lake stage route, and the construction crews of the Union Pacific Railway. Probably established by Captain Henry R. Mizner, 18th U.S. Infantry, by order of Major General John Pope. Originally named Fort John Buford, for Major General John Buford. The post was designated Fort Sanders on September 5, 1866, in honor of Brigadier General William P. Sanders, who died on November 19, 1863, of wounds received at Knoxville. Abandoned on May 22, 1882. The military reservation was transferred to the Interior Department on August 22, 1882.

STAMBAUGH. Established August 20, 1870. Located in Smith's Gulch, between Atlantic City and the Oregon Trail, about eight miles north of the Sweetwater River. Established because the miners of the Sweetwater district demanded protection when the boundaries of the Shoshoni Indian Reservation were drawn almost adjoining the mining district. Established by Major James S. Brisbin, 2nd U.S. Cavalry. The post was named for First Lieutenant Charles B. Stambaugh, 2nd U.S. Cavalry, killed by Indians on May 4, 1870, near Miner's Delight, Wyoming. The post was a camp and was never officially designated a fort. Abandoned on August 17, 1878.

The military reservation, never formally declared, was transferred to the Interior Department on May 3, 1881.

STEELE, FRED. Established June 30, 1868. Located on the left bank of the North Platte River, some fifteen miles east of the present town of Rawlins, where the Union Pacific Railway crossed the river. Established by Major Richard I. Dodge, 30th U.S. Infantry. Established as part of the protective system for the Union Pacific and the Overland Trail, and as partial replacement for the abandoned Bozeman Trail posts. Named for Colonel Frederick Steele, 20th U.S. Infantry, who died on January 12, 1868. Abandoned in 1886, the last troops leaving the post on November 3, except for a small guard which remained until the Interior Department could formally receive the military reservation, which had been transferred on August 9, 1886.

WALBACH. Established September 20, 1858. Located on Lodgepole Creek, east of Cheyenne Pass, about twenty miles east of the present town of Laramie. Established to protect the Lodgepole Creek emigrant route, especially the dangerous crossing through Cheyenne Pass. The post was a camp and was never officially designated a fort. Named for Colonel John De Barth Walbach, 4th U.S. Artillery, who died on June 10, 1857. Abandoned on April 19, 1859.

WARREN, FRANCES E. See D. A. Russell.

WASHAKIE. Established in January, 1871, on a site selected by Captain Robert A. Torrey, 13th U.S. Infantry, who also established the post. Located at the present town of Fort Washakie, about fifteen miles northwest of Lander, on the Wind River (Shoshoni) Indian Reservation, near the confluence of the Little Wind River and the North Fork of the Wind. Established to protect the Shoshoni Indians. Located, as it was, on the southern edge of the Big Horn Basin, the post became an important supply base for those entering the basin from the south. Originally called Camp Brown (see Camp Augur). The post was designated Fort Washakie on December 30, 1878, in honor of Chief Washakie, a Shoshoni Indian. The order to abandon the post was issued in 1899, but Chief Washakie, then more than ninety years of age, objected so strenuously that the order was revoked. Evacuated on May 1, 1907. Reoccupied on June 6, 1907, and again constituted a permanent post on October 14, 1907. Permanently abandoned on March 30, 1909. The post and military reservation were turned over to the Interior Department and became the headquarters for the Shoshoni Agency.

YELLOWSTONE. Established August 17, 1886. Located in Yellowstone Park on Beaver Creek, near Mammoth Hot Springs. Established to protect the park from vandalism, enforce the game laws, and to guard the natural wonders from despoilation. Established by Captain Moses Harris, 1st U.S. Cavalry. Originally called Camp Sheridan, for Lieutenant General Phil Sheridan. The post was designated Fort Yellowstone on May 11, 1891. Abandoned in 1918.

APPENDIX

CIVIL WAR FORTS IN THE TRANS-MISSISSIPPI WEST

A LARGE NUMBER OF POSTS were established by both the Union and Confederacy solely for the purpose of furthering their respective war efforts. Very few of these posts outlived the conflict itself. This period constitutes the major deviation from the normal military policy pursued by the United States in the West. It must be remembered, though, that the normal policy was being applied in most parts of the West even while the Civil War was being fought, and that many forts were established during the period in connection with that policy. The following listing makes no pretense of completeness.

ARKANSAS
   Hindman
   Minor
   Pinney
   Steele

KANSAS
   Blair
   Lincoln
   McKean
   Montgomery
   Simple
   Sully[1]

LOUISIANA
   Banks
   Beauregard
   Berwick
   Bisland
   Brashier
   Buchanan
   Buhlow
   De Russey
   Morganza
   Plaquemine[2]
   Randolph
   Shreveport

[1] Fort Sully was located on the Fort Leavenworth military reservation.
[2] This is not to be confused with Fort San Felipe, or Plaquemines, located below New Orleans on the left bank of the Mississippi River.

MISSOURI
  A, B, C, and
    D (Cape Girardeau)
  Curtis (also called Hovey)
  Davidson
  Dette
  Hamer
  Insley
  New Madrid
  Thompson
  Wyman

OKLAHOMA
  Davis
  McCulloch

TEXAS
  Bankhead
  Chambers
  Debrey
  Esperanza
  Green
  Hebert
  Jackson
  Magruder
  Mannahasset
  Moore
  Murrah
  Quintana
  Sabine
  Scurry
  Velasco

189

BIBLIOGRAPHY

THERE IS AN ABUNDANCE OF PUBLISHED MATERIAL available for the study of western military posts. Full-scale biographies of a few forts have been written, and many more have been the subject of articles, both scholarly and popular. Most western posts, however, have not received individual treatment, and many of them, interesting though their stories may be, were not of sufficient importance to warrant an extended account.

Unpublished materials are voluminous also. The National Archives of the United States contain much correspondence pertinent to western military history, as well as general orders, special orders, order, inspection reports, post returns for individual posts, reports of medical officers, and other documents of a comparable nature. Valuable materials are to be found in the archives of state historical societies and in many public and private libraries. In general, these materials supplement the National Archives, but they often provide information unavailable in the official correspondence and reports. Another considerable body of unpublished writing consists of dissertations, especially at the master's level, in the various institutions of higher education throughout the West. Many contain useful information drawn from local and often obscure sources.

The following bibliography is a listing of published materials found most useful in compiling the data contained herein. Particularly valuable are the annual reports of the secretary of war, especially for the years 1848–98. For the Civil War period, the *War of the Rebellion Records* are essential.

GOVERNMENT PUBLICATIONS

Abel, Annie Heloise, ed. *The Official Correspondence of James S. Calhoun while Indian Agent at Santa Fe and Superintendent of Indian Affairs in New Mexico*. Washington, D. C., 1915. Contains some material for military posts and policy, 1849–52.

American State Papers: Indian Affairs. 2 vols. Washington, D. C., 1832–34.

American State Papers: Military Affairs. 7 vols. Washington, D. C., 1832–61.

Annual Reports of the Secretary of War. 1821–1900.

Atlas to Accompany the Official Records of the Union and Confederate Armies. 3 vols. Washington, D. C., 1891–95.

Belknap, William W. *Letter of the Secretary of War, Communicating . . . a Copy of the Report of Lieutenant Colonel Samuel B. Holabird, of a Reconnoissance Made by Him in the Department of Dakota in 1869*, 41 Cong., 3 sess., *Sen. Exec. Doc. 8*. Washington, D. C., 1870.

Brown, Harvey E., comp. *The Medical Department of the United States Army from 1775 to 1873*. Washington, D. C., 1873.

Buchanan, James. *California and New Mexico*, 31 Cong., 1 sess., *House Exec. Doc. 17*. Washington, D. C., 1850.

Calhoun, John C. *Letter from the Secretary of War Transmitting . . . a Report of the Number and Station of All Military Posts in the United States*, 16 Cong., 2 sess., *House Exec. Doc. 41*. Washington, D. C., 1821. The information contained is for 1820.

Carey, Asa B. *A Sketch of the Organization of the Pay Department of the U. S. Army from 1775 to 1876*. Washington, D. C., 1876.

Conrad, Charles M. *Report of the Secretary of War Communicating . . . Colonel McCall's Reports in Relation to New Mexico*, 31 Cong., 2 sess., *Sen. Exec. Doc. 26*. Washington, D. C., 1851.

Coolidge, Richard H., comp. *Statistical Report on the Sickness and Mortality in the Army of the United States, Compiled from the*

Records of the Surgeon General's Office; Embracing a Period of Sixteen Years, from January, 1839, to January, 1855, 34 Cong., 1 sess., *Sen. Exec. Doc. 96*. Washington, D. C., 1856.

————. *Statistical Report on the Sickness and Mortality in the United States Army, Compiled from the Records of the Surgeon General's Office; Embracing a Period of Five Years, from January, 1855, to January, 1860*, 36 Cong., 1 sess., *Sen. Exec. Doc. 52*. Washington, D. C., 1860.

Crosby, H. T. *Military Sites in Texas*, 43 Cong., 1 sess., *House Exec. Doc. 282*. Washington, D. C., 1874.

Davis, Jefferson. *Report of the Secretary of War Communicating the Several Pacific Railroad Explorations*, 33 Cong., 1 sess., *House Exec. Doc. 129*. 3 vols. and atlas. Washington, D. C., 1855.

Emory, William H. *Notes of a Military Reconnoissance, from Fort Leavenworth in Missouri, to San Diego, in California, Including Part of the Arkansas, del Norte, and Gila Rivers*, 30 Cong., 1 sess., *House Exec. Doc. 41*. Washington, D. C., 1848. Includes the establishment of Fort Marcy, New Mexico, and Fort Moore, California.

Floyd, John B. *Expenditures for Barracks and Quarters*, 35 Cong., 2 sess., *House Exec. Doc. 93*. Washington, D. C., 1859.

Heitman, Francis B. *Historical Register and Dictionary of the United States Army from Its Organization, September 29, 1789, to March 2, 1903*. 2 vols. Washington, D. C., 1903. Privately compiled, but purchased and published by direction of Congress.

Hieb, David L. *Fort Laramie National Monument, Wyoming*. Washington, D. C., 1954.

Hodge, Frederick W. *Handbook of American Indians North of Mexico*. 2 vols. Washington, D. C., 1907–12.

Lawson, Thomas. *Statistical Report on the Sickness and Mortality in the Army of the United States*. Washington, D. C., 1840. The report covers the period 1819–39.

Lincoln, Robert Todd. *A Communication from the Secretary of War* of December 14, 1883, Respecting Abandoned Military Reservations, and Renewing Recommendation for Such Legislation as Will Provide for the Disposal of Military Sites That Are No Longer Needed, 48 Cong., 1 sess., *Sen. Exec. Doc. 25.* Washington, D. C., 1883.

McDowell, Irvin. *Outline Description of Military Posts in the Military Division of the Pacific.* Presidio of San Francisco, 1879.

Marcy, Randolph B. *Outline Descriptions of the Posts and Stations of Troops in the Geographical Divisions and Departments of the United States.* Washington, D. C., 1872.

Orton, Richard H., comp. *Records of California Men in the War of the Rebellion, 1861 to 1867.* Sacramento, 1890.

Pope, John. *Department of Missouri,* 39 Cong., 1 sess., *House Exec. Doc. 76.* Washington, D. C., 1866.

Records of Engagements with Hostile Indians within the Military Division of the Missouri, from 1868 to 1882, Lieutenant-General P. H. Sheridan, Commanding. Washington, D. C., 1882. Includes the Departments of Dakota, Platte, Missouri, Texas, and, briefly, the Gulf. A year-to-year synopsis.

Reports of Explorations and Surveys to Ascertain the Most Practicable and Economical Route for a Railroad from the Mississippi River to the Pacific Ocean, Made under the Direction of the Secretary of War in 1853–6. 12 vols. Washington, D. C., 1855–61.

Risch, Erna. *Quartermaster Support of the Army.* Washington, D. C. 1962.

Schofield, John M. *Sale of Fort Snelling Reservation,* 40 Cong., 3 sess., *House Exec. Doc. 9.* Washington, D. C., 1868.

Sheridan, Philip H. *Outline Descriptions of the Posts in the Military Division of the Missouri, Commanded by Lieutenant General P. H. Sheridan.* Chicago, 1872.

Stanton, Edwin M. *Inspection by Generals Rusling and Hazen,* 39 Cong., 2 sess., *House Exec. Doc. 45.* Washington, D. C., 1867.

————. *Protection across the Continent*, 39 Cong., 2 sess., *House Exec. Doc. 23*. Washington, D. C., 1867. Contains letters of Lieutenant General William T. Sherman, written during a tour of inspection, and inspection reports of Colonel Delos B. Sacket.

Surgeon General's Office. *Circular No. 4. A Report on Barracks and Hospitals with Descriptions of Military Posts*. Washington, D. C., 1870.

————. *Circular No. 8. A Report on the Hygiene of the United States Army, with Descriptions of Military Posts*. Washington, D. C., 1875.

Taft, Alphonso. *Lines of Communication between Southern Colorado and Northern New Mexico*, 44 Cong., 1 sess., *House Exec. Doc. 172*. Washington, D. C. 1876.

Thian, Raphael P. *Notes Illustrating the Military Geography of the United States*. Washington, D. C., 1881.

Tyler, Robert Ogden. *Revised Outlines and Descriptions of Posts and Stations of Troops in the Military Division of the Pacific*. San Francisco, 1872.

Utley, Robert M. *Fort Union National Monument, New Mexico*. Washington, D. C., 1962.

The War of the Rebellion: A Compilation of the Official Records of the Union and Confederate Armies. 70 vols. in 128. Washington, D. C., 1880–1901.

BOOKS AND PAMPHLETS

Alessio Robles, Vito. *Coahuila y Texas desde la consumación de independencia hasta el tratado de paz de Guadalupe Hidalgo*. 2 vols. Mexico, 1945–46.

————. *Coahuila y Texas en la época colonial*. Mexico, 1938.

[Anderson, George B.] *History of New Mexico, Its Resources and People*. 2 vols. Los Angeles, 1907.

Ashburn, Percy M. *A History of the Medical Department of the United States Army*. Boston, 1929.

Bancroft, Hubert Howe. *Works*. 39 vols. San Francisco, 1882–90.

Bandel, Eugene. *Frontier Life in the Army, 1854–1861*. Ed. by Ralph P. Bieber. Glendale, 1932. Bandel was a soldier in the Sixth United States Infantry.

Barker, Eugene C. *Mexico and Texas, 1821–1835*. Dallas, 1928.

Barnes, Will C. *Arizona Place Names*. Revised and enlarged by Byrd H. Granger. Tucson, 1960.

Beers, Henry Putney. *The Western Military Frontier, 1815–1846*. Philadelphia, 1935.

Bender, Averam B. *The March of Empire: Frontier Defense in the Southwest, 1848–1860*. Lawrence, Kansas, 1952.

Bennett, James A. *Forts and Forays*. Ed. by Clinton E. Brooks and Frank D. Reeve. Albuquerque, 1948. A dragoon in New Mexico, 1850–56.

Bieber, Ralph P., ed. *Southern Trails to California in 1849*. Glendale, 1937.

———, and Averam B. Bender, eds. *Exploring Southwestern Trails, 1846–1854*. Glendale, 1938. The journals of Philip St. George Cooke, William H. C. Whiting, and Francis Xavier Aubry.

Binkley, William C. *The Expansionist Movement in Texas, 1836–1850*. Berkeley, 1925.

Bledsoe, A. J. *Indian Wars of the Northwest, a California Sketch*. San Francisco, 1885.

Bourke, John G. *On the Border with Crook*. Chicago. 1962.

Brackett, Albert G. *History of the United States Cavalry, from the Formation of the Federal Government to the 1st of June, 1863*. New York, 1865.

Bradley, James H. *The March of the Montana Column*. Ed. by Edgar I. Stewart. Norman, 1961.

Brandes, Ray. *Frontier Military Posts of Arizona*. Globe, Arizona, 1960.

Brill, Charles J. *Conquest of the Southern Plains*. Oklahoma City, 1938.

Brown, Dee. *Fort Phil Kearny: An American Saga*. New York, 1962.

Carey, Charles H. *A General History of Oregon Prior to 1861*. 2 vols. Portland, Oregon, 1936.

Carroll, H. Bailey, and J. Villasana Haggard, trans. and eds. *Three New Mexico Chronicles*. Albuquerque, 1942.

Castañeda, Carlos E. *Our Catholic Heritage in Texas, 1519–1936*. 7 vols. Austin, 1936–50. Contains useful information in regard to the Spanish presidios.

Caughey, John W. *California*. New York, 1940.

Chandler, Melbourne C. *Of Garry Owen in Glory*. Published by the author, 1960.

Clarke, Dwight L. *Stephen Watts Kearny: Soldier of the West*. Norman, 1961.

Coan, Charles F. *A History of New Mexico*. 3 vols. Chicago, 1925.

Colton, Ray C. *The Civil War in the Western Territories: Arizona, Colorado, New Mexico, and Utah*. Norman, 1959.

Conkling, Roscoe P., and Margaret B. *The Butterfield Overland Mail, 1857–1869*. 3 vols. Glendale, 1947.

Cooke, Philip St. George. *The Conquest of New Mexico and California*. New York, 1878.

———. *Scenes and Adventures in the Army; or the Romance of Military Life*. Philadelphia, 1857.

Cosulich, Bernice. *Tucson*. Tucson, 1953.

Couts, Cave J. *From San Diego to the Colorado in 1849*. Ed. by William McPherson. Los Angeles, 1932. Includes material for Camp Calhoun, the predecessor of Fort Yuma.

Croghan, George. *Army Life on the Western Frontier*. Ed. by Francis Paul Prucha. Norman, 1958. Excerpts from Colonel Croghan's inspection reports, 1826–45.

Crook, George. *General George Crook: His Autobiography*. Ed. by Martin F. Schmitt. Norman, 1960.

Cullimore, Clarence. *Old Adobes of Forgotten Fort Tejon*. Bakersfield, California, 1949.

Danford, Robert M., ed. *Register of Graduates and Former Cadets, United States Military Academy.* New York, 1953.

De Shields, James T. *Border Wars of Texas.* Tioga, Texas, 1912.

Downey, Joseph T. *The Cruise of the Portsmouth, 1845–1847.* Ed. by Howard Lamar. New Haven, 1958. Contains a description of the erection of Fort Montgomery, California.

Du Bois, John Van Deusen. *Campaigns in the West, 1851–1861.* Ed. by George P. Hammond. Tucson, 1949. Du Bois was a second lieutenant, Regiment of Mounted Riflemen.

Dunn, Adrian R. *A History of Old Fort Berthold.*Bismarck, North Dakota, 1964.

Eccleston, Robert. *The Mariposa Indian War, 1850–1851.* Ed. by C. Gregory Crampton. Salt Lake City, 1957. Some material for Fort Miller, California.

Emmett, Chris. *Fort Union and the Winning of the Southwest.* Norman, 1965.

Englehardt, Zephyrin. *San Diego Mission.* San Francisco, 1920. Both San Diego Mission and San Luis Rey Mission served for a time as military posts.

———. *San Luis Rey Mission.* San Francisco, 1921.

Ewers, John C. *The Blackfeet.* Norman, 1958.

Folwell, William Watts. *A History of Minnesota.* 4 vóls. St. Paul, 1921–30.

Foreman, Grant. *Advancing the Frontier, 1830–1860.* Norman, 1933.

———. *Fort Gibson, a Brief History.* Muskogee, Oklahoma, n.d.

———. *A History of Oklahoma.* Norman, 1942.

———. *Marcy & the Gold Seekers.* Norman. 1939.

———. *Pioneer Days in the Early Southwest.* Cleveland, 1926.

Fuller, George W. *A History of the Pacific Northwest.* New York, 1931.

Garrard, Lewis H. *Wah-To-Yah and the Taos Trail*. Glendale, 1938. Contains some material for Fort Mann, Kansas.

Gayarré, Charles, *History of Louisiana*. 4 vols. New Orleans, 1879.

Glisan, R. *Journal of Army Life*. San Francisco, 1874. Rodney Glisan was an assistant surgeon who was stationed at Forts Orford and Yamhill in the 1850's.

Goetzmann, William W. *Army Exploration in the American West, 1803–1863*. New Haven, 1959.

Gudde, Erwin G. *California Place Names*. Berkeley and Los Angeles, 1949.

Guie, H. Dean. *Bugles in the Valley: Garnett's Fort Simcoe*. Yakima, Washington, 1956.

Hafen, LeRoy R. and Ann W., eds. *Powder River Campaigns and Sawyer's Expedition of 1865*. Glendale, 1961.

———. *Relations with the Indians of the Plains, 1857–1861*. Glendale, 1959.

———. *The Utah Expedition, 1857–1858*. Glendale, 1958.

Hafen, LeRoy R., and F. M. Young. *Fort Laramie and the Pageant of the West, 1834–1890*. Glendale, 1938.

Haley, J. Evetts. *Fort Concho and the Texas Frontier*. San Angelo, Texas, 1952.

Hall, Frank. *History of the State of Colorado*. 4 vols. Chicago, 1889–95.

Hall, Martin Hardwick. *Sibley's New Mexico Campaign*. Austin, 1960.

Hamersly, Thomas H. S. *Complete Regular Army Register of the United States for One Hundred Years, (1779 to 1879)*. Washington, D. C., 1880.

Hamilton, Holman. *Zachary Taylor, Soldier of the Republic*. Indianapolis, 1941.

Hammond, John Martin. *Quaint and Historic Forts of North America*. Philadelphia and London, 1915.

Handy, Mary Olivia. *History of Fort Sam Houston.* San Antonio, 1951.

Hanson, Marcus L. *Old Fort Snelling, 1819–1858.* Iowa City, 1918.

Hart, Herbert M. *Old Forts of the Northwest.* Seattle, 1963.

———. *Old Forts of the Southwest.* Seattle, 1964.

Heard, Isaac V. D. *History of the Sioux War.* New York, 1864.

Hebard, Grace. *Washakie.* Glendale, 1930.

———, and A. E. Brininstool. *The Bozeman Trail.* 2 vols. in 1. Glendale, 1960.

Herr, John K., and Edward S. Wallace. *The Story of the U.S. Cavalry, 1775–1942.* Boston, 1953.

Heyman, Max L., Jr. *Prudent Soldier, a Biography of Major General E. R. S. Canby, 1817–1873.* Glendale, 1959.

Hildreth, James. *Dragoon Campaigns to the Rocky Mountains.* New York, 1836.

Hitchcock, Ethan Allen. *A Traveler in Indian Territory.* Ed. by Grant Foreman. Cedar Rapids, Iowa, 1930. The journal of Colonel Hitchcock, Eighth United States Infantry, November 22, 1841—March 16, 1842. Contains some material for Forts Coffee and Wayne, Oklahoma.

———. *Fifty Years in Camp and Field.* Ed. by W. A. Croffut. New York, 1909.

Holmes, Louis A. *Fort McPherson, Nebraska.* Lincoln, Nebraska, 1963.

Houk, Louis. *A History of Missouri.* 3 vols. Chicago, 1908.

———. *The Spanish Regime in Missouri.* 2 vols. Chicago, 1909.

Hunt, Aurora. *The Army of the Pacific.* Glendale, 1951.

———. *Major General James Henry Carleton, 1814–1873, Western Frontier Dragoon.* Glendale, 1958.

Hunt, Elvid. *History of Fort Leavenworth, 1827–1927.* Fort Leavenworth, Kansas, 1926.

Hunt, Rockwell D., ed. *California and Californians.* 5 vols. Chicago, 1926.

Hyde, George E. *Pawnee Indians.* Denver, 1951.

————. *Red Cloud's Folk.* Norman, 1957.

Ickis, Alonzo F. *Bloody Trails along the Rio Grande.* Ed. by Nolie Mumey. Denver, 1958. Ickis was a soldier in the Colorado Volunteers during the Civil War.

Jackson, W. Turentine. *Wagon Roads West: A Study of Federal Road Surveys and Construction in the Trans-Mississippi West, 1846–1869.* Berkeley and Los Angeles, 1952.

Jenkins, John Holland. *Recollections of Early Texas.* Ed. by John Holmes Jenkins III. Austin, 1958.

Jones, Robert Huhn. *The Civil War in the Northwest.* Norman, 1960. Includes the Dakotas, Iowa, Minnesota, Nebraska, and Wisconsin.

Jocelyn, Stephen Perry. *Mostly Alkali.* Caldwell, Idaho, 1953. Jocelyn was an infantry officer who served in various parts of the West in the post–Civil War years.

Kerby, Robert Lee. *The Confederate Invasion of New Mexico and Arizona, 1861–1862.* Los Angeles, 1958.

Keyes, Erasmus Darwin. *Fifty Years' Observation of Men and Events, Civil and Military.* New York, 1884. Major General Keyes served in the army from 1832 to 1864.

King, James T. *War Eagle: A Life of General Eugene A. Carr.* Lincoln, Nebraska, 1963.

Knight, Oliver. *Fort Worth, Outpost on the Trinity.* Norman, 1953.

Lavender, David. *Bent's Fort.* Garden City, 1954.

Leckie, William H. *The Military Conquest of the Southern Plains.* Norman, 1963.

Linford, Velma. *Wyoming, Frontier State.* Denver, 1947.

Lowe, Percival G. *Five Years a Dragoon.* Kansas City, Missouri, 1906. The years are 1849–54.

McArthur, Lewis A. *Oregon Geographic Names.* Portland, Oregon, 1952.

McFarling, Lloyd, ed. *Exploring the Northern Plains, 1804–1876.* Caldwell, Idaho, 1955.

McKee, James Cooper. *Narrative of the Surrender of a Command of U.S. Forces at Fort Fillmore, N.M.* Houston, 1960. McKee was post surgeon at Fort Fillmore.

Mack, Effie Mona. *Nevada: A History of the State from the Earliest Times through the Civil War.* Glendale, 1936.

Mahan, Bruce E. *Old Fort Crawford and the Frontier.* Iowa City, 1926.

Mansfield, Joseph K. F. *Mansfield on the Condition of the Western Forts, 1853–54.* Ed. by Robert W. Frazer. Norman, 1963.

Meeker, Ezra. *Pioneer Reminiscences of Puget Sound.* Seattle, 1905.

Miles, Nelson A. *Serving the Republic.* New York, 1911.

Mockler, Alfred James. *Fort Caspar (Platte Bridge Station).* Casper, Wyoming, 1939.

Morrison, William Brown. *Military Posts and Camps in Oklahoma.* Oklahoma City, 1936.

Murray, Keith A. *The Modocs and Their War.* Norman, 1959.

Nasatir, Abraham P. *Before Lewis and Clark: Documents Illustrating the History of the Missouri, 1785–1804.* 2 vols. St. Louis, 1952.

National Park Service. *Soldier and Brave: Indian and Military Affairs in the Trans-Mississippi West.* New York, 1963.

Nye, Wilbur S. *Carbine and Lance: The Story of Old Fort Sill.* Norman, 1937.

Ocaranza, Fernando. *Crónica de las Provincias Internas de Nueva España.* Mexico, 1939.

Oehler, C. M. *The Great Sioux Uprising.* New York, 1959.

Olson, James C. *History of Nebraska.* Lincoln, 1955.

Ostrander, Alson B. *An Army Boy of the Sixties.* Yonkers-on-Hudson, 1924. Personal reminiscences written many years later.

Paden, Irene D. *In the Wake of the Prairie Schooner.* New York, 1943.

Parker, William Thornton. *Annals of Old Fort Cummings, New Mexico, 1867–8*. Northampton, Massachusetts, 1916.

Pelzer, Louis. *Marches of the Dragoons in the Mississippi Valley*. Iowa City, 1917.

Pettis, George H. *The California Column*. Santa Fe, 1908.

Pichardo, José Antonio. *Pichardo's Treatise on the Limits of Louisiana and Texas*. Ed. by Charles W. Hackett. 4 vols. Austin, 1931–41. Contains some material for the French and Spanish posts.

Pourade, Richard F. *The History of San Diego*, II, *Time of the Bells*. San Diego, 1961. Contains material for the presidio and Castillo Guijarros.

Price, George F. *Across the Continent with the Fifth Cavalry*. New York, 1959.

Pride, W. F. *The History of Fort Riley*. n.p., 1926.

Prince, L. Bradford. *Historical Sketches of New Mexico from the Earliest Records to the American Occupation*. Kansas City, Missouri, 1883.

———. *Old Fort Marcy, Santa Fe, New Mexico*. Santa Fe, 1912.

Prucha, Francis P. *Broadax and Bayonet: The Role of the United States Army in the Development of the Northwest, 1815–1860*. Madison, 1953.

Reavis, L. U. *The Life and Military Service of Gen. William Selby Harney*. St. Louis, 1878.

Reeve, Frank D. *History of New Mexico*. 2 vols. New York, 1961.

Richards, Ralph. *Headquarters House and the Forts of Fort Scott*. Fort Scott, Kansas, 1954.

Richardson, Rupert N. *The Comanche Barrier to South Plains Settlement*. Glendale, 1933.

———. *The Frontier of Northwest Texas, 1846 to 1876*. Glendale, 1963.

Rister, Carl Coke. *Border Command: General Phil Sheridan in the West*. Norman, 1944.

————. *Fort Griffin on the Texas Frontier*. Norman, 1956.

————. *The Southwestern Frontier, 1865–1881*. Glendale, 1928.

Rodenbough, Theophilus F. *From Everglade to Cañon with the Second Dragoons*. New York, 1875.

Rogers, Fred B. *Soldiers of the Overland*. San Francisco, 1938. Biography of Brigadier General Patrick E. Connor.

Rosebush, Waldo E. *Frontier Steel*. Appleton, Wisconsin, 1958.

Rudd, Augustin G. *Histories of Army Posts*. Governors Island, New York, 1925. A collection of articles originally published in *Recruiting News*.

Ruth, Kent. *Great Day in the West*. Norman, 1963.

Scobee, Barry. *Old Fort Davis*. San Antonio, 1947.

Scott, Leslie M. *History of the Oregon Country*. 6 vols. Cambridge, 1924.

Settle, Raymond W. *The March of the Mounted Riflemen*. Glendale, 1940.

Seymour, Flora W. *Indian Agents of the Old Frontier*. New York, 1941.

Sheridan, P. H. *Personal Memoirs of P. H. Sheridan, General, United States Army*. 2 vols. New York, 1888.

Sherman, William T. *Memoirs of General William T. Sherman*. 2 vols. New York, 1887.

Shoemaker, Floyd C. *Missouri and Missourians*. 5 vols. Chicago, 1943.

Sides, Joseph C. *Fort Brown Historical*. San Antonio, 1942.

Snowden, Clinton A. *History of Washington*. 4 vols. New York, 1909.

Stanley, F. [Stanley Francis Louis Crocchiola]. *Fort Bascom: Comanche-Kiowa Barrier*. Pampa, Texas, 1961.

————. *The Fort Conrad New Mexico Story*. Dumas, Texas, 1961.

————. *Fort Craig*. Pep, Texas, 1963.

————. *Fort Union (New Mexico)*. n.p., 1953.

Stevens, Hazard. *The Life of Isaac Ingalls Stevens.* 2 vols. Boston and New York, 1900.

Stone, Wilbur Fisk, ed. *History of Colorado.* 3 vols. Chicago, 1918.

Sullivan, Charles J. *Army Posts and Towns.* Los Angeles, 1942.

Summerhayes, Martha. *Vanished Arizona.* Chicago, 1939. Mrs. Summerhayes was the wife of an infantry officer.

Sweeny, Thomas W. *Journal of Lt. Thomas W. Sweeny, 1849–1853.* Ed. by Arthur Woodward. Los Angeles, 1956. Useful for the early years of Fort Yuma.

Thomas, Alfred B. ed. *Forgotten Frontiers: A Study of the Spanish Indian Policy of Don Juan Bautista de Anza, Governor of New Mexico, 1777–1787.* Norman, 1932.

Thomlinson, M. H. *The Garrison of Fort Bliss, 1849–1916.* El Paso, 1945.

Thwaites, Reuben Gold, ed. *The French Regime in Wisconsin,* II, *Collections of the State Historical Society of Wisconsin,* XVII. Madison, 1906.

Toulouse, Joseph H. and James R. *Pioneer Posts of Texas.* San Antonio, 1936.

Trobriand, Philippe Régis de. *Military Life in Dakota.* Trans. and ed. by Lucile M. Kane. St. Paul, 1951. Deals with the years 1867–69.

Twitchell, Ralph Emerson. *History of the Military Occupation of New Mexico.* Denver, 1909.

———. *The Leading Facts of New Mexican History.* 5 vols. Cedar Rapids, Iowa, 1911–17.

———. *Old Santa Fé, the Story of New Mexico's Ancient Capital.* Santa Fe, 1925.

———. *The Story of the Conquest of Santa Fe, New Mexico, and the Building of Old Fort Marcy, A. D. 1846.* n.p., n.d.

Victor, Frances Fuller. *The Early Indian Wars of Oregon.* Salem, Oregon, 1894.

Wallace, Edward S. *The Great Reconnaissance: Soldiers, Artists and Scientists on the Frontier, 1848–1861.* Boston, 1955.

Ware, Eugene Fitch. *The Indian War of 1864.* Ed. by Clyde C. Walton. Lincoln, 1960. Ware was an officer in the Seventh Iowa Cavalry.

Webb, Walter Prescott. *The Texas Rangers.* Boston and New York, 1935.

Wesley, Edgar Bruce. *Guarding the Frontier, a Study of Frontier Defense from 1815 to 1825.* Minneapolis, 1935.

Whipple, A. W. *A Pathfinder in the Southwest.* Ed. by Grant Foreman. Norman, 1941.

Whiting, J. S. and Richard J. *Forts of the State of California.* Longview, Washington, 1960.

Whitman, S. E. *The Troopers: An Informal History of the Plains Cavalry, 1865–1890.* New York, 1962.

Winther, Oscar O. *The Old Oregon Country.* Bloomington, 1950.

Wood, Dean Earl. *The Old Santa Fe Trail from the Missouri River.* Kansas City, Missouri, 1955. Contains some information about the forts along the trail.

Woodward, Ashbel. *Life of General Nathaniel Lyon.* Hartford, 1862.

Wortham, Louis J. *A History of Texas.* 5 vols. Fort Worth, 1924.

Wyllys, Rufus Kay. *Arizona: The History of a Frontier State.* Phoenix, 1950.

Yoakum, Henderson K. *History of Texas from Its First Settlement in 1685 to Its Annexation to the United States in 1846.* Austin, 1935.

ARTICLES IN PERIODICALS

Abarr, James W. "Fort Ojo Caliente," *Desert Magazine,* Vol. XXII (April, 1959), 19–21. This and the following article are popular accounts of a post which was never officially a fort.

————. "Ojo Caliente, Army Outpost," *New Mexico Magazine,* Vol. XXXVII (November, 1959), 3–7.

Almonte, Juan Nepomuceno. "Statistical Report on Texas," *Southwestern Historical Quarterly*, Vol. XXVIII (January, 1925), 177–221. Trans. by Carlos E. Castañeda. The date of the report is 1834.

Amsden, Charles. "The Navajo Exile at Bosque Redondo," *New Mexico Historical Review*, Vol. VIII (January, 1933), 31–50. Contains some information for Forts Canby and Sumner.

Anderson, Harry H. "A History of the Cheyenne River Indian Agency and Its Military Post, Fort Bennett, 1868–1891," *South Dakota Historical Collections*, Vol. XXVIII (1956), 390–551.

Anderson, James. "Fort Osage," *Bulletin of the Missouri Historical Society*, Vol. IV (April, 1948), 174–76. Discusses the reconstruction of a portion of the post.

Armstrong, A. F. H. "The Case of Major Isaac Lynde," *New Mexico Historical Review*, Vol. XXXVI (January, 1961), 1–35. Fort Fillmore, New Mexico.

Atkins, C. J. "Logs of the Missouri River Steamboat Trips, 1863–1868," *Collections of the State Historical Society of North Dakota*, Vol. II, part 1 (1908), 263–417. The article includes some material for many posts, both military and trading.

Ayres, Mary C. "History of Fort Lewis, Colorado," *Colorado Magazine*, Vol. VIII (May, 1931), 81–92.

Barrett, Arrie. "Western Frontier Forts of Texas, 1845–1861," *West Texas Historical Association Year Book*, Vol. VII (1931), 115–39.

Barrett, Leonora. "Transportation, Supplies, and Quarters for the West Texas Frontier under the Federal Military System, 1848–1861," *West Texas Historical Association Year Book*, Vol. V (1929), 87–99.

Barry, Louise. "The Fort Leavenworth–Fort Gibson Military Road and the Founding of Fort Scott," *Kansas Historical Quarterly*, Vol. XI (May, 1942), 115–29. Contains some information about Forts Coffee and Wayne as well as Scott.

———. ed. "With the First U.S. Cavalry in Indian Country, 1859–1861," *Kansas Historical Quarterly*, Vol. XXIV (Autumn, 1958), 257–84; (Winter, 1958), 399–425.

Bateman, Cephas C. "History of Fort Clark," *Recruiting News*, November 15, 1923, pp. 7, 12. Fort Clark, Texas.

Belden, L. Burr. "Forgotten Army Forts of the Mojave," *The Westerners Brand Book* (Los Angeles Corral), Vol. XI (1964), 93–102.

Bell, Olive W. "The Fabulous Frontier," *New Mexico*, Vol. XVI (June, 1938), 23, 41–42. A popular account containing some information about Fort Webster.

Bender, Averam B. "Opening Routes across West Texas, 1848–1850," *Southwestern Historical Quarterly*, Vol. XXXVII (October, 1933), 116–35.

———. "The Soldier in the Far West, 1848–1860," *Pacific Historical Review*, Vol. VIII (June, 1939), 159–78.

———. "The Texas Frontier, 1848–1861," *Southwestern Historical Quarterly*, Vol. XXXVIII (October, 1934), 135–48.

Bieber, Ralph P. "The Southwestern Trails to California in 1849," *Mississippi Valley Historical Review*, Vol. XII (December, 1925), 342–75.

Bierschwale, Margaret. "Mason County, Texas, 1845–1870," *Southwestern Historical Quarterly*, Vol. LII (April, 1949), 379–97. Fort Mason.

Bitner, Grace. "Early History of the Concho Country and Tom Green County," *West Texas Historical Association Year Book*, Vol. IX (1933), 3–23. Includes material for Forts Chadbourne and Concho.

Blades, Thomas E., and John W. Wike. "Fort Missoula," *Military Affairs*, Vol. XIII Spring, 1949), 29–36.

Blake, R. B. "Locations of the Early Spanish Missions and Presidio in Nacogdoches County," *Southwestern Historical Quarterly*, Vol. XLI (January, 1938), 212–24. The Presidio de Nuestra Señora de los Dolores de los Tejas.

Block, Augusta Hauck. "Lower Boulder and St. Vrain Valley Home Guards and Fort Junction," *Colorado Magazine*, Vol. XVI (September, 1939), 186–91.

Bolton, Herbert E. "The Founding of the Missions on the San Gabriel River, 1745–1749," *Southwestern Historical Quarterly*, Vol. XVII (April, 1914), 323–78. Includes the establishment of the Presidio de San Xavier.

———. "The Location of La Salle's Colony on the Gulf of Mexico," *Southwestern Historical Quarterly*, Vol. XXVII (January, 1924), 171–89.

———. "The Native Tribes about the East Texas Missions," *Texas Historical Association Quarterly*, Vol. XI (April, 1908), 249–76. The Presidio de Nuestra Señora de los Dolores de los Tejas.

———. "Spanish Activities on the Lower Trinity River, 1746–1771," *Southwestern Historical Quarterly*, Vol. XVI (April, 1913), 339–77. The Presidio de San Agustín de Ahumada.

Bonney, W. P. "Captain Maloney at Fort Chehalis," *Washington Historical Quarterly*, Vol. XX (July, 1929), 190–91.

Bouldin, Edna. "Frontier Garrison," *New Mexico*, Vol. XV (October, 1937), 22–23, 37. A popular account of Fort Selden.

Braley, Earl Burk. "Fort Belknap of the Texas Frontier," *West Texas Historical Association Year Book*, Vol. XXX (1954), 83–114.

Brandes, Ray. "A Guide to the History of the U. S. Army Installations in Arizona, 1849–1886," *Arizona and the West*, Vol. I (Spring, 1959), 42–65.

Bright, Verne. "The Lost County, Umpqua, Oregon, and Its Early Settlement," *Oregon Historical Quarterly*, Vol. LI (June, 1950), 111–26. Includes some material for Fort Umpqua.

Brimlow, George F. "The Life of Sarah Winnemucca: the Formative Years," *Oregon Historical Quarterly*, Vol. LIII (June, 1953), 103–34. Contains information about Forts Churchill, Halleck, and McDermit, Nevada.

Burlingame, Merrill C. "The Influence of the Military in the Building of Montana," *Pacific Northwest Quarterly*, Vol. XXIX (April, 1938), 135–50.

Caldwell, Norman W. "Tonty and the Beginning of the Arkansas Post," *Arkansas Historical Quarterly*, Vol. VIII (Autumn, 1949), 189–205.

"Camp Carlin," *Annals of Wyoming*, Vol. XVII (July, 1945), 157. Camp Carlin was associated with Fort D. A. Russell.

Carter, William H. "Fort Sanford, Iowa," *Annals of Iowa*, 3rd Series, Vol. IV (1899–1901), 284–93.

Caum, Norman C. "History of Fort Douglas," *Recruiting News*, December 1, 1923, pp. 7, 15.

Chapman, John. "Old Fort Richardson," *Southwest Review*, Vol. XXXVIII (Winter, 1953) 62–69.

Chappell, Gordon S. "The Fortifications of Old Fort Laramie," *Annals of Wyoming*, Vol. XXXIV (October, 1962), 145–62.

Clark, Dan Elbert. "Frontier Defense in Iowa, 1850–1865," *Iowa Journal of History and Politics*, Vol. XVI (July, 1918), 315–86.

Clark, Robert Carlton. "Military History of Oregon, 1849–1859," *Oregon Historical Quarterly*, Vol. XXXVI (March, 1935), 14–59.

Coan, Charles F. "The Adoption of the Reservation Policy in the Pacific Northwest, 1853–1855," *Quarterly of the Oregon Historical Society*, Vol. XXIII (March, 1922), 1–38.

Cocks, Bert H. "Fort Moore," *Quarterly, Historical Society of Southern California*, Vol. XXVIII (September, 1946), 89–94.

Coffman, Edward M. "Army Life on the Frontier," *Military Affairs*, Vol. XX (Winter, 1956), 193–201.

Coopwood, Bethel. "Notes on the History of La Bahía del Espíritu Santo," *Quarterly of the Texas Historical Association*, Vol. II (October, 1898), 162–69.

Cowell, Theodore Ray. "History of Fort Townsend," *Washington Historical Quarterly*, Vol. XVI (October, 1925), 284–89.

Cox, Isaac Joslin. "The Louisiana-Texas Frontier," *Southwestern Historical Quarterly*, Vol. XVII (July, 1913), 1–60; (October, 1913), 140–87. Parts 2 and 3 of a longer article.

Cox, Jess. "Fort Bayard—Frontier Outpost," *New Mexico Magazine*, Vol. XLII (April, 1964), 6–8.

Crane, R. C. "Some Aspects of the History of West and Northwest Texas since 1845," *Southwestern Historical Quarterly*, Vol. XXVI (July, 1922), 30–43.

Crimmins, Martin Lalor. "Camp Cooper and Fort Griffin, Texas," *West Texas Historical Association Year Book*, Vol. XVII (1941), 32–43.

———. ed. "Colonel J. K. F. Mansfield's Report of the Inspection of the Department of Texas in 1856," *Southwestern Historical Quarterly*, Vol. XLII (October, 1938), 122–48; (January, 1939), 215–57; (April, 1939), 351–87.

———. "The First Line of Army Posts Established in West Texas in 1849," *West Texas Historical Association Year Book*, Vol. XIX (1943), 121–27.

———. "Fort Elliott, Texas," *West Texas Historical Association Year Book*, Vol. XXIII (1947), 3–12.

———. "Fort Fillmore," *New Mexico Historical Review*, Vol. VI (October, 1931), 327–33.

————. "Fort McKavett, Texas," *Southwestern Historical Quarterly*, Vol. XXXVIII (July, 1934), 28–39.

————. "Fort Massachusetts, First United States Military Post in Colorado," *Colorado Magazine*, Vol. XIV (July, 1937), 128–33.

————. "General Mackenzie and Fort Concho," *West Texas Historical Association Year Book*, Vol. X (1934), 16–31.

———— ed. "W. G. Freeman's Report on the Eighth Military Department," *Southwestern Historical Quarterly*, Vol. LI (July, 1947), 54–58; (October, 1947), 167–74; (January, 1948), 252–58; (April, 1948), 350–57; Vol. LII (July, 1948), 100–108; (October, 1948), 227–33; (January, 1949), 349–53; (April, 1949), 444–47; Vol. LIII (July, 1949), 71–77; (October, 1949), 202–208; (January, 1950), 308–19; (April, 1950), 443–73. Brevet Lieutenant Colonel William Grigsby Freeman inspected the Eighth Military Department (Texas) in 1853.

"Dakota Military Posts," *South Dakota Historical Collections*, Vol. VIII (1916), 77–99.

Donohue, J. Augustine. "The Unlucky Jesuit Mission of Bac, 1732–1767," *Arizona and the West*, Vol. II (Summer, 1960), 127–39. Contains some information about the Presidio of Tubac.

Dunn, William Edward. "The Apache Mission on the San Sabá River; Its Founding and Failure," *Southwestern Historical Quarterly*, Vol. XVII (April, 1914), 379–414. Includes material for the Presidio de San Luis de las Amarillas.

"Early Days at Fort Snelling," *Collections of the Minnesota State Historical Society*, Vol. I (1902), 345–59.

Edgar, William F. "Historical Notes of Old Landmarks in California," *Publications of the Historical Society of Southern California*, Vol. III (1893), 22–30. Edgar was post surgeon at various posts in California in the 1850's. His article contains sketches of Forts Miller, Reading and Tejon, and of some camps.

Edwards, Paul M. "Fort Wadsworth and the Friendly Santee Sioux,

1864–1892," *South Dakota Historical Collections*, Vol. XXXI (1962), 74–156.

Eller, W. H. "Old Fort Atkinson," *Transactions and Reports of the Nebraska State Historical Society*, Vol. IV (1892), 18–28.

Favrot, H. Mortimer. "Colonial Forts of Louisiana," *Louisiana Historical Quarterly*, Vol. XXVI (July, 1943), 722–54.

Faye, Stanley. "The Arkansas Post of Louisiana: French Domination," *Louisiana Historical Quarterly*, Vol. XXVI (July, 1943), 633–721.

———. "The Arkansas Post of Louisiana: Spanish Domination," *Louisiana Historical Quarterly*, Vol. XXVII (July, 1944), 629–716.

Fletcher, Mary P. "The Post of Arkansas," *Arkansas Historical Quarterly*, Vol. VII (Summer, 1948), 145–49.

Folmer, Henri. "Etienne Veniard de Bourgmond in the Missouri Country," *Missouri Historical Review*, Vol. XXXVI (April, 1942), 279–98. Includes some information about Fort Orleans.

Folwell, William Watts. "The Sale of Fort Snelling," *Collections of the Minnesota State Historical Society*, Vol. XV (1915), 394–410.

Foreman, Carolyn Thomas. "Colonel James B. Many," *Chronicles of Oklahoma*, Vol. XIX (June, 1941), 119–28. Many played a role in the transfer of the French posts in Louisiana to the United States in 1804.

———. "Lieutenant-General Theophilus Hunter Holmes, C.S.A., Founder of Fort Holmes," *Chronicles of Oklahoma*, Vol. XXXV (Winter, 1957–58), 425–34.

Foreman, Grant. "Fort Davis," *Chronicles of Oklahoma*, Vol. XVII (June, 1939), 147–50. A Confederate fort in Oklahoma.

Forsythe, Thomas. "Fort Snelling. Colonel Leavenworth's Expedition to Establish It, in 1819," *Collections of the Minnesota State Historical Society*, Vol. III (1880), 139–67.

"Fort Abercrombie, 1857–1877," *Collections of the State Historical Society of North Dakota*, Vol. II, Part 2 (1908). The entire Part 2 is devoted to this publication.

"Fort Apache, Arizona," *Recruiting News*, October 15, 1924, p. 7.

"Fort Winfield Scott," *Recruiting News*, August 1, 1924, pp. 7, 15.

Foster, James Monroe, Jr. "Fort Bascom, New Mexico," *New Mexico Historical Review*, Vol. XXXV (January, 1960), 30–62.

Fridley, Russell W. "Fort Snelling from Military Post to Historic Site," *Minnesota History*, Vol. XXXV (December, 1956), 178–92.

Gallaher, Ruth A. "The Military-Indian Frontier, 1830–1835," *Iowa Journal of History and Politics*, Vol. XV (July, 1917), 393–428. The frontier generally from the Great Lakes to the Red River boundary with Texas.

Garfield, Marvin H. "Defense of the Kansas Frontier, 1864–65," *Kansas Historical Quarterly*, Vol. I (February, 1932), 140–52.

———. "Defense of the Kansas Frontier, 1866–1867," *Kansas Historical Quarterly*, Vol. I (August, 1932), 326–44.

———. "Defense of the Kansas Frontier, 1868–1869," *Kansas Historical Quarterly*, Vol. I (November, 1932), 451–73.

———. "The Military Post as a Factor in the Frontier Defense of Kansas, 1865–1869," *Kansas Historical Quarterly*, Vol. I (November, 1931), 50–62.

Garraghan, Gilbert J. "Fort Orleans of the Missoury," *Missouri Historical Review*, Vol. XXXV (April, 1941), 373–84.

George, M. C. "Address Delivered at Dedication of Grand Ronde Military Block House at Dayton City Park, Oregon, Aug. 23, 1912," *Quarterly of the Oregon Historical Society*, Vol. XV (March, 1914), 64–70. Fort Yamhill.

Giffen, Helen F. "Camp Independence—An Owens Valley Outpost," *Quarterly, Historical Society of Southern California*, Vol. XXIV (December, 1942), 128–42.

————. "Fort Miller and Millerton," *Quarterly, Historical Society of Southern California*, Vol. XXI (March, 1939), 5–16.

Goplen, Arnold O. "The Historical Significance of Fort Lincoln State Park," *North Dakota History*, Vol. XIII (October, 1946), 151–221.

Grange, Roger T. "Fort Robinson, Outpost on the Plains," *Nebraska History Magazine*, Vol. XXXIX (September, 1958), 191–240.

Grant, Ben O. "Life in Old Fort Griffin," *West Texas Historical Association Year Book*, Vol. X (1934), 32–41.

Green, Charles Lowell. "The Indian Reservation System of the Dakotas to 1889," *South Dakota Historical Collections*, Vol. XIV (1928), 307–416.

Greenburg, Dan W. "How Fort William, Now Fort Laramie, Was Named," *Annals of Wyoming*, Vol. XII (January, 1940), 56–62.

Gregg, Kate L. "Building of the First American Fort West of the Mississippi," *Missouri Historical Review*, Vol. XXX (July, 1936), 345–64. Fort Bellefontaine.

————. "The History of Fort Osage," *Missouri Historical Review*, Vol. XXXIV (July, 1940), 439–88.

————. "The War of 1812 on the Missouri Frontier," *Missouri Historical Review*, Vol. XXXIII (October, 1938), 3–22; (January, 1939), 184–202; (April, 1939), 326–48.

Gressley, Gene M., ed. "Report on Fort Garland Made by Christopher (Kit) Carson to Major Roger James, June 10, 1866," *Colorado Magazine*, Vol. XXXII (July, 1955), 215–24.

Griswold, Gillett. "Old Fort Sill: the First Seven Years," *Chronicles of Oklahoma*, Vol. XXXVI (Spring, 1958), 2–14.

Guinn, J. M. "Fort Moore," *Publications of the Historical Society of Southern California*, Vol. VI (1903–1905), 7–9.

Hagemann, E. R. "Scout Out from Camp McDowell," *Arizoniana*, Vol. V (Fall, 1964), 29–47.

Harbour, Emma Estill. "A Brief History of the Red River Country

Since 1803," *Chronicles of Oklahoma*, Vol. XVI (March, 1938), 58–88. Includes brief accounts of Forts Washita, Towson, Sill, Arbuckle II, and Cobb.

Hardin, J. Fair. "Don Juan Filhiol and the Founding of Fort Miro, the Modern Monroe, Louisiana," *Louisiana Historical Quarterly*, Vol. XX (April, 1937), 463–85.

————. "Fort Jesup—Fort Selden—Camp Sabine—Camp Salubrity: Four Forgotten Frontier Army Posts of Western Louisiana," *Louisiana Historical Quarterly*, Vol. XVI (January, 1933), 5–26; (April, 1933), 279–92; (July, 1933), 441–53; (October, 1933), 670–80; Vol. XVII (January, 1934), 139–68.

Hastings, James R. "The Tragedy at Camp Grant in 1871," *Arizona and the West*, Vol. I (Summer, 1959), 146–60.

Heald, Weldon F. "Rio Grande Missions: Byways into New Mexico History," *New Mexico Magazine*, Vol. XXXIX (March, 1961), 4–7, 38. Contains some information about the Presidio of San Elizario.

Hickey, James V. "Fort Sam Houston, Texas," *Recruiting News*, September 12, 1924, pp. 4–5, 15.

"History of Old Army Posts—Fort Sill," *Recruiting News*, February 15, 1923, p. 7.

"History of Old Army Posts—Fort Snelling," *Recruiting News*, July 15, 1923, pp. 5–6, 15.

Hodson, Fremont B. "History of Vancouver Barracks," *Recruiting News*, June 1, 1924, pp. 7, 15.

Hoekman, Steven. "The History of Fort Sully," *South Dakota Historical Collections*, Vol. XXVI (1952), 222–77.

Holden, William C. "Frontier Defense, 1846–1860," *West Texas Historical Association Year Book*, Vol. VI (1930), 35–64.

Hoop, Oscar Winslow. "History of Fort Hoskins, 1856–65," *Oregon Historical Quarterly*, Vol. XXX (December, 1929), 346–61.

Hull, Lewis Byram. "Soldiering on the High Plains," *Kansas His-*

torical Quarterly, Vol. VII (February, 1938), 3–53. Hull's diary, 1864–66. Hull was stationed at Forts Connor, Collins, Halleck, and Laramie during the period.

Hummell, Edward A. "The Story of Fort Sisseton," *South Dakota Historical Review*, Vol. II (April, 1937), 126–44.

Ingham, William H. "The Northern Border Brigade of 1862–3," *Annals of Iowa*, 3rd Series, Vol. V (October, 1902), 481–527. Iowa defenses during the Sioux War.

Jackson, W. Turrentine. "The Army Engineers as Road Surveyors and Builders in Kansas and Nebraska, 1854–1858," *Kansas Historical Quarterly*, Vol. XVII (February, 1949), 37–59.

"Jefferson Barracks Closes," *Bulletin of the Missouri Historical Society*, Vol. II (July, 1946), 55–56.

Johnson, Roy P. "Jacob Horner of the 7th Cavalry," *North Dakota History*, Vol. XVI (April, 1949), 75–100. Deals with the period 1876–81.

Johnson, Sally A. "Cantonment Missouri, 1819–1820," *Nebraska History Magazine*, Vol. XXXVII (June, 1956), 121–33. Predecessor of Fort Atkinson, Nebraska.

———. "Fort Atkinson at Council Bluffs," *Nebraska History Magazine*, Vol. XXXVIII (September, 1957), 229–36.

Kendall, Jane R. "History of Fort Francis E. Warren," *Annals of Wyoming*, Vol. XVIII (January, 1946), 3–66. The former Fort D. A. Russell.

Kimball, James P. "Fort Buford," *North Dakota Historical Quarterly*, Vol. IV (January, 1930), 75–77. Early days of Fort Buford.

Koch, Lena Clara. "The Federal Indian Policy in Texas, 1845–1860," *Southwestern Historical Quarterly*, Vol. XXVIII (January, 1925), 223–34; (April, 1925), 259–86; Vol. XXIX (July, 1925), 19–35; (October, 1925), 98–127.

Ledyard, Edgar M. "American Posts," *Utah Historical Quarterly*, Vol. I (April, 1928), 56–64; (July, 1928), 86–96; (October,

1928), 114–27; Vol. II (January, 1929), 25–30; (April, 1929), 55–64; (July, 1929), 90–96; (October, 1929), 127–28; Vol. III (January, 1930), 27–32; (April, 1930), 59–64; (July, 1930), 90–96; Vol. V (April, 1932), 65–80; (July, 1932), 113–28; (October, 1932), 161–76; Vol. VI (January, 1933), 29–48; (April, 1932), 64–80. Ledyard attempted to include all posts, trading and private as well as military. Some military posts are omitted entirely and others are treated superficially.

Lockwood, Frank C. "Early Military Posts in Arizona," *Arizona Historical Review*, Vol. II (January, 1930), 91–97.

Looscan, Adèle B. "The Old Fort at Anahuac," *Quarterly of the Texas Historical Association*, Vol. II (July, 1898), 21–28.

———. "The Old Fort on the San Saba River as Seen by Dr. Ferdinand Roemer in 1847," *Quarterly of the Texas State Historical Association*, Vol. V (October, 1901), 137–41.

———. "The Old Mexican Fort at Velasco," *Quarterly of the Texas State Historical Association*, Vol. I (January, 1898), 282–84.

Lynd, Roy F. "History of Fort D. A. Russell, Wyoming," *Recruiting News*, March 1, 1924, pp. 7, 15.

McElroy, Harold L. "Mercurial Military: A Study of the Central Montana Frontier Army Policy," *Montana Magazine of History*, Vol. IV (Fall, 1954), 9–23. 1865–82.

Mantor, Lyle E. "Fort Kearny and the Westward Movement," *Nebraska History*, Vol. XXIX (September, 1948), 175–207.

Mattes, Merrill J. "Fort Mitchell, Scotts Bluff, Nebraska Territory," *Nebraska History Magazine*, Vol. XXXIII (March, 1952), 1–34.

———. "A History of Old Fort Mitchell," *Nebraska History Magazine*, Vol. XXIV (April–June, 1943), 71–82.

———. "Patrolling the Santa Fe Trail, Reminiscences of John S. Kirwin," *Kansas Historical Quarterly*, Vol. XXI (Winter, 1955), 569–87. Contains material for Camp Kirwin.

———. "Report on Historic Sites in the Fort Randall Reservoir

Area, Missouri River, South Dakota," *South Dakota Historical Collections*, Vol. XXIV (1949), 470–577.

―――. "Report on Historical Aspects of the Oahe Reservoir Area, Missouri River, South and North Dakota," *South Dakota Historical Collections*, Vol. XXVII (1954), 1–159.

―――. "Salvaging Missouri Valley History," *The Westerners Brand Book* (Chicago Posse), Vol. IX (May, 1952), 17–19, 22–24.

―――. "Under the Wide Missouri," *North Dakota History*, Vol. XXI (October, 1954), 145–67.

Mattison, Ray H. "Arkansas Post—the Human Aspect," *Arkansas Historical Quarterly*, Vol. XVI (Summer, 1957), 117–38.

―――. ed. "An Army Wife on the Upper Missouri: The Diary of Sarah E. Canfield, 1866–1868," *North Dakota History*, Vol. XX (October, 1953), 191–220.

―――. "The Army Post on the Northern Plains, 1865–1885," *Nebraska History Magazine*, Vol. XXXV (March, 1954), 17–43.

―――. Fort Rice—North Dakota's First Missouri River Military Post," *North Dakota History*, Vol. XX (April, 1953), 87–108.

―――. "The Indian Reservation System on the Upper Missouri, 1865–1890," *Nebraska History Magazine*, Vol. XXXVI (September, 1955) 141–72.

―――. "The Military Frontier on the Upper Missouri," *Nebraska History Magazine*, Vol. XXXVII (September, 1956), 159–82.

―――. "Old Fort Stevenson—A Typical Missouri River Military Post," *North Dakota History*, Vol. XVIII (April, 1951), 53–91.

―――. "Report on the Historic Sites in the Big Bend Reservoir Area, Missouri River, South Dakota," *South Dakota Historical Collections*, Vol. XXXI (1962), 243–86.

―――. "Report on Historic Sites in the Garrison Reservoir Area, Missouri River," *North Dakota History*, Vol. XXII (January–April, 1955), 5–73.

Montgomery, Mrs. Frank C. "Fort Wallace and Its Relation to the Frontier," *Collections of the Kansas State Historical Society*, Vol. XVII (1928), 189–283.

Moorhead, Max L. "The Presidio Supply Problem of New Mexico in the Eighteenth Century," *New Mexico Historical Review*, Vol. XXXVI (July, 1961), 210–29.

Morehouse, George P. "History of the Kansa or Kaw Indians," *Transactions of the Kansas State Historical Society*, Vol. X (1908), 327–68. Fort Kanses.

Morrison, William B. "Fort Arbuckle," *Chronicles of Oklahoma*, Vol. VI (March, 1928), 26–34. Fort Arbuckle II.

———. "Fort Towson," *Chronicles of Oklahoma*, Vol. VIII (June, 1930), 226–32.

———. "A Visit to Old Fort Washita," *Chronicles of Oklahoma*, Vol. VII (June, 1929), 175–79.

Muckleroy, Anna. "The Indian Policy of the Republic of Texas," *Southwestern Historical Quarterly*, Vol. XXV (April, 1922), 229–60; Vol. XXVI (July, 1922), 1–29; (October, 1922), 128–48; (January, 1923), 184–206.

Mullay, P. H. "History of Fort Missoula, Montana," *Recruiting News*, February 1, 1924, pp. 7, 12.

Mullin, Cora Phoebe. "The Founding of Fort Hartsuff," *Nebraska Historical Magazine*, Vol. XII (April–June, 1931), 129–40.

Murbarger, Nell. "When the Troopers Came to Nevada," *Desert Magazine*, Vol. XVI (December, 1953), 12–18. Material for Forts Churchill and Haven.

Nankivell, John H. "Fort Garland, Colorado," *Colorado Magazine*, Vol. XVI (January, 1939), 13–28.

———. "Fort Crawford, Colorado, 1880–1890," *Colorado Magazine*, Vol. XI (March, 1934), 54–64.

Neill, Edward D. "Occurrences in and around Fort Snelling from

1819–1840," *Collections of the Minnesota State Historical Society*, Vol. II (1889), 102–42.

Noyer, Charles de. "The History of Fort Totten," *Collections of the State Historical Society of North Dakota*, Vol. III (1910), 178–236.

Oswald, James M. "History of Fort Elliott," *Panhandle–Plains Historical Review*, Vol. XXXII (1959), 1–59.

Parker, Mrs. C. F. "Old Julesburg and Fort Sedgwick," *Colorado Magazine*, Vol. VII (July, 1930), 139–46.

Patterson, Nicholas, and John Mason Peck. "The Boon's Lick Country," *Bulletin of the Missouri Historical Society*, Vol. VI (July, 1950), 442–71. Contains material for forts of the War of 1812 period.

Petersen, William J. "Troops and Military Supplies on the Upper Mississippi River Steamboats," *Iowa Journal of History and Politics*, Vol. XXXIII (July, 1935), 260–86.

Peterson, Charles E. "Colonial Saint Louis," part III, *Bulletin of the Missouri Historical Society*, Vol. IV (October, 1947), 11–30. Defensive works.

Pfanner, Robert. "The Genesis of Fort Logan," *Colorado Magazine*, Vol. XIX (March, 1942), 43–50.

———. "Highlights in the History of Fort Logan," *Colorado Magazine*, Vol. XIX (May, 1942), 81–91.

Plaisance, Aloysius. "The Arkansas Factory, 1805–1810," *Arkansas Historical Quarterly*, Vol. XI (Autumn, 1952), 184–200. Arkansas Post.

Prosch, Thomas W. "The Military Roads of Washington Territory," *Washington Historical Quarterly*, Vol. II (January, 1908), 118–26.

Prucha, Francis P. "Fort Ripley: the Post and the Military Reservation," *Minnesota History*, Vol. XXVIII (September, 1947), 205–24.

————. "The Settler and the Army in Frontier Minnesota," *Minnesota History*, Vol. XXIX (September, 1948), 231–46.

Radzyminski, Stanley F. "Charles Radziminski: Patriot, Exile, Pioneer," *Chronicles of Oklahoma*, Vol. XXXVIII (Winter, 1960), 354–68.

"Report of Inspection of the Ninth Military Department, 1819," *Mississippi Valley Historical Review*, Vol. VII (December, 1920), 261–74. The report, which includes Forts Armstrong, Bellefontaine, Crawford, Osage, and Smith, was prepared by Colonel Arthur P. Hayne.

Rister, Carl Coke. "The Border Post of Phantom Hill," *West Texas Historical Association Year Book*, Vol. XIV (1938), 3–13.

————. "Fort Griffin," *West Texas Historical Association Year Book*, Vol. I (1925), 15–24.

Robbins, Harvey. "Journal of the Rogue River War, 1855," *Oregon Historical Quarterly*, Vol. XXXIV (December, 1933), 345–58.

Rogers, Fred B. "Early Military Posts of Del Norte County," *California Historical Society Quarterly*, Vol. XXVI (March, 1947), 1–11. Fort Ter-waw and Camps Lincoln I and II.

————. "Early Military Posts of Mendocino County," *California Historical Society Quarterly*, Vol. XXVIII (September, 1948), 215–28. Forts Bragg and Weller and Camp Wright.

Rogers, R. W. "History of Fort Ringgold," *Recruiting News*, September 1, 1923, pp. 7, 15.

Ross, A. R. "When Fort Morgan Was Really a Fort," *Colorado Magazine*, Vol. XXII (September, 1945), 227–28.

Rowe, Edna. "The Disturbances at Anahuac in 1832," *Quarterly of the Texas State Historical Association*, Vol. VI (April, 1903), 265–99.

Sánchez, José María. "A Trip to Texas in 1828," *Southwestern Historical Quarterly*, Vol. XXIX (April, 1926), 249–88. Trans. by

Carlos E. Castañeda. Sánchez accompanied General Manuel Mier y Terán on his trip of investigation through Texas.

Savage, Laird. "Fort Wingate," *New Mexico Magazine*, Vol. XXXVIII (August, 1960), 33, 37–39.

Scammell, J. M. "Military Units in Southern California, 1853–1862," *California Historical Society Quarterly*, Vol. XXIX (September, 1950), 229–49.

Shirk, George H. "The Site of Old Camp Arbuckle," *Chronicles of Oklahoma*, Vol. XXVII (Autumn, 1949), 313–15.

Shoemaker, Floyd C. "Fort Orleans: the Heritage of Carroll County," *Missouri Historical Review*, Vol. LI (January, 1957), 105–12. Contains a reproduction of a plan of the fort.

———. "New Madrid, Mother of Southeast Missouri," *Missouri Historical Review*, Vol. XLIX (July, 1955), 317–27. Some information of Spanish defenses, including Fort Celeste.

Simmons, India Harris. "Kendall in Early Days," *Kansas Historical Quarterly*, Vol. VII (February, 1938), 67–69. Fort Aubry.

Slaughter, Linda W. "Fort Abercrombie," *Collections of the State Historical Society of North Dakota*, Vol. I (1906), 412–23.

———. "Fort Randall," *Collections of the State Historical Society of North Dakota*, Vol. I (1906), 423–29.

"The Spanish Forts at the Mouth of the Missouri River," *Missouri Historical Society Collections*, Vol. III (1911), 269–74. Document dated 1769. Fort Principe de Asturias and the blockhouse north of the river.

Spring, Agnes Wright. "The Founding of Fort Collins, United States Military Post," *Colorado Magazine*, Vol. X (March, 1933), 47–55.

Stipes, M. F. "Fort Orleans, the First French Post on the Missouri," *Missouri Historical Review*, Vol. VIII (April, 1914), 121–35.

Sweet, J. H. "Old Fort Kearny," *Nebraska Historical Magazine*, Vol. XXVII (October–December, 1946), 233–43. Fort Kearny I.

Tanner, George C. "History of Fort Ripley, 1849–1859," *Collections of the Minnesota Historical Society*, Vol. X, part 1 (1905), 179–202.

Taylor, Fenton. "So They Built Fort Bowie," *Desert Magazine*, Vol. XIV (August, 1951), 4–7.

Temple, Frank M. "Federal Military Defense of the Trans-Pecos Region, 1850–1880," *West Texas Historical Association Year Book*, Vol. XXX (1954), 40–60.

Thoburn, Joseph B. "The Story of Cantonment," *Chronicles of Oklahoma*, Vol. III (April, 1924), 68–73.

Thomas, Chauncey. "The Spanish Fort in Colorado, 1819," *Colorado Magazine*, Vol. XIV (May, 1937), 81–85.

Thomases, Jerome. "Fort Bridger, a Western Community," *Journal of the American Military Institute*, Vol. V (Fall, 1941), 177–88.

Thomlinson, M. H. "Forgotten Fort," *New Mexico*, Vol. XXIII (November, 1945), 14, 39, 41. Fort Webster.

Thompson, Albert W. "Kit Carson's Camp Nichols in No Man's Land," *Colorado Magazine*, Vol. XI (September, 1934), 179–86.

Thompson, Theronne. "Fort Buffalo Springs, Texas Border Post," *West Texas Historical Association Year Book*, Vol. XXXVI (1960), 156–75. Camp Buffalo Springs was a forerunner of Fort Richardson.

Trickett, Dean. "The Civil War in the Indian Territory, 1861," *Chronicles of Oklahoma*, Vol. XVII (September, 1939), 315–27; (December, 1939), 401–12; Vol. XVIII (June, 1940), 142–53; (September, 1940), 266–80.

Trumbo, Theron M. "Waterhole at the Crossroads," *Desert Magazine*, Vol. XII (January, 1949), 19–21. Fort Cummings, New Mexico.

Ullóa, Antonio de. "The Beginnings of Spanish Missouri. Instructions, d'Ulloa to Rui, 1767," *Missouri Historical Society Collections*, Vol. III (April, 1908), 145–69. Instructions of March 24,

1767, for the establishment of forts at the mouth of the Missouri River.

Unrau, William E. "The Story of Fort Larned," *Kansas Historical Quarterly*, Vol. XXIII (Autumn, 1957), 257–80.

Utley, Robert W. "Fort Union and the Santa Fe Trail," *New Mexico Historical Review*, Vol. XXXVI (January, 1961), 36–48.

Van der Zee, Jacob. "Forts in the Iowa Country," *Iowa Journal of History and Politics*, Vol. XII (April, 1914), 163–204.

————. ed. "Old Fort Madison: Some Source Materials," *Iowa Journal of History and Politics*, Vol. XI (October, 1913), 517–45.

Van Zandt, Howard F. "The History of Camp Holmes and Chouteau's Trading Post," *Chronicles of Oklahoma*, Vol. XIII (September, 1935), 316–37. Fort Mason rather than Camp Holmes.

Victor, Frances Fuller. "The First Oregon Cavalry," *Quarterly of the Oregon Historical Society*, Vol. III (June, 1902), 123–63.

Warren, Gouverneur K. "Survey of Military Reserve of Fort Pierre," *South Dakota Historical Review*, Vol. I (July, 1936), 252–55. Second Lieutenant Warren, Topographical Engineers. Document dated August 7, 1855.

Watkins, Albert. "History of Fort Kearny," *Collections of the Nebraska State Historical Society*, Vol. XVI (1911), 227–67.

Wells, Merle W. "Origins of Anti-Mormonism in Idaho, 1872–1880," *Pacific Northwest Quarterly*, Vol. XLVII (October, 1956), 107–16. Some material for the establishment of Camp Connor.

Welty, Raymond L. "The Army Fort of the Frontier (1860–1870)," *North Dakota Historical Quarterly*, Vol. II (April, 1928), 155–67.

————. "The Frontier Army on the Missouri River, 1860–1870," *North Dakota Historical Quarterly*, Vol. II (January, 1928), 85–99.

————. "The Policing of the Frontier by the Army, 1860–1870," *Kansas Historical Quarterly*, Vol. VII (August, 1938), 246–57.

————. "Supplying the Frontier Military Posts," *Kansas Historical Quarterly*, Vol. VII (May, 1938), 154–69.

Wesley, Edgar B. "James Calloway in the War of 1812," *Missouri Historical Society Collections*, Vol. V (October, 1927), 38–81. Some material for the Missouri Ranger posts.

————. "Life in a Frontier Post: Fort Atkinson, 1823–1826," *Journal of the American Military Institute*, Vol. III (Winter, 1939), 203–209.

Wetzel, Charles R. "Monument Station, Gove County," *Kansas Historical Quarterly*, Vol. XXVI (Autumn, 1960), 250–54.

Williams, J. W. "Military Roads of the 1850's in Central West Texas," *West Texas Historical Association Year Book*, Vol. XVIII (1942), 77–91.

————. "The National Road of the Republic of Texas," *Southwestern Historical Quarterly*, Vol. XLVII (January, 1944), 207–24. The road linked Fort Towson with Austin.

Willman, Lillian E. "The History of Fort Kearny," *Publications of the Nebraska State Historical Society*, Vol. XXI (1930), 211–326.

Winans, W. P. "Fort Colville, 1859–1869," *Washington Historical Quarterly*, Vol. III (October, 1908), 78–82.

Winsor, M., and James A. Scarbrough. "Jewell County," *Collections of the Kansas State Historical Society*, Vol. XVII (1928), 389–409. Fort Jewell.

Wood, Asa A. "Fort Benton's Part in the Development of the West," *Washington Historical Quarterly*, Vol. XX (July, 1929), 213–22.

Woodward, Arthur. "Outpost on the Colorado," *Desert Magazine*, Vol. III (November, 1939), 4–8, 34. Fort Mojave.

Wright, Muriel H. "A History of Fort Cobb," *Chronicles of Oklahoma*, Vol. XXXIV (Spring, 1956), 53–71.

Young, Donald A. "History of Old Army Posts—Fort Riley," *Recruiting News*, March 1, 1923, pp. 7, 16.

INDEX

THIS INDEX does not list forts which appear in alphabetical sequence by states in the text unless there are other references to them.

A

Abercrombie, Fort, N.D.: 67
Abercrombie, John J.: 109, 157
Abiquiu, N.M.: 99
Adai Indians: 59
Adams-Onís Treaty: 42
Ahumada y Villalón, Agustín de, Marqués de las Amarillas: 160, 161
Alamo, the, Tex.: 160
Alamosa River, N.M., post on: 101
Alarcón, Martín de: 160
Albuquerque, N.M., post at: *xxn.*
Alcatraz Island, Calif., post on: *xxii, xxvii*
Alden, Bradford R.: 131
Alden, Camp, Ore.: 131
Alden, Fort, Wash.: 170
Alden, James: 170
Alert, Camp, Kan.: 55
Allen, James: 49, 50
Altar, Tex., alleged post: 139
Alvarado, Juan Bautista: 31
Álvarez de Pineda, Alonzo: *vii, viii*
Alvord, Benjamin: 42, 45, 48, 130, 171
American Fur Company: 50; posts of, 79, 109, 110, 115
American River, Calif.: 32
Anadarko Indians: 150
Anderson, Allen L.: 19
Anderson, William: 181
Andrews, George L.: 138
Angel Island, Calif., post on: *xxvii,* 25
Angelina River, Tex., post on: 163
Anza, Juan Bautista de: 30
Apache, Camp, Ariz.: 3

Apache Indians: *xxv,* 4, 6, 8, 9, 10, 11, 98, 99, 102, 104, 105, 107, 108, 148
Apache Pass, Ariz.: 4, 98
Applegate Cutoff: 93
Arapaho Indians: 118, 182
Aravaipa, Fort, Ariz.: 4
Arbuckle, Fort, Okla.: 119
Arbuckle, Matthew: 116, 117, 120
Arcata, Calif.: 25
Arikara Indians: 110
Arkansas, Fort, Wash.: 171
Arkansas Post, Ark.: *xxn.*
Arkansas River: 37, 42, 51, 55, 59; posts on, 15, 16, 39, 41, 50, 52, 56, 116, 119
Armistead, Lewis A.: 12
Armstrong, Fort, Ill.: *xxix*
Armstrong, John: *xxv,* 46
Arnold, Ripley A.: 150, 164
Arrow Rock, Mo.: 71, 76
Ash Hollow, Neb., post at: 86
Ashley Creek, Utah, post on: 167
Assiniboine, Fort, Mont.: 110
Astoria, Ore.: 132
Atkinson, Camp, Iowa: 47
Atkinson, Fort, Kan.: 56, 57
Atkinson, Fort, Neb.: 76
Atkinson, Fort, N.D.: 109
Atkinson, Henry: 47, 50, 85
Atlantic City, Wyo.: 185
Aubry Cutoff: 51
Aubry, Francis X.: *xxv,* 51
Auburn, Mo.: 74
Augur, Camp, Wyo.: 187
Augur, Christopher C.: 129, 177, 184
Austin, John: 164

Index

Hitchcock, Ethan Allen: 29
Hoffman, William: 12, 50, 178
Hollenbush, Calvin G.: 22
Hollenbush, Camp, Calif.: 22
Holmes, Theophilus Hunter: 121
Hoopa Valley Reservation, Calif.: 23
Horse Creek, N.M., post at: 105
Hoskins, Charles: 130
Houston, Sam: 152, 159
Howard, Benjamin: 72
Howard, Fort, Mo.: 72
Howard, Oliver Otis: 46
Howe, Marshall S.: 96
Howell, François: 72
Howell's Fort, Mo.: 71, 72
Howie, Fort, Mont.: 80n.
Hualpai Indians: 10
Hudson, Camp, Tex.: 159
Hudson, Walter W.: 152
Hudson's Bay Company posts: 44, 45, 173, 174, 176
Humboldt, Fort, Calif.: *xxix*, 25, 31
Humboldt Bay, Calif., posts on: 24, 25
Hungate, Nathan W.: 38
Hunt, Thomas: 68
Huntt, George G.: 147
Huston, Daniel: 112
Hutchins, Benjamin T.: 158
Hydesville, Calif.: 19

I

Iaqua, Camp, Calif.: 20
Illinois, Camp, Okla.: 126
Illinois River, Okla., post on: 126
Independence, Camp (Colorado River), Calif.: 35
Indian Factories: *xiii*, 16, 46, 49, 63, 68, 76
Ingalls, Rufus: 176
Inge, Zebulon M. P.: 62, 152
Ingham, Fort, Iowa: 48
Ingham, Schuyler R.: 48
Ingham, William H.: 48
Iowa Indians: 76

J

Jacksboro, Tex.: 158
Jackson, Andrew: *xxv*, 60, 120
James, Fort, S.D.: *xxix*
James River: 137; posts on, 114, 135

Jamestown, N.D.: 114
Jefferson Barracks, Mo.: *xiii, xxi, xxiii,* 69, 85
Jesup, Cantonment, La.: 61
Jesup, Fort, La.: 125
Jesup, Thomas Sydney: 62
Jicarilla Apache Indians: 37, 40, 96, 105
Jocko Reservation, Mont.: 83
John, Fort, Wyo.: 182
John Buford, Fort, Wyo.: 185
Johnson, Andrew: 183n.
Johnson, Benjamin H.: 153
Johnson, Edward: 33
Johnston, Albert Sidney: 152, 166, 178
Jones, Roger: *xxi*, 25, 181
Jones, Walter: 162
Jornada del Muerto, N.M.: 98, 100, 102
José María village, Tex.: 150
Joseph (Nez Percé Indian): 80
Julesburg, Colo.: 41

K

Kanapolis, Kan.: 53
Kansa Indians: 55, 76
Kansas Pacific Railway: 53, 54, 56
Kansas River: 52, 55, 56; post on, 57
Karankawa Indians: 140
Kautz, August V.: 9, 12
Kaycee, Wyo.: 183
Kearney, Neb.: 87
Kearny I, Fort, Neb.: *xiv*
Kearny II, Neb.: 57, 86, 89
Kearny, Philip: 131, 183
Kearny, Stephen Watts: xiii, 28, 47, 48, 57, 87, 101, 125
Kelley, James K.: 168
Kelly, Camp, Tex.: 147
Kelly, Michael J.: 147
Kelly, William: 130
Kennedy's Fort, Mo.: 72
Keogh, Myles W.: 82
Ketcham, Thomas E.: 19
Kettle (Fort) Lakes, S.D., post at: 137
Keyes, Erasmus Darwin: 169
Kichai Indians: 124
Kickapoo Indians: 56, 117
Kidd, James H.: 184
King, Benjamin: 135
Kingsbury, Jacob: 68

235

Index